*Mary Wollstonecraft
and 200 Years of Feminisms*

Mary Wollstonecraft

AND 200 YEARS OF FEMINISMS

edited by Eileen Janes Yeo

RIVERS ORAM PRESS
LONDON AND NEW YORK

First published in 1997 by
Rivers Oram Press, 144 Hemingford Road, London N1 1DE

Distributed in the United States by
New York University Press, Elmer Holmes Bobst Library,
70 Washington Square South, New York NY 10012-1091

Set in Baskerville by NJ Design Associates, Romsey
and printed in Great Britain by
T.J. Press (Padstow) Ltd

This edition copyright © Eileen Janes Yeo 1997
The articles are copyright © 1997 Himani Bannerji,
Françoise Basch, Moira Ferguson, Muriel Fielding, Gerry
Holloway, Rachel Holmes, Delia Jarrett-Macauley, Joan B.
Landes, Min Dongchao, Mary Nyquist, Dimitrina Petrova,
Gillian Scott, Joan Wallach Scott, Kate Soper, Barbara Taylor,
Eileen Janes Yeo

No part of this book may be produced in any form except
for the quotation of brief passages in criticism without the
written permission of the publishers

British Library Cataloguing in Publication Data
A catalogue record for this book is available from the British
Library

ISBN 1 85489 060 3 (hbk)
ISBN 1 85489 061 1 (pbk)

Contents

Preface vii
Notes on Contributors ix
Introduction 1
Eileen Janes Yeo

Imagination and the Politics of Gender Difference

1. For the Love of God 15
   Religion and the Erotic Imagination in Wollstonecraft's Feminism
Barbara Taylor
2. The Imagination of Olympe de Gouges 36
Joan W. Scott

Reason and Romance

3. Mary Does, Alice Doesn't 49
   The Paradox of Female Reason in and for Feminist Theory
Joan Landes
4. Wanting Protection 61
   Fair Ladies, Sensibility and Romance
Mary Nyquist

Feminism and Race

5. Mary Wollstonecraft and the Problematic of Slavery 89
Moira Ferguson
6. It Ain't All Black and White 104
Delia Jarrett-Macauley

Feminism and Class

7. Some Contradictions of Social Motherhood   121
Eileen Janes Yeo

8. Working-Class Feminism?   134
   The Women's Co-operative Guild, 1880s-1914
Gillian Scott

Inconvenient Feminists

9. Ernestine Rose (1810-92) and her Multiple Identities   147
Françoise Basch

10. Ignota, the Unknown Woman   152
    Elizabeth Clarke Wolstenholme Elmy, 1833-1918
Muriel Fielding

11. Ada Nield Chew   156
    An Uncomfortable Feminist
Gerry Holloway

Engendering Politics Today

12. Leading a Normal Family?   163
    Sexuality and Nation in the 1991 Winnie Mandela Trial
Rachel Holmes

13. The Farewell Dance   180
    Women in the Bulgarian Transition
Dimitrina Petrova

14. From Asexuality to Gender Differences in Modern China   193
Min Dongchao

Humanity and Difference

15. Naked Human Nature and the Draperies of Custom   207
    Wollstonecraft on Equality and Democracy
Kate Soper

16. Mary Wollstonecraft, Feminism and Humanism   222
    A Spectrum of Reading
Himani Bannerji

Reference Notes   243

Index   273

Preface

This book grew out of a Conference on Mary Wollstonecraft and 200 Years of Feminism which celebrated the anniversary of the publication of *A Vindication of the Rights of Woman*. The international and interdisciplinary gathering of academics and activists, with over 70 speakers and 400 attenders, took place at the University of Sussex in December 1992. This book cannot be a complete record of such a large event, which contained not only plenary sessions and many parallel workshops, but a performance of *A Dangerous Reputation* and a finale of fireworks. The chapters that follow come from feminist historians, literary scholars, cultural critics and political philosophers, many of whom are also activists, who have chosen either to contribute their original Conference papers or submit further developments of their work. Although wide-ranging, they are still a small selection of voices.

I thank everyone who participated in the Conference and especially those whose papers are not included here because only a limited number of themes could be represented. I also wish to thank Gerry Holloway, Gill Scott, Kate Soper and Barbara Taylor for reading and advising on the Introduction. A Visiting Fellowship at the History Division of the Research School of Social Sciences, Australian National University, made time available for some of the editing work. The Conference and therefore this book was made possible by financial and administrative support from the Centre for Continuing Education, the History Subject Group, the Gender and Feminist History Group and the Research Centre in Women's Studies all of the University of Sussex as well as from the British Academy, the Equal Opportunities Unit of the Commission of the European Communities and the Lipman Trust to whom acknowledgement and appreciation are due.

Notes on Contributors

Himani Bannerji teaches in the Department of Sociology at York University, Toronto, in the areas of anti-racist feminism, Marxist cultural theories, gender, colonialism and imperialism. Her recent publications include *Thinking Through: Essays on Feminism, Marxism and Anti-Racism* (1995), *The Writing on the Wall: Essays on Culture and Politics* (1993), and the edited anthology *Returning the Gaze: Essays on Racism, Feminism and Politics* (1993). She has also published two books of poetry, *A Separate Sky* and *Doing Time*, and is involved in anti-racist and feminist activism.

Françoise Basch is Professor of British and American Civilisation at the University Paris 7-Denis Diderot in France. She has written on women in both literature and history in nineteenth-century Britain and America and more recently on the history of modern France (the Rights of Man, the Occupation, Nazism). Her books include *Relative Creatures: Victorian Women in Society and the Novel* (1970), *Theresa Malkiel: The Diary of a Shirtwaist Striker* (1990); *Rebelles Américaines au 19ème Siècle* (1990) and *Victor Basch, de l'affaire Dreyfus au crime de la Milice* (1994).

Moira Ferguson was born and raised in Glasgow. She took her BA at the University of London, Birkbeck College, and her MA and PhD from the University of Washington, Seattle. She holds the James E. Ryan Chair in English and Women's Literature at the University of Nebraska-Lincoln and is the founding co-ordinator of the Women's Studies programme. Her recent books include *Subject to Others. British Women Writers and Colonial Slavery 1678-1834* (1992), *Colonial and Gender Relations from Mary Wollstonecraft to Jamaica Kincaid* (1993), *Jamaica Kincaid: Where the Land Meets the Body* (1994) and *Eighteenth-Century Women Poets* (1995).

She is a member of the Feminist Press publications board and vice-president of Nebraskans Against the Death Penalty, and was an NGO delegate to the UN Fourth World Conference on Women in Beijing.

Muriel Fielding was a mature student at Staffordshire Polytechnic and then did a Master of Letters degree at Keele University. Elizabeth Wolstenholme Elmy was the subject of her final thesis. She notes parallels between Elmy and herself: `the denial of her right to a decent education, mirrored my own experiences, as my elementary education ended at the age of 15: a product of the belief that education for girls was wasteful'. Fielding was born in the same area of Manchester as Elmy and has attempted to raise the profile of this ardent feminist in lectures, particularly in Congleton, her home for over 50 years. Fielding taught history part-time at Staffordshire University. She was also a voluntary adviser at the Citizens Advice Bureau, becoming deputy manager in 1992. She is a primary school governor, concerned to see an equal opportunities policy pursued and is attempting to introduce women into the history syllabus.

Gerry Holloway is a feminist historian and course convenor for Women's Studies at the Centre for Continuing Education at the University of Sussex. She recently completed her PhD thesis, 'A Common Cause? Class Dynamics in the Industrial Women's Movement, 1888-1918'. Her published work includes a contribution on dynamics in the Women's Studies classroom in Mary Stuart and Alistair Thomson (eds), *Engaging with Difference: The Other in Adult Education* (1995) and her own life history as a working-class academic in Pat Mahoney and Christine Zmroczek (eds), *Class Matters* (1997). Particularly interested in the way women organise formally and informally, she is on the steering committee of the Women's History Network both nationally and in the Southern Region, where she helps to organise conferences and other events. She also worked with Eileen Yeo organising the Wollstonecraft 200 Conference.

Rachel Holmes is Lecturer in Lesbian Studies at the University of Sussex. She was brought up in KwaZulu Natal, South Africa, and completed her education at the University of London. She has taught at the London School of Contemporary Dance, and the University of London. In 1990 and 1991 she was an organiser of the international Questions of Homosexuality: Lesbian and Gay Studies Conferences held at London University. Her published work includes a contribution to Mark Bevisser and Edwin Cameron (eds), *Defiant Desire: Gay and Lesbian Lives in South Africa* (1994), and she is currently writing a queer critical biography of Dr James Barry. During the course of her research on sexuality in South Africa, she has been hosted by the Department of English at the University of the Western Cape. Her earlier activities in South Africa focused around the End of Conscription Campaign and United Democratic Front in Natal, whilst in more recent years she has worked with the Association of Bisexuals, Gays and Lesbians (ABIGALE) in Cape Town. Her favourite assignment was to be one of the judges on the panel for the Miss Gay South Africa drag queen contest held in Guguletu township in August 1993.

Delia Jarrett-Macauley edited the first British black women's studies anthology, *Reconstructing Womanhood, Reconstructing Feminism: Writings on Black Women* (1995). During the 1980s, she was an active member of the now defunct Brixton Black Women's Group and a researcher for Women Working Worldwide. Delia taught at the Universities of Kent and London from 1989 to 1994 and now works as a management consultant. She has written *A Life of Una Marson 1905-65* (1997), about a black British feminist writer and activist, and has edited a collection of Marson's writings. She is now writing a book on black women in Britain.

Joan B. Landes is Professor of Women's Studies and History at the Pennsylvania State University, where she teaches feminist theory, women's history and modern European cultural and intellectual history. Her numerous writings address the antecedents of contemporary feminist argument, the historical relationship of feminist theory and feminist movements, and the genesis of modern feminism in the West. She is the author of *Women and the Public Sphere in the Age of the French Revolution* (1988). She has edited a volume of essays on *Feminism the Public and the Private* (1998), is completing a forthcoming book *Visualizing Freedom: Gender, Politics and Culture in Eighteenth-Century France* and planning a larger study on the topic of women and reason.

Min Dongchao is an Associate Professor of History at Tianjin Normal University, People's Republic of China and, before coming to the UK as a visiting scholar, was co-director of their Centre of Women's Studies. As a visiting scholar, she has carried out research at the Institute of

Development Studies at Sussex, later moving to Leeds. Her research interests include feminist theory, women's history, women and development, and women and culture. Her present work is an analysis of the sinolisation of Western feminism and women's studies in China. She is author of a book on *The International Women's Movement, 1789-1989*, and of several articles on women's studies and history.

Mary Nyquist teaches in the Women's Studies Programme and the Department of English at the University of Toronto. She has been involved in feminist and anti-racist organisations for twenty-odd years, and has recently been facilitating groups for survivors of domestic violence. The co-editor, with Margaret Ferguson, of *Re-Membering Milton* (1987), she has published several essays on Milton and other early modern writers, and has also written on numerous nineteenth-century, modern and contemporary women authors.

Dimitrina Petrova was born in Bulgaria and is now director of the European Roma Rights Center in Budapest, an international human rights organisation devoted to monitoring the rights of Roma (gypsies) in Europe and providing legal defence for victims of human rights violations. From 1992 to 1995, she chaired the Human Rights Project in Bulgaria. Before 1989, she was involved in human rights and environmental opposition against the communist regime and, in 1990-1, was a member of the first democratically elected parliament after communism. Between 1982 and 1994, she taught philosophy at the University of Sofia and, in 1995, taught human rights and gender at the University of Oregon. She has published in the field of political science, human rights (particularly minority rights) and philosophy, and her PhD thesis (1993) is on utopia and the philosophy of values.

Gillian Scott teaches in the School of Historical and Critical Studies at the University of Brighton and previously did educational work in the co-operative movement. She first became involved with the women's movement as a student in the 1970s, and it was as a result of that activity that she began to investigate the relationship between feminism and working-class women historically. She is currently completing a book on the Women's Co-operative Guild.

Joan Wallach Scott is Professor of Social Science at the Institute for Advanced Study in Princeton, New Jersey. Her recent books include:

Gender and the Politics of History (1988) and *Only Paradoxes to Offer: French Feminists and the Rights of Man* (1996). She has edited *Feminists Theorize the Political* (1992) with Judith Butler, and *Feminism and History* (1996).

Kate Soper is a Senior Lecturer in Philosophy at the University of North London. Her own writings include *On Human Needs* (1981), *Humanism and Anti-Humanism* (1986), *Troubled Pleasures: Essays on Politics, Gender and Hedonism* (1990) and *What is Nature? Culture, Politics and the Non-Human* (1995). She has also worked as a translator of texts by Bobbio, Castoriadis, Foucault, Carlo Ginzburg and Timpanaro among others. She has been very active in the peace movement, and in the mid-1980s served as chairperson of European Nuclear Disarmament (END). She has written for the *New Left Review*, is a regular contributor to *Feminist Review*, and is a long-standing member of the *Radical Philosophy* collective.

Barbara Taylor is the author of *Eve and the New Jerusalem: Socialism and Feminism in the Nineteenth Century* (1983) and numerous articles in the history of feminism. She is now writing a book on the feminist philosophy of Mary Wollstonecraft, provisionally titled *A Wild Wish: Mary Wollstonecraft and the Feminist Imagination*. Barbara Taylor is currently a Senior Lecturer in Cultural History at the University of East London, and a member of the editorial board of *History Workshop Journal*.

Eileen Janes Yeo teaches history and women's studies at the University of Sussex and helped to organise the Wollstonecraft 200 Conference there. She has published widely on the history of radical culture, has been active in community publishing and is chairperson of the Society for the Study of Labour History. Her most recent books are *The Contest for Social Science: Relations and Representations of Gender and Class* (1996) and, with Barbara Einhorn (eds), *Women and Market Societies: Crisis and Opportunity* (1995), written by scholars from Sussex and East Asia and presented at the UN Fourth World Conference on Women. She is currently writing a book on *Meanings of Motherhood in Europe and America, 1750 to the present*.

Introduction
Eileen Janes Yeo

Mary Wollstonecraft has been hailed as the founder or foremother of Western feminism. Her bicentenaries invite us to review such judgements as well as to take stock of current concerns. Conceived at a conference marking the two-hundredth anniversary of the publication of *A Vindication of the Rights of Woman*, and appearing two hundred years after her death, this book reveals the mixture of celebration and troubled reflection which has produced particularly complex assessments. Taking little for granted, the chapters that follow explore tensions in Wollstonecraft's texts, problematise the process of reading, interrogate the writing of history and examine the difficult issues involved in extending the limits of the possible for women and men in Wollstonecraft's present, in later movements and in our own time.

That such complexity should characterise scholarship in the present political moment is only to be expected. Our experience of the instability of the current context parallels our concern about the instability of texts. The dismantling of familiar frameworks, especially the collapse of Communist states in the East and the restructuring of economies and welfare states in the West, has created crises for women and men worldwide, and, it is to be hoped, opportunities as well. The directions ahead are not clear. Several chapters below indicate just how problematic gender politics have become in some of the most dynamic parts of the world, for instance, East Central Europe, China and South Africa, let alone in Western capitalist societies.

This book makes no pretension to offer answers to pressing problems. It does, however, provide insights into how present concerns make us resonant to themes in Wollstonecraft's writing, such as her handling of the politics of gender difference, her awareness of sexuality and romance, her valuation of imagination and fantasy, her passionate wrestling with reason, and the relevance of her version of the Enlightenment humanist project to women's citizenship today. On a more sombre note, this book makes very clear how much exclusion and subjugation of women has taken place within Western feminist 'tradition' from Wollstonecraft onwards and how attentive we need to be to decolonising the thinking in our own heads while we dream of liberating wider worlds.

Feminism, Identity and Imagination

Complex conversations between past and present are involved in any attempt to read Wollstonecraft's texts or to write the history of feminisms. In the first two chapters, Barbara Taylor and Joan Scott plunge back into the unfamiliar historical context of the Enlightenment to explore how Mary Wollstonecraft and her French contemporary Olympe de Gouges created their feminist identities. These chapters are not so much interested in constructing chronological histories or traditions of feminism, as in probing, in Scott's words 'how women tried to move within and beyond cultural constraints of their own day by exploiting ambiguities in politics and representations of the moment'. The scrupulous historical work of these chapters is informed by an issue of current feminist concern. In the politics of sexual difference, our subjective sense of self and our resources for self-representation are critical for empowering us to transcend present conventions about gender. How can women create personal and collective identities which expand our possibilities, not only on the conscious level of ideas and self-representation but also on the more intractable psychic levels of fantasy and desire?

The role of imagination and of fantasy in bringing about an enlargement of gender roles concerns several chapters here. Both Barbara Taylor and Joan Scott analyse concepts of the imagination in Wollstonecraft's time, which, paradoxically, could function in both highly creative and destructive ways. Scott shows how imagination was an ambiguous concept for the Enlightenment, at once the source of creativity in learning and politics and the antithesis of reason, leading to madness. Using her imagination, Olympe de Gouges could speak in many voices, representing herself as 'a great man' and active citizen or as a woman. By a tragic irony, the ambivalence of imagination was bent the other way and used to defeat her in the end: her execution by guillotine in 1793 reportedly punished her for 'exalted imagination' amounting to 'delirium'.

Barbara Taylor's chapter engages with the most unfamiliar and possibly alien aspect of Wollstonecraft's thought, her piety. Taylor shows how Wollstonecraft tried to discriminate between the proper and improper channelling of the erotic imagination, not only in her fiction and in her social thought but also on the psychological level of desire. The 'vivifying principle' of creative mind and religious belief, Wollstonecraft felt that imagination could be debauched by being directed towards mortal objects. Instead, she placed God at the centre of an authentic female subjectivity and used the religious erotic imagination to internalise a Father God and create the possibility for self-reverence, on the basis of which 'women's ethical selfhood can emerge, beyond the eroticising male gaze'.

Mary Nyquist, in chapter 4, also explores the dangers of misdirecting the romantic imagination which can lead to obsessional behaviour and deliver neither the protection nor liberation that women truly desire. Nyquist focuses upon another subversion by Wollstonecraft and radical novelists of her period, who attempt to refashion the chivalry which is integral to the genre of romance. Women wanting protection (that is both needing and desiring protection) are revealed to be lacking such protection not only from men but from the law and the conduct of social institutions. In this present state of affairs, effective rescue comes not so much from upper-class gallants as from ladies themselves, or from more or less worthy lower-class persons of both sexes. Nyquist also notes how the mismatch between the want of protection and the desire for gallant rescue has persisted into today's popular romance, despite the vast 'structural adjustments' in consumer capitalism which have feminised poverty as well as the labour market.

Fantasy enters into the discussion of Wollstonecraft and the history of feminisms in yet another way. Scott, in chapter 2, and Barbara Taylor, in her Sussex conference talk suggested that to look at Wollstonecraft's place in any feminist 'tradition' is really to see what generations of feminists made of her, and especially how they fantasised about her. Later activists shaped Wollstonecraft into a magnetic icon with strong powers of attraction or repulsion. Taylor reviewed the many different Wollstonecrafts who, by the 1980s,

> had marched across feminism's imagination — from the wild woman who had so fascinated and frightened the mid-Victorians, to the domestic paragon of [Millicent] Fawcett's creation, to the heroically iconoclastic figure of fin-de-siècle radicalism, to the middle-class

liberal, rather narrow and complacent despite her unconventional sexual history, who dominates much recent writing....And to these, the advocates of feminine *écriture* have most recently added yet another — the woman writer into whose texts, particularly her novels, is inscribed the transgressive feminine gesture which reaches past the masculinist logic of her politics.[1]

To explore why these fantasies of Wollstonecraft have changed over the years, it would be necessary to consider the aspirations, struggles and angles of vision of later generations of feminists in their historical contexts.

If past contexts need recapturing, present vantage points also require careful placing. Himani Bannerji closes this book with a chapter exploring the process of active reading which sees a text as 'a sort of social relation' between a socially located writer and a socially situated reader. She traces how her own understanding of *A Vindication of the Rights of Woman* has changed three times during her life as her position in social systems, which are also power systems has changed. Thus, as an upper-caste girl in India, she responded to the gender politics of the text, but when she moved to Canada, and became docketed as an immigrant Other by widespread racist thinking, she became angrily aware of its contradictory use of metaphors of slavery and orientalism. Now, disappointed with the results of a politics of difference, she proposes another reading, which, while acknowledging the previous two, finds positive value in Wollstonecraft's rationality, which argues for a full humanity not on abstract grounds but from the real lived experience of its having been denied.

Feminism and Race

It is no longer possible to accept the idea of a self-evident feminist history or tradition. We are now very aware that traditions are not only invented but highly selective.[2] Even the term 'feminism' has been contested and often rejected by women's movements or invoked at moments of fracture to conjure up a spurious unity.[3] In this book, as at the Wollstonecraft 200 Conference, there is a great emphasis on the women who have been excluded, because of their race, class, ethnicity or creed, from previous versions of a feminist past. Apart from treatments of Wollstonecraft herself, there are few narratives about 'sheroes'. As chapters 9 to 11 below indicate, the spotlight has fallen rather on inconvenient feminists such as Ernestine Rose and 'Ignota', who were active in organised women's movements but were pilloried for their atheistic views, while Rose was further attacked for her Polish accent and Elizabeth Wolstenholme Elmy for her principled but dissident sexual behaviour. Together with Ada Nield Chew, a working-class activist, all were in one way or another concealed by a feminist amnesia which sometimes wrote them out of the historical record.

Several chapters here consider feminism and race, and point to Wollstonecraft's ambivalent position in both recognising the oppression of slavery and at the same time being implicated in racialising women's sensibility and potential. In chapter 4, Mary Nyquist shows how Wollstonecraft satirised false sensibility precisely by pointing to 'fair ladies' who invent 'unheard-of tortures for captive negroes'. Nonetheless, Wollstonecraft believed in the superior qualities of an educated British bourgeois sensibility, which she implicitly denied to women of other races and explicitly to women from other classes, such as ex-prostitute Jemima in *Maria, or The Wrongs of Woman*.

Moira Ferguson, in chapter 5, shows how the discourse of slavery, which was already widely used in relation to marriage, became recontextualised in the 1790s in terms of colonial slavery. By associating colonial slavery with female subjugation, Wollstonecraft opened new political possibilities, which could be signalled obliquely by analogy with crowd uprisings and slave rebellion. But Bannerji (chapter 16), in her angrier second reading of *The Rights of Woman*, argues that the use of slavery as a rhetorical device to dramatise the oppression of British women 'leads to an erasure of slavery as an actual practice as well as of African experiences and histories in bondage'. Bannerji also derides the use of orientalist imagery to depict degeneration in a static, hypersexualised space, from which there is no exit because women collude with their own subjection. These metaphoric devices function to devalue the peoples whom Europe sought to dominate, and to privilege European men and women in the name of all humanity. 'Once more,' she insists, 'the slave serves the cause of the master class.'

Precisely this kind of qualified ethnocentricity, as well as its more flagrant racist forms, were challenged at the Sussex conference plenary session on Feminism and Race. Catherine Hall pointed to the end of empire as the key difference between the 1790s and 1990s, and urged feminists to tackle the question: 'What contribution can we make to the decolonisation of knowledge, including our own knowledges in relation to feminist discourses?'[4]

Determined to be optimistic, Delia Jarrett-Macauley, in chapter 6 below, wants to prevent difference from setting into hard division and to move beyond what she considers a calcified debate on feminism and race, locked in a polarisation between black and white, First and Third worlds, privileged against underprivileged, powerful against voiceless.

Jarrett-Macauley suggests that 'we do not always need to acknowledge a history of polarisation more firmly and more tenaciously than our shared history and present troubles', and proposes a number of ways to see the past which will also help to create the conditions for a more co-operative future. She asks that we focus on the presence of black women within British activities and communities as well as rehabilitating anti-racist feminist traditions. She insists on making black women visible and audible, allowing articulation, if need be, to take the form of screams of rage. She insists on validating 'discredited knowledge' and on reclaiming a black feminist intellectual tradition in which a woman like Sojourner Truth is recognised as 'a formidable intellectual, though she was a former slave who had never learnt to read and write'. In this way, we might begin to influence each other and, in a world where identities are 'changing, unfixed, renewable possibilities', to 'think in terms of an interculturation of feminist thought'.

Feminism and Class

Another pivotal tension in feminism has revolved around class differences among women. In chapter 4, Mary Nyquist shows how Wollstonecraft, in her novel, *The Wrongs of Woman*, did not emphasise the commonality between Jemima, the working-class character, and Maria, the heroine, so much as the differences in their class and therefore their education, which in turn created differences in sensibility. Sexual slumming with prostitutes is what confirmed the degeneracy of Maria's husband Venables, and Maria felt disgusted at his consorting with 'squalid inhabitants of some of the lanes and back streets of the metropolis, mortified at being compelled to consider them as my fellow-creatures, as if an ape had claimed kindred with me'. And yet, despite all this, in a final innovative scene of rescue it is Jemima, not a chivalrous protective male, who leads Maria out of the prison madhouse through the garden gate to freedom.

Such ambiguity, containing solidarity but also hierarchy, has riddled class relations between women since Wollstonecraft's time. Catherine Hall called for a new phase of work in women's history which would 'develop further understanding of interconnections between the hierarchies of power in any social formation' and particularly place understandings of gender power 'in articulation with class/race/ethnicity'. She drew attention to the fact that women, particularly in the anti-slavery movement, constructed their political identities differently from men, and to how the language of family was central to their thinking about 'race' as well as 'gender'. Abolitionist women identified with slaves not only in terms of mutual weakness and dependence but as suffering mothers, although the white abolitionists put words into the mouths of slave mothers rather than allowing them to speak for themselves.[5]

I extend the discussion in chapter 7 to explore how a language of social motherhood was prevalent in the relations between women of different classes in Britain, Germany and the United States in the period around the First World War (and still resonates today). Examining its contradictory nature, I show how creating an identity as a social mother paid dividends for women activists and professionals in their negotiations with men for public space, but also restricted the educational and occupational chances they gained. Moreover, the discourse of social motherhood became very problematic in relations with women of other class, ethnic and racial groups, and could function as a woman's language of subordination, where maternal authority figures prevailed over and spoke for putative children. In a discussion of different types of social motherhood, I try to distinguish between the more and less empowering varieties of familial language.

Gillian Scott, too, in chapter 8, shows the creative ways in which gender tensions within a working-class movement and class tensions within feminism were addressed by the Women's Co-operative Guild. Guided by general secretary Margaret Llewelyn Davies who had direct family links to the mid-century middle-class women's movement, the Guild found that most feminist demands for equality with men of their class, except in the case of the vote, offered only limited gains. Guildswomen maintained a class struggle for social justice, together with a focus upon sexual inequality and suffering in marriage and childbirth, raising issues which ramified into public life, where 'official men of the Board can't stand our acting independently. It is just the same feeling as between husband and wife.' Welcoming women of leisure to work in the movement, Davies made it clear that they had to identify themselves with working-class interests and to facilitate working women's self-representation. She was aware of the continual need for a balancing act, believing, as Scott puts it, that 'working women could no more afford to give up their class solidarity in pursuit of women's rights than they could sacrifice their feminist principles to the imperatives of a male-dominated labour movement'.

Engendering Politics Today

Moving from the past to present, in some of the most dynamic parts of the world today, women are wrestling with many of the same issues about balancing class, race and gender priorities, about using existing (and even shrinking) cultural materials to remake gender models and about achieving meaningful protection in situations of very rapid change. The transition to market economies in the East has accelerated crises in femininity. In chapters 13 and 14, Dimitrina Petrova, writing on Bulgaria, and Min Dongchao, writing about China, both speak of the recoil from the asexual or masculine woman of post-war communism, identified by Petrova as 'woman on a tractor' who carried the too-heavy burden of 'three watermelons' under her arm: as asexual worker in the public labour market, as wife and mother and as political activist. Even before the fall of Eastern European communism, women were trying to shed the political 'watermelon' and become the attractive woman secretary, the auxiliary either at home or in the workplace, under the protection of their male bosses. Yet this complicated move towards dependent femininity comes just at the time when legislative protections are being repealed, when women are bearing the brunt of the economic transition and when femininity is being used symbolically, as in Wollstonecraft's time, to characterise decadent humanity, and more specifically to denigrate the evil, corrupt communist past. Despite the fact that communism has a masculine gender in the Bulgarian language, Petrova shows how it is being portrayed as an evil woman in popular songs such as 'Give Me Divorce' and 'The Farewell Dance'.[6]

Min Dongchao explores how Chinese women are currently trying to marry elements of femininity from the old Confucian past (retaining an emphasis on dedicated work and service but shedding the insistence on total obedience) to concepts of self-development from the West. The difficulties of blending these opposites is conveyed in the much-discussed case of a local authority governor who also tried to be the exemplary wife and mother but was nonetheless rejected by her husband who held to the old belief that men should have higher status — or, as Confucius said, 'husband high, wife glorious'. Min Dongchao's oral history interviews point to the rewards and problems that women are experiencing as they live through the new conceptual coupling of East and West.

Rachel Holmes, in chapter 12, shows how the South African nationalist movement identified Nelson and Winnie Mandela as an icon of a heterosexual national family. Intimately connected was the idea that homosexuality was a waste product of imperialism, a reflection of a corrupted social order, as in Wollstonecraft's time, with colonialism the culprit in this case. Winnie Mandela's defence at her trial on charges of abduction and assault presented her as the mother of the nation, protecting endangered youth from sexual perversion. Yet, when she was later exposed as an unfaithful wife, this representation transformed from mother to sexualised 'mugger of the nation'. These shifting representations are just a part of the story, where there are layers of discourse and a constant flux in identities, as indicated by the fact that she has kept her popular following among the youth in the townships. Nonetheless, Holmes argues that the symbolic reliance on iconographic heterosexual families to represent the emancipatory social order can function to shrink real choice about sexuality and shut down dignified space for the lesbian, gay and bisexual movements.

Politics of Knowledge: Knowledge and Politics

As this is a volume written mainly by feminist scholars, it is to be expected that there would be a concern with feminist reason not least in a period when intellectual work has itself become a battleground. Joan Landes, in chapter 3, expresses the feminist desire to get beyond 'masculinist' reason, which she feels that Wollstonecraft was obstructed by her context from ever being able to do. Landes explores the possibilities suggested by Alice in Wonderland, who (despite her creator being a middle-aged don with a penchant for little girls) goes into the interior realm and there, independent and masterless, shows a brilliant capacity to solve problems and to play on the boundaries between sense and nonsense.

Bannerji, in chapter 16, argues that Wollstonecraft reworked the Enlightenment rationalist discourse in ways that are still pertinent. Already, in her time, the discourse of reason was 'a code word for a critical apparatus which is used to...interpret prevailing social and political conditions, and thus it ceases to be only a name for a faculty which transcends the social'. Her emancipatory concept of reason refused a dualist split and retained a connection with experience ('embodiment and location in society and history') and with subjectivity. It became at once a moral, creative and critical faculty. Taylor and Nyquist, in their chapters, contribute further dimensions to Wollstonecraft's construct of an imaginative, passionate and caring reason.

Bannerji argues that Wollstonecraft's interest in humanism or universal rights was not derived simply from a priori principle but rather 'from her empirical knowledge and personal experience of injustice peculiar to lives of women'. Wollstonecraft thus approaches the universal from the standpoint of difference: an 'unorthodox premise for a universalist thinker'. Yet, as Kate Soper also argues in chapter 15, it is precisely this kind of contradictory position that we need to learn to inhabit more comfortably at this time. Soper calls for a political philosophy which includes both universal sameness and entitlement, together with specific and different cultural histories, needs and desires. Exploring several of the instabilities in Wollstonecraft's writing, which help account for its continued fascination, she assigns Wollstonecraft an ambiguous place in the tradition of liberalism, and uses Wollstonecraft's attack on Burke (a champion of cultural difference, or 'the draperies of custom') to challenge postmodern political theorists. Soper argues that democracy depends on assumptions of sameness and equality, and that some philosophies of difference can be as subjugating as the tricks of the Enlightenment, which preached universal human rights but practised exclusion.

The issue of power keeps reappearing in this book: between genders, between classes, between races, between women ourselves. One new form of hierarchy against which we need particularly to guard is the kind that can result from our positions and indeed struggles as university academics which, as Jarrett-Macauley reminds us, can turn 'feminist thought into a highly sophisticated, academic and frequently elitist business'. The kinds of inclusions that we are keen to make as we construct the past and the present require that previously muffled voices should now be heard loud and clear in whichever way they choose to speak. This involves creating comfortable settings for dialogue where we can learn from each other. The issue is not only of access to university-type institutions, but of the kind of 'practical and caring approach' that Jarrett-Macauley exemplified in the actions of young Anna, who was trying to build bridges between Jewish women and the immigrant women who are current targets of German racism.[7] Problems cannot be resolved or mutual learning take place only on the level of thought. Alongside our attempts to create a more shared past and to analyse the challenges of the present, Jarrett-Macauley counsels us to explore 'what kind of practical action we are prepared to engage with together'. A divorce of academic feminism from political engagement would be very dangerous now. We live in turbulent times, and, like Mary Wollstonecraft in her revolutionary moment, we need to be committed to understandings which facilitate transformation.

Imagination and the Politics of Gender Difference

1. For the Love of God
Religion and the Erotic Imagination in Wollstonecraft's Feminism
Barbara Taylor

In the chapter of *A Vindication of the Rights of Woman* entitled 'The State of Degradation to Which Woman is Reduced', Mary Wollstonecraft suddenly breaks away from addressing the reader, usually presumed by her to be a man, to address the only male she acknowledged as her natural superior:

> Gracious Creator of the whole human race! hast thou created such a being as woman, who can trace Thy wisdom in Thy works, and feel that Thou alone art by Thy nature exalted above her, for no better purpose...[than] to submit to man, her equal — a being who, like her, was sent into the world to acquire virtue? Can she consent to be occupied merely to please him — merely to adorn the earth — when her soul is capable of rising to Thee?

Wollstonecraft, never short of an answer, then goes on to reply to her own question: 'if [women] be moral beings, let them have a chance to become intelligent; and let love to man be only a part of that glowing flame of universal love, which, after encircling humanity, mounts in graceful incense to God.'[1]

Several years ago the feminist critic Ann Snitow, commenting on the many 'appeals to God and virtue' which are to be found throughout Wollstonecraft's writings, noted that these are of course 'a dead letter to feminists now'.[2] If by 'dead letter' is meant a failed communication, then it is certainly true that of all aspects of Wollstonecraft's thought it is her piety which has failed to speak to late twentieth-century feminists. We have found it so difficult even to hear the profound religious commitment which shapes Wollstonecraft's credo that within the now very large literature on her it is rarely mentioned. Her earliest works are acknowledged to be encumbered to a certain extent with some of the conventional pieties of the age, but the two *Vindications* — the *Rights of Men* and the *Rights of Woman* — are viewed as severely rationalist texts. *A Vindication of the Rights of Woman* in particular is almost invariably located within a tradition of Enlightenment liberalism which is assumed to be at least indifferent to religion if not actively hostile to it. So it is startling, on looking again at the *Rights of Woman*, to find that it contains at least 50 discussions of religious themes, ranging from brief statements on one or other doctrinal point to extended analyses of women's place within a divinely ordered moral universe. Nor are these discussions in any sense peripheral to the main message of the text. If Wollstonecraft's faith becomes a dead letter to us then so does much of her feminism, so closely are they harnessed together. And what locks them together, I plan to show, is a concept of the erotic imagination which places the love of God at the centre of an authentic female subjectivity — and thus at the centre of the feminist project as Wollstonecraft defined it.

Mary Wollstonecraft's family were inactive members of the Church of England, and according to her husband and biographer, William Godwin, she 'received few lessons of religion in her youth'.[3] Nonetheless, for the first 28 years of her life she was a regular churchgoer, and her first published work, *Thoughts on the Education of Daughters*, was steeped in orthodox attitudes, advocating 'fixed principles of religion' and warning of the dangers of rationalist speculation and deism. For women in particular, the young Wollstonecraft argued, clear-cut religious views were essential: 'for a little refinement only leads a woman into the wilds of romance, if she is not religious; nay more, there is no true sentiment without it, nor perhaps any other effectual check to the passions.'[4] In the same year that *Thoughts* was published, however, Wollstonecraft stopped attending church, and by the time she produced her last book, *A Short Residence in Sweden*, she had performed an apparent *volte-face*, writing approvingly of freethinkers who 'deny the divinity of Jesus Christ, and...question the necessity or utility of the christian system'.[5] The abandonment of Christian orthodoxy, however, only served to underline her commitment to what had become a highly personal vision of God. 'Her religion,' as Godwin wrote in his *Memoir* of her shortly after her death, 'was almost entirely of her own creation. But she was not on that account less attached to it, or the less scrupulous in discharging what she considered as its duties.'[6]

At the time Godwin met Wollstonecraft she had not been a church-goer for over four years. Nonetheless, on that occasion they managed to have a row about religion in which, as Godwin recalled, 'her opinions approached much nearer to the received one, than mine'.[7] By the time they met again, in 1796, Godwin was an atheist. This meeting was much more successful than the first: they became friends, then lovers, then husband and wife — and meanwhile went on disagreeing about religion. 'How can you blame me for taking refuge in the idea of a God, when I despair of finding sincerity here on earth?' Wollstonecraft demanded at one low point two months before her death.[8] At any rate, little as he would have wanted it, it was Godwin who had the last word, since after his wife's premature death it was left to him to produce an account of her religious beliefs in his *Memoir*. Wollstonecraft's religion, he wrote, was 'in reality, little allied to any system of forms' and 'was founded rather in taste, than in the niceties of polemical discussion':

> Her mind constitutionally attached itself to the sublime and the amiable. She found an inexpressible delight in the beauties of nature, and in the splendid reveries of the imagination. But nature itself, she thought, would be no better than a vast blank, if the mind of the observer did not supply it with an animating soul. When she walked amidst the wonders of nature, she was accustomed to converse with her God. To her mind he was pictured as not less amiable, generous and kind, than great, wise and exalted.[9]

Further on in his text, Godwin linked this style of religious belief to what he described as a faculty of intuition 'possessed [by Mary] in a degree superior to any other person I ever knew':

> She adopted one opinion, and rejected another, spontaneously, by a sort of tact, and the force of a cultivated imagination; and yet, though perhaps, in the strict sense of the term, she reasoned little, it is surprising what a degree of soundness is to be found in her determinations.[10]

'She reasoned little': — this of the woman who had translated and reviewed theological works in three languages, who was familiar with most of the major theological writings of her century, and who consistently argued that true religion was not a mere matter of enthusiastic sentiment but rather 'a governing principle of conduct, drawn from self-knowledge, and rational opinion respecting the attributes of God'.[11]

Godwin's difficulty in taking seriously the intellectual basis of Wollstonecraft's theology reflected more than just a rather tacky set of male prejudices. In fact it was symptomatic of important underlying shifts of attitude in the late eighteenth century, as religious belief became increasingly aligned with the feminine and as both came under the rule of sentiment, what Godwin described as the 'empire of feeling'. In the second edition of his *Memoir*, Godwin revised his account of Wollstonecraft's 'intellectual character' so as to make some of these connections more explicit. The difference between the sexes, he argued there, corresponds to the psychological opposition between reason and emotion. He and Wollstonecraft, he believed, exemplified this divide, he being dominated by 'habits of deduction', while she enjoyed an 'intuitive sense of the pleasures of the imagination', which eventually aroused his own emotions as well: 'Her taste awakened mine; her sensibility determined me to a careful development of my feelings.'[12] So, while the philosopher could not follow his wife into her religious beliefs, he nonetheless became a convert to the deep sense of personal truth reflected in them, the 'fearless and unstudied veracity' of Wollstonecraft's womanly heart.

This portrait of the woman of sensibility (at one point Godwin called Wollstonecraft a 'female Werther') tells us less about Wollstonecraft than it does about prevailing sexual mores — and Godwin's haphazard attempts to keep his wife's stormy history within the boundaries of them. This is not to deny that Wollstonecraft enjoyed donning the cloak of female Wertherism at times, but the idea of a uniquely feminine emotionality was of course anathema to her, a central target of her feminism. It is an unhappy irony that much of the *Rights of Woman* is taken up with denouncing precisely the type of hyper-idealisation of womanhood that Godwin produced in his eulogy. Nonetheless, there is an important moment in Wollstonecraft's own writings where she appears in a guise very similar to Godwin's sentimentalised portrayal. This is as the eponymous heroine of her first, semi-autobiographical, novel — *Mary, a Fiction* (1788) — the story of a young woman of 'great soul', whose tale of youthful passions and exquisite enthusiasms was told by its young author with a blend of sympathetic respect and ironic detachment. 'I have lately written a fiction,' Wollstonecraft wrote to a friend at the time, 'to illustrate an opinion of mine, that a genius will educate itself. I have drawn from nature.'[13] The genius is her own; the tale is of the education of a female self through suffering — a woman's inchoate, traumatic search for a position from which she may know and speak herself. The book is crammed with voyages, but all with one ultimate destination: the discovery of a 'being...whose grandeur is derived from the operation of its own faculties, not subjugated to opinion'.[14] And the core faculty through which this sense of authentic self is realised is the imagination:

> Those chosen few wish to speak for themselves, not to be an echo — even of the sweetest sounds....The paradise they ramble in, must be of their own creating — or the prospect soon grows insipid, and not varied by a vivifying principle, fades and dies.[15]

The relationship between this 'vivifying principle' of the creative mind and religious belief is a central theme of the book. The fictive Mary's life, particularly in her early years, is dominated by what Wollstonecraft describes as 'enthusiastic sentiments of devotion':

> Sublime ideas filled her young mind — always connected with devotional sentiments....The wandering spirits, which she imagined inhabited every part of nature, were her constant friends and confidants. She began to consider the Great First Cause, formed just notions of his attributes, and, in particular, dwelt on his wisdom and goodness.[16]

At night the adolescent Mary 'converses' with God and sings hymns 'of her own composing' until at times she almost hallucinates her Creator: 'only an infinite being could fill the human soul'.[17] At fifteen, she decides to receive the holy sacrament and in order to prepare herself 'would sit up half the night', 'perusing the scriptures, and discussing some points of doctrine which puzzled her'. The oscillation between an almost ecstatic communion with God and the fierce intellectualism of the student of theology vividly calls up the adolescent Wollstonecraft. In the life of the fictive Mary, it climaxes in the great day of her 'baptismal vow':

> ...she hailed the morn, and sung with wild delight, Glory to God on high, good will towards men. She was indeed so much affected when she joined in the prayer for her eternal preservation, that she could hardly conceal her violent emotions; and the recollection never failed to wake her dormant piety when earthly passions made it grow languid.[18]

But alas for bright young hopes: Mary's unloving parents contract her to a mercenary marriage, from which she flees to female friendship and the love of a dying man, combined with various nerve-wracking adventures and the doing of good works. It ends with Mary left with 'a heart in which there was a void, that even benevolence and religion could not fill' and the eager anticipation of an early death.[19] It is hard not to agree with Wollstonecraft's later verdict that the book was 'a crude production',[20] yet also an audacious and fascinating one, not least in its anticipation of many of the key themes of the *Rights of Woman*. Central to these is the connection established between religion, eroticism and female subjectivity.

Throughout most of her history, the fictive Mary — like her author — is a virgin: she and her young husband separate before the marriage is consummated and remain apart until the penultimate chapter. The man she loves touches her soul but never her body, and when she finally does join her husband it is only to deliver herself to him in a fugue of despair: 'when her husband would take her hand, or mention anything like love, she would instantly feel a sickness, a faintness at her heart, and wish...that the earth would open and swallow her'.[21] In the end it is religion only which makes life 'supportable', and Mary is left with her only 'gleam of joy' being the thought that 'she was hastening to that world, where there is neither marrying, nor giving in marriage'. The message is direct: a loveless marriage can produce only sexual revulsion. Yet when it comes to Henry, the sensitive invalid whom Mary does love, Wollstonecraft's position is much hazier. That Henry is loved with passion is made explicit, but just what the source and character of this passion is, is much more ambiguous. It is at this point in the text that Wollstonecraft's prose, never particularly lucid throughout the novel, becomes tortuously congested and difficult to follow. Why it is so hard for her to get something coherent on to the page becomes clearer, however, when we look carefully at the ideas with which she was struggling. Here is her account of the moment when Mary realises the strength of her feeling for Henry, at the point when he has just told her of his fatherly affection for her, his wish to view her as his 'darling child'. Mary is overwhelmed:

> He had called her his dear girl...his child! His child, what an association of ideas! If I had a father, such a father! — She could not dwell on the thoughts, the wishes which obtruded themselves. Her mind was unhinged, and passion unperceived filled her whole soul.[22]

The reader barely has time to draw breath from this extraordinary passage before Mary tackles Henry directly about her views on love. Henry has previously told her of his own propensity towards romantic fantasy — 'my fancy has too frequently delighted to form a creature that I could love, that could convey to my soul sensations which the gross part of mankind have not any conception of' — and now Mary reciprocates with an account of her own 'flights of the imagination' and the 'tumultuous passions' which give them wing. In her case, however — and here Wollstonecraft ties together the enthusiastically devout young theologian with the loving woman — these passions are ultimately divinely inspired and divinely directed. The erotic imagination is directed towards mortal man only as a 'faint image' of a much greater love. She begins her peroration with a quotation: 'Milton has asserted, That earthly love is the scale by which to heavenly we may ascend' and then elaborates:

> The same turn of mind which leads me to adore the Author of all Perfection — which leads me to conclude that he only can fill my soul, forces me to admire the faint image — the shadows of his attributes here below; and my imagination gives still bolder strokes to them. I know I am in some degree under the influence of a delusion — but does not this strong delusion prove that I myself 'am of subtiler essence than the trodden clod'; these flights of imagination point to futurity; I cannot banish them.

The tone then alters:

> Every cause in nature produces an effect; and am I an exception to the general rule? have I desires implanted in me only to make me miserable? will they never be gratified? shall I never be happy? My feelings do not accord with the notion of solitary happiness. In a state of bliss, it will be the society of beings we can love, without the alloy that earthly infirmities mix with our best affections, that will constitute great part of our happiness.[23]

'With these notions can I conform to the maxims of worldly wisdom?' she concludes by demanding, in what amounts to a virtual manifesto for the rights of the heart as against the 'cold dictates of worldly wisdom'. She concludes with a terrific flourish: 'My conscience does not smite me, and that Being who is greater than the internal monitor, may approve of what the world condemns.' But what exactly it is that God condones while the world condemns is never clear: is Mary propositioning Henry, reflecting on her separation from her husband, or simply embracing the inevitable martyrdom of a romantic spirit in a cynical world? Or should the post-Freudian reader also begin to speculate about the alignment between love of Henry, with all his fatherly affection for her, and love of the Divine Father (into whose hands, Wollstonecraft tells us, Mary nightly delivers her soul)? Clearly Wollstonecraft herself did not know; and her unhappy heroine, bewildered by misfortune, can only conclude with a sigh: 'the world...is ever hostile and armed against the feeling heart!'[24]

But it was not only worldly opinion which needed to arm itself against feeling hearts and impassioned imaginings. By the time Wollstonecraft wrote the *Rights of Woman* — and the argument is implicit in her first novel as well — she thought that it was women in particular who needed to defend themselves against romantic passion. Rather than identifying with her fictive Mary's views on love, Wollstonecraft implies that these views are excessive: Mary has been 'unhinged', love has 'blotted out' 'every other remembrance and wish'. But even in her unhinged state, Mary too reveals an ambivalence about sexuality. It is expressed, however, not in terms of her feelings for Henry but rather in terms of her attitude towards the erotic imagination: 'I know I am in some degree under the influence of a delusion.' But what exactly is this delusion, and what are its implications for women's psychology? And, perhaps even more important for the purposes of this chapter, what non-delusional mode of perception is it being set against? The answer to the last, at least, the fictive Mary herself gives us. 'You may tell me I follow a fleeting good, an *ignis fatuus*; but this chase, these struggles prepare me for eternity,' she tells Henry, quoting Corinthians: 'when I no longer see through a glass darkly I shall not reason about, but *feel* in what happiness consists'.[25] Erotic illusion becomes eternal truth only in the presence of God.

I return to the relationship between Wollstonecraft's theism and her sexual philosophy below. But first a look at the ideological setting in which *Mary, a Fiction* was written.

That one of feminism's earliest fictional heroines should appear draped in the mantle of piety is unsurprising if we recall the centuries of religious proto-feminism which preceded Wollstonecraft's novel. In England, the spiritual equality of women had been a contested theme within Protestantism since the Reformation. Puritanism in particular, with its fierce emphasis on the democracy of God's grace, had long provided female believers with a language of spiritual self-assertion, and even the Church of England harboured godly feminists. 'Whatever....Reasons Men may have for despising Women, and keeping them in Ignorance and Slavery, it can't be from their having learnt to do so in Holy Scripture,' the High Anglican Mary Astell claimed in 1700, adding stoutly that 'the Bible is for, and not against us.'[26] Calls to a higher life — whether it meant an intensification of female piety in the home or even, as in the case of seventeenth- and eighteenth-century women preachers, leaving their households to spread God's Word — was a route to enhanced self-esteem and moral status, and sometimes to the potential subversion of Female Duty. 'I chose to obey God rather than man,' one female preacher wrote on abandoning her husband in order to serve her Maker,[27] and the appeal of such forms of religious obedience to many insubordinate female spirits is easily imagined.

The religious revival which had swept Britain from the 1730s onwards carried such aspirations in its wake, although with diminishing force. The decline of the militant spirit which had fostered the revival, combined with stricter policing of sexual divisions within its ranks, led to women's spiritual claims being pushed either to the margins of the movement or outside evangelicalism entirely. So, while the 'enthusiastic' religious impulses of the fictive Mary are clearly revivalist in tone, by the time the book was written her bossy pronouncements on spiritual matters — so reminiscent of early Puritan women preachers — would certainly have been deemed improper by most evangelicals.

Moreover, although Wollstonecraft's young heroine is represented as belonging to the Established Church, she is hardly orthodox in her opinions, displaying many of the deistical sentiments characteristic of the liberal Enlightenment. In the mid 1780s Wollstonecraft had begun attending the chapel of Reverend Richard Price, the leading figure in the radical community of Rational Dissenters (or Unitarians, as they became known) living in Newington Green, north of London. Wollstonecraft never joined Price's flock, but the impact of his brand of radical nonconformity on her first novel is easily recognised. Mary's lack of interest in Christ; her reverential attitude towards Nature; her view of God as a benign and reasonable Author of All Things rather than an all-powerful Jehovah: all these point to the 'rational religious sentiments' which by the time the *Rights of Woman* was published had become a linchpin of Wollstonecraft's feminism. 'In treating of the manners of women,' an early chapter uncompromisingly sets out, 'let us, disregarding sexual arguments, trace what we should endeavour to make them in order to co-operate...with the Supreme Being.'[28] And what they should be made was free, in the sense in which Price and his associates advocated it. Liberty, as Price had written in a book Wollstonecraft knew well, was 'the power of acting and determining. And it is self-evident, that where such a power is wanting, there can be no moral capacities.' Liberty and reason, he argued, 'constitute the capacity of virtue'.[29] Or as Wollstonecraft put it: 'the conduct of an accountable being must be regulated by the operations of its own reason; or on what foundation rests the throne of God?...Liberty is the mother of virtue.'[30] Without freedom to act and think for themselves, women could not attain their full status as moral beings; without that status they could not save their immortal souls. The enslavement of women is their damnation both in this life and in the hereafter.

Women's rights, in other words, are an essential prerequisite to women's redemption. This emphasis in Wollstonecraft's thought on secular gains as a means to spiritual goals is possibly one of the most difficult for Western feminists to appreciate today; yet both her first novel and the *Rights of Woman* are suffused with it. The case is clearly put: if the human soul were not immortal — if our brief existence terminated at death — then female oppression, however censurable in itself, would be only one more of those infinite woes which make up our lot in this vale of tears. Social revolution throws into relief the injustice of women's subordinate status and offers opportunities for change, but it is the prospect of life beyond all such mortal contrivances which makes women's sufferings as a sex wholly reprehensible — for in enslaving women on earth men have also been denying them heaven. Only a free soul can seek and know God; but women have been either regarded as soulless (like most Europeans, Wollstonecraft thought Muslims were particularly culpable in this respect) or refused the spiritual and intellectual freedom from which true devotion arises. Yet, if we are all made in the image of God, how can the profane distinction of sex override the sacred equality of souls? 'It be not philosophical to speak of sex when the soul is mentioned,' Wollstonecraft insisted in staunch Augustinian fashion,[31] in contradiction to many who held otherwise — notably Milton, whose poetic vision of Eve's spiritual subordination to Adam Wollstonecraft constantly invoked and repudiated. 'God is thy law, thou mine:' she quotes Milton's Eve: 'to know no more/ Is woman's happiest knowledge and her praise'. Such advice, she comments typically, is 'that I have used to children' and is surely not appropriate to adult women:

For if it be allowed that women were destined by Providence to acquire human virtues, and, by the exercise of their understandings, that stability of character which is the firmest ground to rest our future hopes upon, they must be permitted to turn to the foundation of light, and not forced to shape their course by the twinkling of a mere satellite.[32]

Women owe fealty to none but God, and even to Him true devotion is self-willed rather than externally dictated. The 'common father' commands us through our own rationality. 'Rational religion...is a submission to the will of a being so perfectly wise, that all he wills must be directed by the proper motive — must be reasonable.'[33] Why should women offer to mere mortal men the blind devotion which enlightened men would themselves never be willing to offer — even to God? 'Let us then, as children of the same parent...reason together, and learn to submit to the authority of Reason...they alone are subject to blind authority who have no reliance on their own strength. They are free — who will be free!'[34]

Wollstonecraft's insistent representation of God as paternal had many meanings, of which the most obvious was as a rhetorical weapon against secular male authority. As spiritual sisters and brothers, with equal status in God's sight, neither men nor women are entitled to ascendancy over the other, yet both may claim respect 'founded on the same principle' as is our devotion to God Himself, that is on reverence for those virtues — wisdom, goodness and mercy — which are the basis of all ethical life, human or divine. We love and worship God, Wollstonecraft argues, for these virtues, rather than for His omnipotence. Worship is not a submission to divine power; it is a product of our own impassioned rationality and idealising imagination which bring us to the loving comprehension of our Divine Father's righteousness.[35] Wollstonecraft insists on this — and for a very good reason: it provides her with an alternative model of relations between men and women. 'It were to be wished that women would cherish an affection for their husbands,' she writes, 'founded on the same principle that devotion [to God] ought to rest upon.'[36] This sounds shockingly retrograde until one realises exactly what she is saying. Men should be loved inasmuch — and only inasmuch — as they possess those virtues to which their wives and daughters may freely and rationally accord respect, and just so also should women be respected and loved. Power alone, whether of man, woman, or God, is entitled to nothing.

But 'a king is always a king, and a woman always a woman'.[37] Rank and sex deform the natural community of humanity, fomenting 'false distinctions' and preventing the 'rational converse' which links individuals to each other and to God. 'The stamen of immortality...is the perfectibility of human reason' but 'outwardly ornamented with elaborate care, and so adorned to delight man, "that with honour he may love", the soul of woman is not allowed to have this distinction.' Thus the female sex is disendowed not only of its natural freedom but also of its ethical integrity. 'They were made to be loved, and must not aim at respect, lest they should be hunted out of society as masculine.'[38]

Throughout Wollstonecraft's writings this moral privation is attributed chiefly to the cultural inscription of femininity as a state of eroticised infantilism. Little women are trained to become 'coquettes', in the term most often used in the *Rights of Woman*; the 'pretty play things' of men, as Wollstonecraft dubbed them in *Mary, a Fiction*. Chapter 5 of the *Rights of Woman*, entitled 'Animadversions on Some of the Writers Who Have Rendered Women Objects of Pity, Bordering on Contempt', scrutinised some of the popular prescriptions for sexual modesty offered to women by bestselling male moralists, to show how often high-minded sentiments masked lubricity. The text marked out for particular opprobrium here was Rousseau's *Emile*, in which he had painted a hugely influential portrait of ideal femininity in the person of Sophie, lover and wife of the eponymous boy citizen. Wollstonecraft quoted his account of Sophie's deportment at length:

> Her dress is extremely modest in appearance, and yet very coquettish in fact: she does not make a display of her charms, she conceals them; but in concealing them, she knows how to affect your imagination. Everyone who sees her will say, There is a modest and discreet girl; but while you are near her, your eyes and affections wander all over her person, so that you cannot withdraw them; and you would conclude, that every part of her dress, simple as it seems, was only put in its proper order to be taken to pieces by the imagination.[39]

'Is this modesty?' Wollstonecraft wants to know. 'Is this a preparation for immortality?' In fact, she concluded, a girl educated to such behaviour is better suited for an 'Eastern harem' than decent womanhood. 'I cannot see why women should always be made subservient to love or lust.'[40]

This sexual objectification of women was a target of all Wollstonecraft's writings, but its most far-reaching critique is to be found in the *Rights of Woman* where it is not only the exploitation of women within sexual relations which stands condemned, but physical sexuality in general. 'The depravity of the appetite which brings the sexes together', in Wollstonecraft's words, corrupts both sexes. 'Nature must ever be the standard of taste...' she writes, 'yet how grossly is nature insulted by the voluptuary' which renders women 'the slaves of casual lust'. Sexual pleasure is always and everywhere lascivious, even within marriage:

> In order to fulfil the duties of life, and to be able to pursue with vigour the various employments which form the moral character, a master and mistress of a family ought not to continue to love each other with passion. I mean to say that they ought not to indulge those emotions which disturb the order of society, and engross the thoughts that should otherwise be employed....I will go still further, and advance, without dreaming of a paradox, that an unhappy marriage is often advantageous to a family, and that the neglected wife is, in general, the best mother.[41]

Statements like these — and the *Rights of Woman* is littered with them — have led a number of commentators, unsurprisingly, to describe Wollstonecraft as a sexual puritan. The *Rights of Woman*, Cora Kaplan has argued, 'expresses a violent antagonism to the sexual, it exaggerates the importance of the sensual in the everyday life of women and betrays the most profound anxiety about the rupturing force of female sexuality'.[42] Mary Poovey, in her major study of Wollstonecraft's relationship to eighteenth-century sexual ideology, makes a similar point, arguing that Wollstonecraft's sexual outlook was heavily inflected by the repressive codes of propriety characteristic of the new middle class.[43] At one level this is clearly right, although much more needs to be said on the subject than is possible here. But the picture is incomplete. For, alongside this aversion to the physical erotic in Wollstonecraft's early writings, there also exists, as we have seen, an equally important emphasis on love as a primary spiritual force. Far from turning away from Eros, Wollstonecraft persistently celebrates it as the dynamic centre of the human psyche whose source, however, is the creative mind, not the body, and whose direction must be heavenward. A soul in love has only one right object. 'I see the sons and daughters of men pursuing shadows, and anxiously wasting their powers to feed passions which have no adequate object,' Wollstonecraft writes, and then, more satirically:

> To see a mortal adorn an object with imaginary charms, and then fall down and worship the idol which he had himself set up — how ridiculous!... Would not all the purposes of life have been much better fulfilled if he had only felt what has been termed physical love? And would not the sight of the object, not seen through the medium of the imagination, soon reduce the passion to an appetite if reflection, the noble distinction of man, did not give it force, and make it an instrument to raise him above this earthly dross, by teaching him to love the centre of all perfection...?[44]

The 'deification of the beloved object' in erotic love is a shadowy intimation of our love of the Deity; the erotic imagination is implanted in us by God to lead us towards Him. If directed exclusively toward mortal objects, the imagination becomes — in the term Wollstonecraft used to describe both Rousseau and Burke's fantasies about women — 'debauched': delusional, corrupting, and particularly invidious in its consequences for women. When directed toward the divine, however, it illuminates the soul and gives us clear evidence of our immortality.

This concept of the divinely oriented erotic imagination was inherited by Wollstonecraft, via Milton and Rousseau, from the long tradition of Christian Platonism. References to Plato's love philosophy appear in Wollstonecraft's writings from 1787 onwards. If women are merely to be loved for their 'animal perfection', she rebuked Burke in 1790, then 'Plato and Milton were grossly mistaken in asserting that human love led to heavenly', but if one accepts the Platonic view that love of the divine is 'only an exaltation of [earthly] affection' then women too must be loved for their rational virtues rather than their physical attributes.[45] The feminist twist was new, but the general argument had its source in what James Turner, in his fine study of Christian sexual theorising, has described as the 'Christianisation of the Platonic Eros' to be found in Augustine and many varieties of post-Augustinian theology, leading up to Milton.[46] 'Thy affections are the steps; thy will the way;' Augustine had written, 'by loving thou mountest, by neglect thou descendest.'[47] Desires that ascend towards God are to be radically distinguished from those that descend toward earthly things, yet both are designated as Eros — the love that links humanity to the divine. Those moralists who would disdain earthly affections, Christian Platonists thus argued, are in fact apostates, denying their connection to God. 'They...who complain of the delusions of passion,' Wollstonecraft wrote, 'do not recollect that they are exclaiming against a strong proof of the immortality of the soul.'[48]

This valorisation of love points to one of the most abiding tensions within Christian morality. On the one hand, sexual love has functioned as the key trope for relations between God and the church across the entire Judeao-Christian tradition, and marriage as the central metaphor for the consummation of all things. On the other hand, love's physical expression, with a few heretical exceptions, has been either condemned *in toto* or confined to the marital bed. Christian Platonism, with its celebration of earthly affections as the vehicle for transcendent devotion, elevated this ambivalence into a primary theological principle. Milton, as so often, brings the dilemma into focus. In *Paradise Lost*, Adam, confronted with Eve, finds himself yearning for more than just intimations of the divine, and is scolded by the Archangel:

> What higher in her society thou find'st
> Attractive, human, rational, love still;
> In loving thou dost well, in passion not,
> Wherein true Love consists not; love refines
> The thoughts, and heart enlarges, hath his seat
> In Reason, and is judicious, is the scale
> By which to heav'nly Love thou may'st ascend,
> Not sunk in carnal pleasure.

Wollstonecraft quotes from these lines repeatedly, returning to the text apparently for its anti-erotic message, but also, one begins to suspect, for its libidinal intensity — a suspicion heightened by her insistent recourse to one of the most sexily Miltonic books of the age, Rousseau's *La Nouvelle Héloïse*, in which the adulterous passion of two lovers becomes transmuted into divine ardour and the promise of love beyond the grave. While Milton, however, had called upon the will to re-orient desire from its earthly to its transcendent object, Rousseau's Platonism relied on the workings of the erotic imagination to draw love towards its source — the theme which became so central to Wollstonecraft's writing.

In his writings on sexuality Rousseau famously distinguished between two varieties of eroticism: 'physical love', based on instinctual sexual appetite, and 'moral love', based on the fantasisation of an ideal love object. One of the central psychological lessons of both *La Nouvelle Héloïse* and *Emile* is that it is moral love, not physical, which acts as the *primum mobile* of human affective life. Sexual desire is a product of fantasy.

The senses are awakened by the imagination alone. Their need is not properly a physical need. It is not true that it is a true need. If no lewd object had ever struck our eyes, if no indecent idea had ever entered our minds, perhaps this alleged need would never have made itself felt to us, and we would have remained chaste without temptation, without effort, and without merit.[49]

Emile's love for Sophie — like the adulterous desire of St Preux for the heroine, Julie, in *La Nouvelle Héloïse* — is based on a passionate erotic idealisation. Men imaginatively create the women they desire. Women on the other hand, Rousseau mostly wants to suggest, must take what they can get in the way of husbands, so their imaginations are best confined to their wardrobes. But as always in Rousseau's writings on women, other ideas surface, apparently without the author's intention. In Sophie's case, this happens when a second Sophie, an alter-Sophie, suddenly appears in the text, only to disappear into her bedroom with a copy of Fenelon's romantic novel *Telemachus*. There this new Sophie remains, lost in erotic fantasies of Fenelon's hero, until her parents despair and Rousseau himself — alarmed at the fate of his little heroine — steps in to eliminate the Rousseauite interloper and restore the original Sophie, happily a less imaginative creature. Rousseau's conclusion to this peculiar episode demonstrated very clearly the paradoxes in his thought, of which Wollstonecraft claimed she was so fond. The alter-Sophie interlude was, he declared,

> a striking example that, in spite of the prejudices born of the morals of our age, enthusiasm for the decent and the fine is no more foreign to women than to men, and that there is nothing that cannot be obtained under nature's direction from women as well as from men.[50]

Certainly, the example seems to have struck Wollstonecraft. She was reading *Emile* when she was writing *Mary, a Fiction*, and, although the preface to the novel explicitly declared that her heroine was 'not a Sophie', it does not seem farfetched to suggest that the fictive Mary probably owes much to Sophie mark two. At any rate, both Mary and her author were clearly indebted to Rousseau for their views on the erotic imagination, as was the heroine of Wollstonecraft's last, unfinished novel, *The Wrongs of Woman: or, Maria*. *Maria*, published posthumously in 1798, is a gothic tale of love and betrayal, in which Wollstonecraft, having resurrected the Mary of her first novel, sets her on another stony path. Like her predecessor, Maria is an inveterate fantasist: imprisoned by her wicked husband in a lunatic asylum, she spends her time in imaginative reverie, until eventually she encounters a fellow prisoner, another sensitive man of large soul, again named Henry. Like Mary before her, she proceeds to construct him as an erotic object: 'Maria's imagination found repose in portraying the possible virtues the world might contain. Pygmalion formed an ivory maid, and longed for a informing soul. She, on the contrary, combined all the qualities of a hero's mind, and fate presented a statue in which she might enshrine them.'[51] This Henry even lends her a copy of Rousseau's *La Nouvelle Héloïse* to underline the point. 'We see what we wish, and make a world of our own,' Wollstonecraft told her readers; 'Maria now, imagining that she had found a being of celestial mould — was happy.'[52]

'True voluptuousness must proceed from the mind,' the *Rights of Woman* declared in the best Rousseauite fashion,[53] and the minds of such cerebral voluptuaries are inevitably superior to those absorbed in pleasures of a less ethereal variety. Here Wollstonecraft's heroines, like their author, joined that veritable army of eighteenth-century middle-class sentimentalists preoccupied with distinguishing their high-minded enthusiasms from the crasser desires of lesser mortals. The fictive Mary and Maria's other-worldly imaginings are not appreciated, much less shared, by most of the people around them, and even their romantic Henries either expire or turn out to have feet of clay. Men in general, Wollstonecraft explained in 1792, are coarser and more animal-like in their natures than women: an argument with formidable staying power in the feminist tradition. Nor was the man of her own dreams exempt from such a charge. A letter to Gilbert Imlay in 1794 accused him of lacking the 'magic wand' of the imagination which 'convert[s] appetite into love'.

> Ah! my friend, you know not the ineffable delight, the exquisite pleasure, which arises from a unison of affection and desire, when the whole soul and senses are abandoned to a lively imagination, that renders every emotion delicate and rapturous. Yes; these are emotions, over which satiety has no power...[emotions which] appear to me to be the distinctive characteristic of genius, the foundation of taste, of that exquisite relish for the beauties of nature, of which the common herd of eaters and drinkers and *child-begeters* [*sic* and her emphasis], certainly have no idea.[54]

Women, the letter implies — or at least women like Wollstonecraft — are as much in touch with the higher part of their nature as men are: a direct rebuttal of the Augustinian dichotomy between masculine spirit and female flesh. In claiming for herself the potential for imaginative 'genius', Wollstonecraft was thus explicitly defying the equation between femininity and animal carnality which dominated so much Christian thinking, insisting instead on a psycho-moral equality rooted in the common possession of soul, reason and the impassioned imagination — the capacities that link us to God. In 1790, responding to Burke's suggestion that women should mimic infantile tottering and lisping in order to enhance their sexual attractiveness, Wollstonecraft pointed out that such advice denies women not only the virtues which prepare them for heaven but also the self-respect to which they are entitled on earth. 'If beautiful weakness be interwoven in a woman's frame, if the chief business of her life be...to inspire love...her duty and happiness in this life must clash with any preparation for a more exalted state...for the love of the Deity, which is mixed with most profound reverence, must be love of perfection, and not compassion for weakness.' 'What can make us reverence ourselves' she demanded, 'but a reverence for that Being of whom we are but a faint image?' 'I FEAR God...[and] this fear of God makes me reverence myself.'[55]

But female self-reverence, as Wollstonecraft knew all too well, is hard-won, easily lost. 'You know my opinion of men in general;' she wrote to Imlay in 1794 as he was drifting away from her after the birth of their daughter, 'you know that I think them systematic tyrants, and that it is the rarest thing in the world, to meet with a man with sufficient delicacy of feeling to govern desire.'[56] But for this man it was she who felt an ungovernable desire, a passionate sexual love which ultimately became an agony of self-destructive humiliation. No suggestion to Imlay that they two should transfer their devotions from each other to God — far from it. 'My friend — my dearest friend — ' she writes in 1795, 'I feel my fate united to yours by the most sacred principles of my soul...'[57] And for the fate that followed, the loss of Imlay, not even religious faith could console her. 'I have loved with my whole soul, only to discover that I had no chance of return — and that existence is a burden without it.'[58] To escape that burden she was prepared to lose perhaps her soul as well as her life, in a suicidal plunge from Putney Bridge.

For women it seems, divine love is a much more reliable bet than the profane variety. 'When friends are unkind,' as Wollstonecraft wrote, 'and the heart has not the prop on which it fondly leaned, where can the tender suffering being fly but to the Searcher of hearts?'[59] The figure to whom her own suffering soul flew, as we have seen, was almost invariably paternal: an image of divine fatherhood, perfect in his power and his love. This fantasy found echoes in her idealising affection for a number of benevolent older men in her life — most notably Richard Price and the publisher Joseph Johnson — and also in the imagery of ideal manhood which dominated her early political rhetoric, particularly *A Vindication of the Rights of Men*. To love liberty, as she argued typically there, is a 'masculine godlike affection'.[60] The identification with such fantasies of phallic perfection, so evident in the *Rights of Men*, was clearly an important source of her theism; and certainly as an ego-ideal the vision of an omniscient, omnipotent Father of Love served her much better than memories of her own drunken father and withdrawn, ineffectual mother. 'That civilisation, that the cultivation of the understanding, and refinement of the affections, naturally make a man religious, I am proud to acknowledge,' she wrote in the *Rights of Men*. 'What else can fill the aching void in the heart, that human pleasures, human friendships can never fill? What but a profound reverence for the model of all perfection, and the mysterious tie which arises from a love of goodness? What can make us reverence ourselves, but a reverence for that Being, of whom we are a faint image?'[61] Such self-reverence, 'enlightened self-love' as she described it elsewhere, had not been a lesson taught at home. 'Could she have loved her father or mother, had they returned her affection' she wrote of the fictive Mary, 'she would not so soon, perhaps, have sought out a new world'[62] and perhaps would have been able to find within her own troubled self the image of a loving, regarding presence which no parent, or lover, ever provided. 'I have lived in an ideal world,' she told Imlay in 1795, 'and fostered sentiments that you do not comprehend — or you would not treat me thus. Forget that I exist: I will never remind you.'[63]

And it is these contradictions — painful confusions — in Wollstonecraft's thought and feelings which point to what I believe, finally, to be the real key to her theology — the dilemmas of women's sexual subjectivity as she lived and understood them. 'I have examined myself with more care than formerly,' Wollstonecraft wrote to Imlay at one point, 'and find...that aiming at tranquillity, I have almost destroyed all the energy of my soul.' 'Love is a want of my heart.[64]' This energy of heart and soul, which Freud later dubbed libido, is the erotic core of the personality — the 'enthusiastic' portion of her character, as Wollstonecraft described it. This eroticism, as Freud demonstrated, does not simply draw us toward others — mortal or divine — but in fact forms us as women or men — as psychically gendered individuals — through an amorous identification with the images of our desire. As children, we turn to our fathers and mothers with the idealising love which inscribes on our psyches the images of masculinity and femininity which are the basis of our sexual self-identity. This worshipful identification with our parents — every child's personal gods — forms the threads from which our subjectivity is woven. In this sense, Wollstonecraft's preference for divine images over human ones is no more exotic or archaic than the unconscious ego itself, built on the history of its *amours*. We all become what we have loved.

Identifying with our early loves, as adults we turn to new ones. But for women who love men, this turn is a route into relations of power as well as of desire. Today, perhaps, this is beginning to change, but two hundred years ago the situation for women of Wollstonecraft's class was, in certain respects at least, actually worsening. Although the century had seen some slow erosion of gender barriers in areas of intellectual and professional life — witness Wollstonecraft's own career as a literary lady — this was countered by a discursive hardening of gender definitions within genteel culture. Being a woman, as Wollstonecraft so bitterly complained, had become being nothing *but* a woman, that is a being defined by its sexual functions. Even the idea of a gender-free spirituality was deeply suspect, so pervasive was the hyperfeminisation of womanhood.

'The soul of a perfect woman and a perfect man ought to be no more alike than their faces,' as Rousseau had one of his female characters state in *La Nouvelle Héloïse*, 'All our vain imitations of your sex are absurd...and discourage the tender passion we were made to inspire.'[65] Denied any space outside eroticised femininity, finding their image only in male eyes, where were women to turn for a sense of self which affirmed the integrity of mind and emotion? 'A wild wish has just flown from my heart to my head.' Wollstonecraft wrote in the *Rights of Woman*, 'I do earnestly wish to see the distinction of sex confounded'[66] and it was through the loving identification with 'the image of God implanted in our nature' that this emancipation from the feminine could occur. 'What can make us reverence ourselves,' she demanded, 'but a reverence for that Being, of whom we are a faint image?' It is only on this basis of this righteous self-worship that women's ethical selfhood can emerge, beyond the eroticising male gaze. 'It is not sufficient to view ourselves as we suppose that we are viewed by others....We should rather endeavour to view ourselves as we suppose that Being views us who seeeth each thought ripen into action, and whose judgement never swerves from the eternal rule of right.'[67]

Such ethical submission to God will free women from masculine pretensions to moral hegemony, just as the amorous subjugation of the feminine heart to divine love will redeem women from the corrosive power relations of human sexuality. 'These may be termed Utopian dreams,' Wollstonecraft writes, but 'Thanks to that Being who impressed them on my soul, and gave me sufficient strength of mind to dare to exert my own reason, till, becoming dependent only on Him for the support of my virtue, I view, with indignation, the mistaken notions that enslave my sex.'[68] For these notions she would substitute the 'dignity of a rational will that only bows to God and forgets that the universe contains any being but itself and the model of perfection to which its ardent gaze is turned':[69] a form of subjection — simultaneously rational, impassioned and imaginative — by which women may achieve an authentic moral subjectivity. To our secular imaginations, such a dream may indeed seem utopian, but if we allow it to become, in Ann Snitow's phrase, a 'dead letter', then we disregard not only the dream but the dreamer — the Mary Wollstonecraft whose hopes for women were inseparable from her spiritual ambitions, and for whom the free female soul was one bound by the love of God.

2. The Imagination of Olympe de Gouges
Joan W. Scott

The last 20 or so years have shown us that there are many ways to write the history of feminism, and it is probably fair to say that most or all of these were exemplified at the Sussex conference. That is as it should be. Mary Wollstonecraft is, after all, a great rallying point for feminist history and feminist iconography. Her *Vindication of the Rights of Woman*, written in the context of debates during the French Revolution, is one of those foundational texts whose arguments have become synonymous with feminism. Whether or not the term 'feminist' was used in her time, and whether or not she applied the label to herself, there is no question that her defence of women's rights and her protests against the exclusion of women from republican citizenship articulated a position that future generations identified as a precursor to their own feminist programmes, however different the historical circumstances within which they operated. Mary Wollstonecraft's feminism is the result of the meaning given to it by subsequent generations of activists and historians of the women's movement. We are in no position to question this by now quite well-established fact of history.

We are, however, in a position to write about Wollstonecraft as the product of a long history of feminism which created (or invented) a continuous tradition for itself. How Wollstonecraft has figured in that tradition, what purposes her work has served and the ways in which her writing has become a vehicle for expressing women's highest aspirations for democracy — these kinds of questions make the history of feminism itself the object of our inquiry and allow us to go beyond a simple reiteration of its premises and conclusions.

I want to argue that great figures like Wollstonecraft become great through their incorporation into a feminist tradition, and that we can learn a great deal about them by studying the creation of that tradition, rather than by assuming that it simply reflects the self-evident and continuous history of women or feminism. Attention to the creation of feminist traditions is attention to the imaginative identifications women make with the past in order to inspire and legitimise their own actions. Indeed, it is the retrospective identification that provides unity and continuity to otherwise disparate and discontinuous movements by and on behalf of women. The history of Wollstonecraft as a feminist, from this perspective, is the history of the uses made of her by subsequent generations.

This is, of course, not the only history of Wollstonecraft or of feminism that one can write. There is another kind of history of feminism for which I want to argue as well: one that focuses on feminists in their own epochs rather than on the place made for them by subsequent movements. This is a history that asks how what comes to be seen as 'feminism' — a claim for the end to women's subordination — is formulated in the context of its times. What makes possible the oppositional stance taken by feminists at any particular moment? Out of what conceptual materials is it fashioned? Feminism, in this approach, is taken to be at once oppositional, but also integral to its time. It is not invented out of whole cloth, but strategically fashioned to exploit inconsistencies, contradictions, and possibilities inherent in the politics of the moment. It is a stance taken with and against the grain of a political theory, system or regime — from the eighteenth century onward, that would be republicanism, democracy, liberal individualism, and democratic socialism.

This second kind of history of feminism — the study of feminists in context — is crucial for the first — the study of the creation of feminist traditions — for it insists on specificity and refuses transcendence. It understands feminism in terms not of teleology, but of discontinuous political strategies, not as an enduring identity of Woman (or women), but as the temporary collective association of many differently positioned females seeking a specific and commonly agreed-upon goal. Such a history asks how collective identities are formed, rather than assuming they already exist, and it understands the agency of subjects to be discursively attributed, rather than an expression of innate individual will. It thus questions many of the assumptions that have been built into notions of a feminist tradition, notions that were ahistorical even as they constructed a history of and for women.

The occasion of the celebration of Mary Wollstonecraft's *Rights of Woman* gave me the opportunity to think about the history of feminism, but I want to illustrate the points I have made about the writing of that history with examples from the life of one of her contemporaries, Olympe de Gouges, the French woman who produced scores of plays, pamphlets and treatises commenting on the events of the Revolution. De Gouges and Wollstonecraft were contemporaries, and they shared a feminist agenda, though they never seem to have met or to have read one another's work. The similarities between them had less to do with the influence of one on the other than with the political framework within which they both operated, one that (despite the obvious and many differences between the politics and political traditions of France and England in the 1790s) was shaped by the French Revolution. By writing about Olympe de Gouges, I can introduce the context of the Revolution, a context which also bears on an appreciation of Mary Wollstonecraft.

De Gouges's career as a revolutionary activist was short. Born in 1748 in Montauban, she had moved to Paris by the early 1770s. There she mingled in opposition circles in the 1780s, writing plays and agitating for their production by the Comédie Française. But it was in 1788 that her first political pamphlet appeared; in it she called for the creation of a 'patriotic fund', consisting of donations from the public, to solve the financial crisis of the realm. In 1791, as the Constitution was being debated, she wrote the piece that was to establish her place in feminist history: the *Declaration of the Rights of Woman and Citizen*. The declaration paralleled the 1789 *Declaration of the Rights of Man and Citizen* article for article, claiming for women the universal rights already recognised for men. In the annals of feminist history, the most frequently cited line in this declaration comes from article 10, which stated that 'no-one ought to be disturbed even for his most fundamental beliefs' and then added, 'if woman has the right to mount to the scaffold, she ought equally to have the right to mount to the tribune' (the tribune being the rostrum in the Assembly and in any public, political arena). De Gouges's death in 1793, at the hands of the Jacobins made this ringing claim a fatal prophecy. From 1788 to 1793 she was a publicist and political activist. At least once, she rushed to the speaker's podium in the Assembly. Outspoken about her views, she was finally guillotined (according to the formal charges brought against her) for threatening the unity of the republic 'one and indivisible' by advocating federalism. But the charges also suggest that she was punished for transgressing the lines of gender so critical for Jacobin hegemony by describing herself, and behaving, as 'a man of state.'[1] Pleading, by turns, patriotism, illness and pregnancy, she failed to overturn her conviction. According to the final report on her case, 'while mounting the scaffold, the condemned, looking at the people, cried out, "Children of the Fatherland, you will avenge my death." Universal cries [none of them ironic, I'm sure] of "Vive la République" were heard among the spectators waving hats in the air.'[2]

Nineteenth-century feminists made de Gouges's phrase one of the slogans of their movement, and the scene of her martyrdom at the hands of the republic became in feminist recountings of it the figure for the recurring fate of feminism. Here was a woman who insisted that the rights of citizenship belonged to anyone who was subject to the law; here was a woman whose claim for that citizenship brought her the full punishment of the law. Born of the republic, feminism was repeatedly sentenced to death by that same republic. The utopian socialist Jeanne Deroin, looking back on her own attempts to insert feminist claims into the Second Republic after the Revolution of 1848, wrote of the many women of her generation who, 'following the example of Olympe de Gouges, had to pay with their lives for their devotion to Justice and Truth.'[3] Deroin thought herself to have been in de Gouges's situation in 1849 when she faced a jeering, all-male crowd during her (unconstitutional) campaign for a legislative seat.[4]

Although de Gouges was eccentric and something of a loner, and although there were other women at the time who equalled her productivity and activism, she became in feminist stories an originary or prototypical figure, an example of defiant womanhood asserting rights she had been unjustly denied. Important details of her political life were lost from view. Her strong monarchist sympathies were ignored or obscured. No one read or cited her many writings other than the *Declaration*; these would have produced a far more complex picture of her ideas since they were a mixed and often contradictory set of proposals for reform. Contradiction and inconsistency were read out of de Gouges's legacy, and she became instead a republican (and later a socialist) heroine, seeking only to realise fully the promises of liberty, equality and fraternity. With this stripped down version of transcendent republican feminism, de Gouges's successors gave their followers an ancestor in their own image, one they could use to inspire actions by infusing them with historical meaning as the connection between the past and the future.

The de Gouges who emerges in this kind of history is hard to place in the context of her times. And yet it is exactly that context that can begin to account for her ability to undertake the kind of action she did. If, instead of assuming that feminism is an inevitable response to the subordination of women, we ask how it appears, under what conditions and in what terms, we can produce the kind of analytical history that not only treats the past historically, but also sharpens our own strategic formulations.

What enabled the articulation of de Gouges's feminism? With what concepts did she represent her self? These two questions are intimately connected, for the question of self-representation is at the heart of feminist practice. Self-representation has to do not only with independence and agency, but with the ways in which an individual gets access to those capacities. It is about subjectivity, as well as about voting; it is at once a conceptual and a practical issue, the link between theory and politics. In the framework of the French Revolution, the right to self-representation was the right of the active citizen; women, who were barred from citizenship because they were deemed incapable of acting on their own behalf, had the right only to be represented by someone else.[5] How, then, could a woman become a citizen, when the law denied her that status?

De Gouges appealed to the universal principles of the Revolution, about which there were conflicting interpretations. It was precisely this conflict or ambiguity that she exploited to make the case for women's citizenship. The individual whose rights were recognised by the Revolution was an abstraction, a colourless, genderless person meant to signify the universal human being. References to this individual as a 'Man' did not have to be taken literally (although the majority of legislators did so), and they were not taken literally by those who argued that women and blacks (slave and free) ought to have the same liberty enjoyed by white men. While some revolutionaries argued that biological or sociological characteristics mattered for the exercise of political rights, others (like Condorcet) insisted that politics was not a total identity but an activity (one of many in a person's varied life), in which all individuals must be allowed to participate.[6] To make her case, de Gouges took advantage of the disagreement and of the ambiguities inherent in the ideas of the individual and of natural rights. She also presented herself as a member of and spokesperson for the Public, that body of literate opinion which had emerged during the eighteenth century as an institutional counter to absolute royal authority.[7]

There was nothing unusual about identifying herself as a member of the Public. During the Old Regime, women were very much a part of the opposition to absolutism, and their activity took more or less overtly political forms. The salons, run by elite women, sponsored the discussions that contributed to what became a critical and dissenting 'public opinion'. This Public included women, but only those of wealth, education and social grace. De Gouges was not a *salonnière*, and she did not participate in these polite, learned centres of sociability, although they provided one example of a public role for women. Rather, she was associated with the more activist circles of women journalists, whose newspapers appealed to a wider and more disaffected constituency than did the salons. Historian Nina Gelbart sees this oppositional journalism — exemplified by *Le Journal des Dames* in its twenty -year history (1759-78) — as the wellspring not only of de Gouges's demands that women participate in politics, but of much of the republican feminism of the Revolution.[8]

De Gouges crafted an identity as a member of the Public and she assumed that women, like men, were rights-bearing individuals. She threw herself into politics, eager to demonstrate women's capacity in this arena. De Gouges's statements confound historians who want to categorise their feminists as proponents of either equality or difference. Neither label fits the strategy she evolved. Sometimes she insisted that she was like a man in her actions. (She told Robespierre that she was '*un grand homme*', while he was a vile slave.)[9] At other times, she reminded her listeners that a woman was speaking. (When she offered to defend the king during his trial, she reminded her audience that 'heroism and generosity are also women's portion, and the Revolution offers more than one example of it.')[10] On still other occasions, she mixed the two: the title of one of her brochures was '*Le Cri du Sage, par une Femme*'.[11] The point was not to establish women's likeness to men in order to qualify for citizenship, but to refute the prevailing equation of active citizenship with masculinity, to make sexual difference irrelevant for politics *and*, at the same time, to associate women — explicitly as women — with the right to self-representation, to citizenship. This apparent contradiction between the relevance and irrelevance of sexual difference was at the heart of the feminist project of constructing a subjective identity for women that would define them as citizens. It was a commentary on the contradiction of the individualism implemented by the Revolution, an individualism that was at once universal in its promise and restricted in its practice (to white men initially, then after 1794 to all men), an individualism that took man to be the representative human and established the sexual desire of man for woman as the normative way to confirm the existence of the self.

Most interestingly, de Gouges explained her ability to act in terms of her imagination. In this she drew on a long-standing discussion of imagination, pursued by Enlightenment philosophers but with many echoes among the general population. Imagination was a varied and ambiguous concept for the Enlightenment. It was seen as the antithesis of reason, the synonym for desire: controlling desire (or imagination) was the reason for reason's existence. Imagination was also taken to be both the source of creativity in the arts, sciences and mathematics and, at the same time, the cause of madness — when fantasy displaced all sense of reality. Writing in the *Encyclopedia*, Voltaire distinguished two kinds of imagination, the active and the passive. The passive imagination was reflective: it imposed images and sensations on the mind, taking over an individual. As with a dream one had while sleeping, no control could be exercised over it. The active imagination involved considered thought, the modification of received images and ideas, the surpassing of what was given in nature by the art of man.[12] Ultimately, the active imagination involved the representation of the self, a presentation to the world that was not a reproduction of something else but an authentic production. Diderot thought women were incapable of such originality; Rousseau thought they were, and that was precisely the problem — women's potential for desire, imagination and originality had to be curbed so that they would only reflect the desire of men.[13] Voltaire made no comment on gender; he worried instead about whether the active imagination could be subject to rational control, whether the distinction could be maintained between benign exercises of fantasy and dangerous departures from reality, and whether the mind could be controlled to prevent the chaos of dreams (which need to be confined to sleep) from taking over while one was awake during the day. The line between fiction and reality, error and truth, madness and sanity, disorder and order needed constant policing by internal mechanisms of self-government. Those who lacked these internal mechanisms needed to be regulated by those who had them, by those reasonable people who understood, respected and embodied the law. Self-regulation was thus the means by which self-representation was realised; here, again, subjectivity and politics defined one another.

The ambiguities of imagination made it both appealing and risky as a way of justifying one's behaviour. It was by means of 'imagination' that de Gouges portrayed herself as the possessor of the rights of man and citizen, and explained her interventions in politics in a period when the political rights of women were highly contested. When she wrote about the origins of human society, she likened herself to Rousseau, to whom she referred as her 'spiritual father'. Like him and like Voltaire, she had imagined her ideas; her proposals for reform came, like theirs she said, from 'dreams', the inspired visions of a creative imagination.[14] (And these proposals were legion: a new national theatre for women, clean streets in Paris, divorce, a revision of marriage laws to end the distinction between legitimate and illegitimate children, the right to vote for women, and many more.) In her actions, as in her writing, de Gouges represented herself, not as the reflection of others' views of her, but as she imagined she should be. She described herself as a second Cassandra, a sage, Rousseau's imitator and his better, a lawyer who would defend the king at his trial. She was Homer and Joan of Arc. In a pamphlet denouncing the crimes of Robespierre, she signed herself with the anagram Polyme, 'an amphibious animal'. 'I am neither man nor woman. I have all the courage of one and the weaknesses of the other.' Elsewhere she wrote, 'I am a woman and I have served my country as a great man.'[15] She represented herself always as an active citizen, fully in control of her self.

This is not the place for an exhaustive review of the ways in which de Gouges construed her actions in terms of imagination. It was the concept that allowed her room to dissent from prevailing views about the capacities of women for politics, to enter the debates about women's rights on the side of the small minority around Condorcet. It allowed her to speak in many voices, to imagine herself in the position of men, even as she was a woman. In one pamphlet she spoke first as herself, then as the Duke of Orleans, then as the king. She had the king defend his insistence that the Constitution provide him with a veto and the duke proclaim his support for women's rights as writers and as citizens. She called the pamphlet 'Patriotic Dreams', but coyly suggested that these dreams, these imaginings, might also influence reality.[16] Like her contemporaries, she believed in the power of imagination to produce change.

But imagination was also the concept that ultimately led to her destruction. For imagination, ambiguous concept that it was, carried risks as well as benefits for those seeking to stretch the boundaries of political and social discourse.

From 1789 to 1793, de Gouges's interventions were tolerated, and though little came of her proposals for reform and few responded to her *Declaration of the Rights of Woman and Citizen*, she did gain a hearing. Sometimes — as when she was allowed to organise a massive festival of women to honour the martyrdom of an assassinated mayor in 1792 — she even played a part in official events.[17] The period from 1789 to 1793 was relatively open; debate was possible, and people regularly floated practical and utopian proposals for reform. In that context, Olympe de Gouges's imagination did not single her out as unusual, and certainly not as dangerous. But by 1793, as the Jacobins consolidated their rule and Terror became government policy, de Gouges's behaviour, especially her appeal to imagination, was taken as transgressive or, worse, as mad. Her attempt to enact the role of citizen as a woman was defined as a flight from reality so dangerous that it had to be punished by death. For the Jacobins, truth was transparent to the virtuous: its meaning must be literal and unambiguous. There was no room even for Voltaire's active imagination, that creative recombination that might produce new ideas, but that might also confuse fiction and reality. Instead, ideas must be direct readings of nature; imagination was ruled out of order lest it misrepresent the truth. And, for the Jacobins, one clear truth of nature was that men were meant to be active in public, while women's destiny was to stay at home and nurture babies. Exploding at the request by women petitioners to have restored their right to meet in political clubs, Pierre-Gaspard Chaumette ridiculed them this way: 'Since when is it permitted to give up one's sex?...Is it to men that nature confided domestic cares? Has she given us breasts to feed our children?'[18]

In this context, de Gouges's claims to be a 'man of state' were taken literally, as a sign of the play of that now illicit imagination. Her support of federalism as an alternative to Jacobin centralism was taken as another indicator of her craziness: she sought, it was averred, to dismember France, to sow disunity in the republic 'one and indivisible.' This was how the official newspaper reported her guillotining in November, 1793:

> Olympe de Gouges, born with an exalted imagination, took her delirium for a reflection of nature. She wanted to be a man of state. She adopted perfidious projects that sought to divide France. The law has punished this conspirator for having forgotten the virtues that belong to her sex.[19]

All of de Gouges's crimes were connected: her transgression of the republic was finally a transgression of her gender. Her 'exalted imagination' — excessive, fervid, tumultuous, disorderly — had led her to advocate the dismemberment of the republic, to threaten not only its inviolate geographic boundaries but also the so-called natural boundaries of gender on which a rational social order, in the eyes of the

Jacobins, must depend. Unable any longer to regulate herself, overtaken by her imagination, de Gouges was brought to order by the representative of the state, the authority of the law.

In a very fundamental way, imagination enabled de Gouges to act as a public, political figure. But there came a time when it outlived its usefulness as a justifying concept. De Gouges recognised this as she protested her sentence of death, insisting that her criticisms of Robespierre's government were not those of an 'exalted imagination', but a clear reflection of his obvious corruption.[20]

It is the lot of feminism to work with ambiguous concepts that are at once empowering and dangerous, to run always the risk of being indicted for the very ideas that give one the strength to challenge prevailing arrangements. This is surely true of the very concept of 'women' itself, which, as Denise Riley has so brilliantly pointed out, has been simultaneously in its negative and positive meanings the rallying cry for feminists.[21] It is the condition of feminism, I would argue, to have to deal with such ambiguity, for feminism itself is born of liberalism's inherent contradiction: on the one hand there is the abstract individual, dissolving all difference, and on the other hand, there is the need for difference (for an Other) to confirm any individual's sense of self. If this is the case, it is not the task of the history of feminism to root out the concepts that have miraculously evaded ambiguity and to offer them as the corrective for all time (as has been done with endlessly dreary arguments about whether it has been more effective to argue for equality or for difference). Rather, historians of feminism can most usefully track the ways in which feminists have exploited ambiguity, have attempted to evade its most obvious traps, and have, through extraordinarily inventive means, managed to enlarge for themselves and for posterity the limits of the possible.

Reason and Romance

3. Mary Does, Alice Doesn't
The Paradox of Female Reason in and for Feminist Theory
Joan B. Landes

The lapse of two hundred years seems to have restored Mary Wollstonecraft's much-deserved reputation as a woman of great intelligence and remarkable courage. Yet in her own lifetime Wollstonecraft paid dearly with her life and good name for challenging the punishing taboos against female independence. Writing in a 'disinterested spirit', pleading not for herself but for her sex, she held up a mirror to enlightenment and its most high-minded advocates, and in its glass were revealed the female victims of a world in which equality was not yet habit nor likely ideal despite the universalistic pretensions of an enlightened age.[1] She called for a revolution in manners, a cultural revolution capable of transforming the individual, the family and the market place to the same degree as the changes wrought by the great political and social revolution to which she bore personal witness. Only on the basis of educational and cultural reform, she believed, could the rights of women and the moral equality of the sexes be guaranteed. Only with the institutionalisation of sexual rights could society be said to accord with the principles of human reason. Certainly, it is because of her bold, uncompromising vision that Wollstonecraft has been awarded the celebrated position of mother to modern feminism, a woman whose life and philosophy embodied the principle that the 'personal is political'.

Still, we need no special recourse to psychoanalytic theory to make sense of the striking discord between duty and rebellion shaping the ambivalent response to Wollstonecraft among her erstwhile daughters. On the one hand, tributes to Wollstonecraft persist in an ever-expanding feminist scholarly literature registering her thought and life; on the other hand, doubts are expressed by a new generation of feminists (post-humanist, post-modernist, post-structuralist), who debate the value of a feminist contribution burdened by enlightened reason and its dualities, and who dispute the utility of a concept of the female subject which disguises class and race prejudices in the name of the universal. It is no secret that, as Rosi Braidotti has advised, ours is an age marked by two not unrelated crises: first, that of philosophical modernity, or the crisis of the rational subject, and second, the question of the feminine and therefore of women within philosophy[2] — or, to speak more broadly, of women's relationship to reason. Certainly, the ambivalence towards Wollstonecraft's version of feminism is a mark of the troubles we've seen.

With this in mind, I propose to revisit *A Vindication of the Rights of Woman* alongside a brief excursion to the underground world travelled by Lewis Carroll's dream child.[3] For if Mary expresses an adult woman's vexed relationship to reason and passion, Alice symbolises the possible freedom and fear of a pre-adolescent child's desire set free in a world beyond reason. Indeed, the invitation to pass 'through the looking glass' beckons in the writings of 'second-stage' feminist writers, most notably Sheila Rowbotham, Teresa de Lauretis and Luce Irigaray. More than Mary, the fictional Alice haunts our feminist consciousness, despite the fact that she is a character invented by a celibate Oxford don with peculiar Victorian sensibilities and a compulsive attachment to little girls.

Wollstonecraft launches her defence of women's rights with a forceful sally directed at Talleyrand (a member of the French Constituent Assembly and author of an influential report on public education) and, by implication, at all his contemporaries who advocated human progress and reason: 'Who made man the exclusive judge,' she asks, 'if woman partake with him the gift of reason?'[4] At face value, her argument is elegantly simple and logically indisputable: if reason is admitted to be a universal human attribute, then by definition no members of the human race may arrogate its privileges for themselves to the detriment of others. However, Wollstonecraft qualifies the original premise. She argues for the virtues and duties as well as the rights of women.[5] For want of a proper education, she believes, women have been reduced to a condition of misery and deficiency:

> The conduct and manners of women, in fact, evidently prove that their minds are not in a healthy state; for, like the flowers which are planted in too rich a soil, strength and usefulness are sacrificed to beauty; and the flaunting leaves, after having pleased a fastidious eye, fade, disregarded on the stalk, long before the season when they ought to have

arrived at maturity. One cause of this barren blooming I attribute to a false system of education, gathered from the books written on this subject by men, who considering females rather as women than human creatures, have been more anxious to make them alluring mistresses than affectionate wives and rational mothers.[6]

Thus, with a proper education, women will turn away from their false, artificial affectations and, to continue her metaphor, blossom in a natural soil. They will cultivate in themselves and their daughters the virtuous duties of rational motherhood. Wollstonecraft is quite explicit on this point. She speaks of women choosing to spend time in the nursery, rather than at 'their glass'.[7] She imagines a new duty for fathers as well, as man is called upon to leave behind the harlot and return to the family, where he will unite with a modest and sensible spouse. Waving aside narcissistic, vain, coquettish femininity, Wollstonecraft projects a reformed system of marriage based on friendship and happiness rather than lust, pleasure and fleeting desire; and she yokes this vision to a reformed education of the senses. In effect, she joins both Protestant and Lockean strains of English moral philosophy to make her case for the education and rights of women.

Following the liberal philosophical view of man (*sic*) as a passionate being, simultaneously endowed with God-given powers of reason (sensation and reflection) found out through experience, Wollstonecraft observes that men (like women) are malleable creatures, subject to social influences. The solution to the wayward direction of the senses for both sexes would seem to be a process of radical self-discipline, as in Puritanism. Borrowing from Rousseau's programme to rationalise opinion in the general will, Wollstonecraft came to believe that all sensuous, reflective and rational human beings might achieve the highest standards of morality through the workings of opinion, the very source, according to Rousseau, for women's questionable virtue. However, according to Wollstonecraft, once opinion is elevated through the progressive education of humankind, and thereby endowed with appropriate content, woman's susceptibility to social opinion would no longer be a detriment, but instead an essential mechanism of morality.[8]

So far, we have been speaking as if there were no difference in the moral status of men and women. Indeed, as Carol Kay has observed, the radical implication of Hobbes's epistemological revolution with its emphasis on opinion and passion, was to turn all moral beings into 'women'.[9] Yet most mid-eighteenth century moralists tended 'to avoid

Hobbes's tone, his mock-heroic humiliation of classical masculinity'. First, some took a more positive view of women's sensitiveness, thus lessening the difficulty for men to share it. Second, in a contradictory move, but more important for our purposes, 'they reintroduced a masculine difference, a masculine virtue that would once again contrast with female subservience to opinion, but which would also conform to modern sceptical theory. This neoclassicizing reintroduction to virtue [Kay calls] the "remasculinization" of moral theory (putting the vir...back into virtue).'[10]

The 'remasculinization' of moral theory, especially in Rousseau's hands, occasioned Wollstonecraft's protest and her accompanying plea to grant women the same independence, the 'basis of every virtue', as allowed to men. She went further, warning against the dire consequences if women were to be excluded from equal rights: 'If she be not prepared by education to become the companion of man, she will stop the progress of knowledge and virtue....If children are to be educated to understand the true principle of patriotism, their mother must be a patriot'[11] Moreover, Wollstonecraft states, if women are to remain slaves, 'immured in their families, groping in the dark', they will degrade not only themselves but their masters as well.[12] So it is in the interest of enlightened men to advance the cause of women. But Wollstonecraft is careful to reassure her male readers that women's liberty will be tied to the duty of performing their patriotic tasks as virtuous mothers. She even flatters men, proposing that by acting on women's behalf they will advance not only the common interest but their own interest as well: 'I presume that rational men will excuse me for endeavouring to persuade them to become more masculine and respectable.' Wollstonecraft strikes an austere bargain with men: although they will need to become 'more chaste and modest', women will 'grow wiser' in the same ratio and will leave off their propensity to tyrannise through cunning or to undermine men by exciting their desires.[13] While protesting against the double standard in moral theory, Wollstonecraft participates in the very same project of 'remasculinization' of virtue — allowing for a gendered redistribution of virtue.

Wollstonecraft prises open the possibility that once reason prevails, men will abandon their domination of women; she boldly challenges men to test their claims of superiority against the possibility of common human rationality. However, she is careful not to prejudge the outcome of reason's trials — that is, whether women will occupy themselves with different, more private tasks and duties than will men. Her own ambivalence is manifested in her rhetoric.[14] Wollstonecraft reassures her readers that she does not 'wish to invert the order of things'. She acknowledges, and at the same time doubts, the necessary order of existence. She grants that 'from the constitution of their bodies, men seem to be designed by Providence to attain a greater degree of virtue', only to ask next whether 'their virtues should differ in respect to their nature', especially 'if virtue has only one eternal standard'.[15] Whereas Wollstonecraft posits that neither virtue nor reason is in itself gendered, she also holds to the view that '"as a sex women are more chaste than men", and as modesty is associated with chastity this is an important way in which a virtue is achieved. But here, Wollstonecraft insists, this achievement is not the result of activity (the "virtue is ascribed"), whereas men "produce" modesty through the action of reason.'[16] Moreover, while positing the role of convention in sexual arrangements, she contends that a natural division of labour will reassert itself in the absence of social pressure: 'Let there be no coercion established in society, and the common law of gravity prevailing, the sexes will fall into their proper places.'[17] At one and the same time, Wollstonecraft dismisses and reinscribes sexual division, stating: 'I here throw down my gauntlet, and deny the existence of sexual virtues, not excepting modesty. For man and woman, truth, if I understand the meaning of the word, must be the same.' Yet, she continues, 'Women, I allow, may have different duties to fulfil; but they are human duties, and the principles that should regulate the discharge of them, I sturdily maintain, must be the same.' For Wollstonecraft, as for so many of her contemporaries, it is difficult to shake free from the possibility that reason itself dictates that human duties are to be distributed along gender lines.[18]

The irony in Wollstonecraft's double gesture and her resulting recuperation of a masculine standard for rationality is compounded further by her position as a female author. It has been noted how in the eighteenth century, 'female authorship — with all the authority the term implies — was more or less explicitly assimilated to female sexuality, and both were discouraged'.[19] As I have argued elsewhere, however, Wollstonecraft's absorption in matters of linguistic style is as much a consequence of her stated ambivalence toward words and the women who employ them as it is a reflection of the distrust of her own sexuality and desire noted by Mary Poovey and Cora Kaplan.[20] Wollstonecraft worries over women's wilful, artificial and unnatural control over language. She celebrates the virtues of reason and utility over feeling and flowery diction, of writing over conversation:

> I shall disdain to cull my phrases or polish my style; — I aim at being useful, and sincerity will render me unaffected; for, wishing rather to persuade by the force of my arguments, than dazzle by the elegance of my language, I shall not waste my time in rounding periods, or in fabricating the turgid bombast of artificial feelings, which, coming from the head, never reach the heart. — I shall be employed about things, not words! —and, anxious to render my sex more respectable members of society, I shall try to avoid that flowery diction which has slided from essays into novels, and from novels into familiar letters and conversation.[21]

Wollstonecraft registers her discomfort with the culture of cultivated sensibility, in the mixed estimation of French salon society which appears on the first page of her dedication. She begins affirmatively, stating: 'In France there is undoubtedly a more general diffusion of knowledge than in any part of the European world, and I attribute it, in a great measure, to the social intercourse which has long subsisted between the sexes.' But, she continues in a less flattering vein, 'modesty, the fairest garb of virtue! has been more grossly insulted in France than even in England, till their women have treated as prudish that attention to decency, which brutes instinctively observe'.[22] Thus, for Wollstonecraft, the liberal society of mixed company which she so admires and which has enabled her own authorship is mired by the supposed existence of adulterous unions and immodest behaviour among its members.

By the revolutionary decades of the eighteenth century, the tradition of liberal philosophical culture had become polarised, thereby further complicating Wollstonecraft's position as a woman writer. Earlier in the century, in the hands of Addison and Steele the essay form was associated with an image of a 'feminised' man — one who loves peace, sympathises with women and participates in a discourse appropriate to a mixed audience. However, Edmund Burke —Wollstonecraft's political and intellectual adversary — had upset this progressive tradition by his reactionary style: 'Burke transformed the sociable, polite man of feeling into a figure of violent and irrational attachments, and the woman who had been "friend" in the scene of refinement became a sheltered symbol of the fragility of the whole social order.' In this context, Kay notes, Wollstonecraft's male identification is a very complex affair:

> The woman writer, invited into the culture of femininized modern male refinement, criticizes this effeminacy (even though it has licensed

her activity), but she hopes to give the project of remasculinization, the renovation of virtue, a female leadership. The slave of mere feeling becomes the heroine of true feeling who will 'rise' by strength of mind above the subservient state of woman and raise man's virtue above opinion by first bringing him to acknowledge her superiority to the common opinion of her sex.[23]

Indeed, at moments in the text, Wollstonecraft appears to talk to a vanguard of women 'who will assemble the men of abilities around them'.[24]

In order to succeed in persuading by 'force of argument', Wollstonecraft requires the perfect interlocutor: one who is mature, rational, free and knowledgeable. Despite her own ardent passions and sincere feelings, Mary does want to believe in the positive force of reason and the possibility of reasonable humanity. But were such predictable, enlightened subjects to exist, her own efforts would become redundant. Nor is reason itself indifferent to gender. As we have seen, Mary is never entirely convinced of the unqualified equality of women whose cause she advocates; at least, she cannot imagine a world in which duty would not divide the sexes into appropriate public and private zones. In her fiction *The Wrongs of Woman: or, Maria*, Wollstonecraft explores the dark underside of the culture of enlightened public rationality, exposing the reality of woman's bondage to male passion in the sphere of intimacy. As Moira Gatens recognises, the problem posed by Wollstonecraft's liberal feminism is that 'fair and equal treatment for women will only apply to those activities which stimulate the neutral subject....The ultimate irony of the liberal state is revealed....[T]he right and freedom to use one's bodily capacities as one sees fit, is denied to women with regard to the specific character of their bodies.'[25]

Finding paradoxes in Wollstonecraft's and so many other versions of liberal feminism, today's feminist philosophers of difference defend the specificity of the embodied, female subject as 'a theoretical, libidinal, ethical and political agent'.[26] Likewise, in place of Wollstonecraft's faith in reason, feminists of a post-modernist persuasion cast suspicion on the concept of the human subject as a conscious, rational or self-transparent entity. Many would even link abstract reason to masculine forms of violence. In this atmosphere, Mary seems hopelessly trapped by the antinomies of a modern consciousness — not an agent, but a victim of modernity's ruses. In contrast, Lewis Carroll's dream child and her experiences 'through the looking glass' resonate with feminism's denial of the 'givenness' of material and cultural reality and with women's desire for agency.[27]

The little girl in question is well tutored in her lessons, educated to balance self-interest and altruism, and taught to appreciate reasonable, sensible, moderate outcomes. But as has been often noticed, except for her proper manners, Alice is by no means a good little girl in mid-Victorian terms. She doesn't always behave reasonably — but neither do those around her. As Alison Lurie observes,

> She is not gentle, timid, and docile, but active, brave, and impatient; she is highly critical of her surroundings and of the adults she meets. At the end of both books she fights back, reducing the Queen of Hearts' court to a pack of playing cards and the Red Queen to a kitten, crying 'Who cares for you?' and 'I can't stand this any longer!'[28]

By a feminist account, the body is not an essence or some anatomical destiny but 'one's primary location in the world, one's primary situation in reality'.[29] But what happens when our senses no longer seem to anchor that reality; when, to paraphrase Deleuze, the discovery of sense forebodes nonsense?[30] In this context, we might recall that Alice's body is what is called into question. In one unforgettable exchange, Alice is challenged by Humpty Dumpty to contemplate whether proper names mean anything about the nature of the things to which they refer. Why is it that her name does not signify anything about her body (or its shape)? In answer to Alice's retort, '*Must* a name mean something?', Humpty Dumpty replies with a short laugh: 'Of course it must, my name means the shape I am — and a good handsome shape it is, too. With a name like yours, you might be any shape, almost.' More perplexing is the fact that Alice's size and shape are constantly changing, as a response in good measure to what she ingests. Thus, when the Caterpillar asks, 'Who are *you*?', Alice, at a loss, replies, 'I — I hardly know, Sir, just at present — a least I know who I was when I got up this morning, but I think I must have changed several times since then'. She is also unable to convince the pigeon that she is not a serpent but a little girl, or rather that there is a difference between the two; that is a difference which 'signifies', as she admits to also eating eggs (though she prefers hers cooked).[31] It is not her sex that is called into question in Wonderland. But, then, she is a pre-adolescent child: a creature of desire, but a child whose desires are not yet anchored to the object choices of adult heterosexuality. As William Empson once observed, the Alice books are haunted by sex and death, especially the connection between the marriage bed and the death of childhood.[32]

It could be said that Alice comes to the same radical distrust of the senses which motivated Hobbes's (modernist) break with objectivist theories of truth some two centuries earlier,[33] though sense here is the occasion for nonsense — not something Hobbes would have entertained with comfort. In any event, Alice does learn through her experience. As Jan Gordon notes, playing with the notion of a university curriculum, 'Alice's entire world underground comes to exist as a college of stories'.[34] In that sense, therefore, she prefigures a new post-disciplinary eclipse of the boundaries between literature and philosophy, and an appreciation for the value of storytelling as a vehicle to knowledge. Though Alice is no philosopher, she is a little girl who is being tutored by the author of a textbook for the new symbolic logic, a gentleman who much prefers teaching young girls to his official male charges.[35] Generations of readers have delighted, as does Alice, in Carroll's logic puzzles. We are amused when the 'rationalist' game of chess becomes a theatre of the irrational. Like Alice, readers of *Through the Looking-Glass* are forced to ponder whether the dream is Alice's or the Red King's. Alice's exchange with Tweedledum and Tweedledee leaves us wondering who has the last laugh, the sensible little girl (who finally regains her composure) or the ludicrous twins:

> 'Well, it's no use *your* talking about waking him,' said Tweedledum [referring to the Red King], 'when you're only one of the things in his dream. You know very well you're not real.'
> 'I *am* real!' said Alice, and began to cry.
> 'You won't make yourself a bit realler by crying,' Tweedledee remarked: 'there's nothing to cry about.'
> 'If I wasn't real,' Alice said — half-laughing through her tears, it all seemed so ridiculous — 'I shouldn't be able to cry.'
> 'I hope you don't suppose those are real tears?' Tweedledum interrupted in a tone of great contempt.
> 'I know they're talking nonsense,' Alice thought to herself; 'and it's foolish to cry about it.' So she brushed away her tears, and went on, as cheerfully as she could...[36]

The books return repeatedly to the tutorial motif. Carroll playfully subverts the role and practice of education, as in the especially irrational episode in Wonderland where Alice encounters the Mock Turtle and the Griffin and is asked to tell them her stories. Altogether, the questions of who is tutoring whom, who is eating whom, and who stole the tarts produce a radical discourse on justice and power. Furthermore, Carroll's own paradoxical relationship to gender and reason is highlighted by the fact that he is instructing Alice (and other little girls) in logic games and stories in the grounds of a university which she cannot attend — nor, by all accounts, would he have preferred that she be able to enrol!

Feminists have investigated the pedagogical dimension of philosophy, especially the erotics of the master-disciple relationship in post-Cartesian philosophy. There is a charged relationship between the master who possesses the truth and the disciple who desires to possess it, a relationship made all the more complicated when the master is male and the disciple is female. Moreover, in the post-Cartesian universe, the cultural assignment of women to the side of the senses and the irrational was institutionalised in the segregated educational institutions of the modern world.[37] In this context, it is interesting to consider Alice (along with Carroll's erotic interest in Alice Liddell and other little girls). Not only does Alice explore the beyond — the zone of madness, error, passion (and women?) — but she is 'masterless': she proceeds alone. She mocks the presumed teachers and masters she encounters on her journeys. Carroll, a Victorian eccentric, makes a 'love-gift' of these stories to a real little girl, whose reason is exhibited by her ability to solve logic puzzles and to play with words. He parodies Victorian England's moralistic educational programme for girls, demonstrating that the best instruction involves making logic into a game.

After Wollstonecraft's death, the salon culture which she simultaneously admired and abhorred split into two halves: public space, men's special province, and the interior realm, a domain of women and children. Without too much exaggeration, it is possible to say that Victorian men intended their women to be maintained in a kind of purdah. The bourgeois masculine mind desired nothing more than to keep these two spheres apart, so that only men could cross the threshold at will (spiritually and practically).[38] We have found that Mary Wollstonecraft failed to find a satisfactory way for women to circumnavigate that division in Western bourgeois culture. Yet we have also discovered a countercultural strain in Western man's approach to reason. Carroll's writing testifies to the fact that, though formally repressed, logic returns to the interior. Alice is wholly a creature of the interior, the preferred family domain and its adjacent grounds. There, however, she explores the boundaries of sense, and demonstrates that little girls can also be puzzle-solvers. She appears to be the pure paragon of rationality, rebelling against the insanity of the creatures she meets. At the same time, she is revealed to be a desiring, impure being who is constantly reflecting on how she has just eaten another being.

In a letter to William Godwin, Mary Wollstonecraft implied that by the end of her life she was willing to forfeit passion and sensuality for 'a convenient part of the furniture of a house'.[39] In contrast, in Lewis Carroll's hand, the 'furniture of existence' of the domestic interior become the counters for a game in which a little girl exercises her knowledge and power. Alice falls through a tunnel filled with bric-à-brac into another interior. But she soon breaks out of the claustrophobic confinement which fills the domestic enclosure. By exercising her freedom of movement, Alice goes beyond the garden in *Wonderland* and visits some very strange creatures. In *Looking-Glass*, she goes further into a public domain as she traverses and surveys the countryside of some universe where she plays for a crown. In each of her adventures, she must test the bounds of sense and non-sense, and she discovers that what she has been taught is rational does not always avail her. In any event, Alice's singular power derives from the fact that she is no-one's child. But perhaps that is why so many of us desire to claim her as our own.

But what about Mary? The difficulties she experienced in reconciling her passionate and her reasoning self, her subjective desires and her hopes for social transformation, confirm her place in the history of feminist thought, or what Teresa de Lauretis terms a 'developing theory of the female-embodied social subject that is based on its specific, emergent, conflictual history'.[40] Mary Wollstonecraft's texts cannot be separated from her life. They testify to her concerted efforts to enter the public world of reason and argument — to perform intellectual work and to participate in the new public spheres of eighteenth-century Europe. More generally, her words and actions suggest how it is that 'our politics begins with our desires, and our desires are that which evade us, in the very act of propelling us forth, leaving as the only indicator the traces of where we have already been, that is to say, of what we have already ceased to be.'[41] Wollstonecraft's struggles to define a new gendered subjectivity for herself and other women, to think in new ways about change and transformation, are reflected in the unresolved antinomies in her writings between the body and reason, passion and intellect, nature and convention. These are not dilemmas which admit of easy solutions, then or now. As Rosi Braidotti contends, 'feminism shares with other philosophies of modernity...the dubious privilege of having an unresolved relationship toward both subjectivity and materialism'.[42] On those grounds alone — and notwithstanding who is real and who is not — it would be preposterous to presume that Alice's refusals wholly succeed whereas Mary's affirmations failed. However fraught with contradictions, Mary's relationship to reason is better comprehended as something like Alice's practice of thinking, as a powerful 'desire to know'.[43] Accordingly, both the eighteenth-century feminist author and the nineteenth-century fictional child continue to claim the attention of feminists as we approach the twenty-first century.

4. Wanting Protection
Fair Ladies, Sensibility and Romance
Mary Nyquist

How are emotion and political action related? If feeling is shaped by socio-economic experience, what inspires effective resistance to injustice? Such questions — often eagerly taken up by both activists and theorists — have in recent feminist discussions tended to focus on how internalised privilege perpetuates inequalities among women. Related questions were posed in the 1790s when Mary Wollstonecraft, Mary Hays and other British feminists joined their fellow Jacobins in debating the basis for a new, egalitarian society. 'Sensibility' — a volatile compound of sensation, emotional responsiveness and imagination — figures prominently in these debates. Used in a variety of competing contexts, an implicitly racialised 'sensibility' can be an attribute of revolutionary genius, a properly educated bourgeois consciousness, the hypercivilised refinement of a decadent aristocracy, or the middle-class woman's femininity. Whatever its connotations, 'sensibility' is inextricably bound up with the paternalistic ideology which radical writers critique in both polemical and fictional texts. Sensibility and chivalry go together like, well, love and marriage, but also in more complex ways, which only fiction seems able to capture. In this essay, I recontextualise Wollstonecraft's unfinished *The Wrongs of Woman: or, Maria*, by placing it in the company of other Jacobin novels that call attention to the class- and gender-inflected significance of romantic, chivalric codes. (Don't worry, dear late twentieth-century, unleisured reader, I won't assume knowledge of the texts under discussion.) In the process, I hope to trace the genealogy of certain features — both oppressive and liberatory — of contemporary feminist discourse.

A rationalist committed to revolutionary change, Wollstonecraft holds that progressive action results from sound, virtuous principles. But, as a proto-Romantic, Wollstonecraft also believes that such principles will be grounded in unsophisticated, empathic feeling, in what she calls 'true' sensibility. That unjust social relations are maintained by debased sensibilities is suggested in Wollstonecraft's first polemical treatise, *A Vindication of the Rights of Men* (1790), written in response to Edmund Burke's *Reflections on the Revolution in France* (1790). Portraying Burke as an apologist for sentimentalised feudal relations or, more simply, for chivalry (referred to as 'Gothic affability' or 'Gothic gallantry'), Wollstonecraft takes him to task for promoting emotive social bonds among unequals in his defense of the *status quo*. Shamelessly, Burke encourages his readers to identify the transient experience of sensible feelings with real virtue. As momentary feeling, however, chivalrous sensibility is very much dependent on its immediate stimulus, Wollstonecraft argues — 'the sight of distress, or an affecting narrative' — and must therefore be distinguished from the fixed, rational principles that give rise to genuine, 'masculine' goodness. Throughout the *Rights of Men*, Wollstonecraft opposes chivalrous sentiments to the principled eradication of inequalities based on property and title that will result in true social progress. The biting, satiric edge of the following passage is meant to pierce through Burke's duplicitous defence of the naturalness — and consequent rightness — of existing emotional ties:

> Where is the dignity, the infallibility of sensibility, in the fair ladies, whom, if the voice of rumour is to be credited, the captive negroes curse in all the agony of bodily pain, for the unheard of tortures they invent? It is probable that some of them, after the sight of a flagellation, compose their ruffled spirits and exercise their tender feelings by the perusal of the last imported novel. How true these tears are to nature, I leave you to determine. But these ladies may have read your Enquiry concerning the origin of our ideas of the Sublime and Beautiful, and, convinced by your arguments, may have laboured to be pretty, by counterfeiting weakness.[1]

The effects of a vitiated sensibility are dramatically, even sensationally, displayed by the 'fair ladies' Wollstonecraft polemically represents — inverting the terms of colonialist discourse — as sadistic barbarians. In the story Wollstonecraft tells, the women of the colonial slave-owning classes are not merely complicit in the brutalities of slavery. They actively invent *and* oversee the unheard of bodily tortures savagely inflicted on their slaves. Far from expressing true sensibility, their tears — released, later, in response to an affecting narrative — represent the perverted indulgence of self-pleasing sentiments typical of tyranny (the term used in republicanist discourse to signify an assumption of arbitrary, illegitimate power).

The presumed naturalness of both colonial slavery and feminine sensibility is sent up here. In effect, both are corrupt institutions. Significantly, however, there is no suggestion of an analogy between slavery and womanhood. That analogy — with whose racist legacy contemporary feminisms continue to contend — does not come into its own until *A Vindication of the Rights of Woman* (1792). In the *Rights of Men*, Wollstonecraft's 'fair ladies' occupy *only* a position of unearned, illegitimate privilege: tyrants themselves, they are in no way slaves. Because slavery in a loose sense is the polar opposite of tyranny in republicanist discourse, Wollstonecraft's later comparison of women and slaves generally does not refer directly to colonial slavery as a historically specific phenomenon. Yet its implicit privileging of white, bourgeois experience all the more effectively occludes the specificity of other forms of gendered oppression, most notably that experienced by female African slaves.[2] Such biases are less strikingly present in this early passage, which is nevertheless pivotal in bringing together ideas later developed in the *Rights of Woman*. For in it white, leisured femininity itself appears as a construct, while sensibility is implicitly racialised. In the scene of novel-reading Wollstonecraft creates for the *Rights of Men*, the act of 'perusing the last imported novel' is the product of an underoccupied, consumerist condition, one most immediately characteristic of a decadent aristocracy. But novel-reading is also engaged in by women of the middle classes, and in the *Rights of Woman* frequently appears as a signifier of their equally hypercivilised parasitism. In Wollstonecraft's feminist tract, the reading of romantic fiction — the kind of literature most sought after by minds schooled in weakness and frivolity — contracts interests to the smallest possible sphere, thereby sustaining a state of self-enslaved, overstimulated sensibility. Together with the ideology of romantic love it promulgates, romantic fiction reconciles otherwise privileged women to their civil non-existence.

In Euro-American societies from Wollstonecraft's time to the present, patriarchal and romantic ideologies have developed in ways that have actually strengthened their interdependence. The very continuity of this interrelationship makes it difficult to register historical changes and class- and race-specific differences. There have, however, been significant changes since the end of the eighteenth century, most notably around issues relating to protection. In contemporary, capitalist-patriarchal societies, women still experience a need for protection, which now, as then, continues to rationalise patriarchally organised heterosexuality. Women of all classes, ages and racial or ethnic backgrounds are encouraged to believe that protection against male violence can best be provided by a male partner or lover. (If circles can be vicious, surely this one is.) Further, the desire for protection continues to be exploited by popular romance, thereby reinforcing what are, in origin, white, middle-class, notions of feminine weakness. Scenes of gallant rescue, timely intervention and protective advice are standard features of today's contemporary mass-produced romance (increasingly exported to the 'Third World'). Sexy as it continues to be, patriarchal protection no longer has the same status ideologically, though. Liberal ideology, the rise and demise of the Welfare State, the feminisation of poverty and the wrenching socio-economic changes brought about by advanced consumer capitalism (under the guise of 'structural adjustment') have co-signed its death warrant. In spite of concerted neo-conservative attempts to prolong chivalry's life, the ideology of patriarchal protection may soon be struggling for its final, illusion-shattering breath.

In Wollstonecraft's time, unlike in ours, a man's responsibility to provide protection was explicitly part of Euro-American patriarchal ideology. Early modern bourgeois marriage and conduct books specified 'protection' as a husband's natural obligation, often spelling out in considerable detail just what it entailed. In a debate on the relations of the sexes in Richardson's popular *Sir Charles Grandison* (1753-4), the gallant Sir Charles presents the provision of protection as the veritable cornerstone of white, bourgeois, patriarchal relations:

> I, for my part, would only contend, that we men should have power and right given us to protect and serve your Sex; that we purchase and build for them; travel and toil for them; run through...dangers and difficulties; and, at last, lay our trophies...at your feet; enough rewarded in the conscience of duty done, and your favourable acceptance.[3]

Patriarchal protection is here — and everywhere — made to seem irresistibly attractive, its assumed naturalness best expressed in idealising language. As part of this strategy, Richardson's novel — like its predecessor, chivalric romance, and today's popular romantic fiction — links the exercise of this patriarchal 'right' to upper-class standing.

For Jacobin writers, this perpetuation of what are essentially feudal ideals is a serious problem. In the social landscape represented in radical novels, characters of all classes may at times need to claim or to benefit from protection, something that those considered social superiors are often best able to provide. In and of itself, protection is a definite social good. But the legitimacy of a presumed 'right' to grant protection is subject to critique. Thomas Holcroft, intellectual comrade of both Wollstonecraft and Godwin, systematically challenges the outmoded, chivalric codes embraced by aristocratic white male characters in *Anna St. Ives* (1792). *Anna St. Ives* abounds with scenes of dramatic rescue, sensitively bestowed ethical guidance, modestly transacted monetary aid and preventative protection. But in scene after scene the gallant protector is none other than the lower-class Frank Henley, whose father is Sir Arthur St. Ives's servant. Following fully articulated egalitarian principles, Holcroft's novel makes the principled Frank its true hero, presenting Anna's more privileged suitor, the upper-class Coke Clifton, as a useless — and increasingly dangerous — rake. Just as significantly, *Anna St. Ives* does not focus the hero's protective function on the heroine. Indeed, Henley's most spectacular feat of daring involves a leap into rocky waters to save his rival from death by drowning, a death Clifton risks in a foolhardy bid to establish his love of honour in the eyes of another rival, Count de Beaunoir. Like the Count, who is steeped in chivalric lore, Clifton has adopted 'high' but 'false' notions of honour. When his desire to perform another act of gallantry once again brings about conditions that permit Frank to perform the offices of true, other-directed heroism, Clifton succumbs to a desire to revenge himself upon the upstart gardener's son and Anna. To owe his very life to one of such low birth, the force of whose visionary energy even he cannot deny, so offends the overcharged sensibility of the narcissistic Clifton that he devotes himself with satanic relish to destroying the two lovers.

Central to Holcroft's critique of paternalism is the principle, repeatedly dramatised, that reciprocal duties provide the basis of individual integrity and of human ties. To feel oppressed by a sense of obligation, as Clifton does, is to be caught up in one-upmanship and the hierarchical *status quo*. Nor should the ability to provide protection automatically create indebtedness or establish special claims. Frank's unpretentious opinion of his own acts of gallantry demonstrates this, as does Anna's sense of her own autonomy *vis à vis* her protector. Frank struggles with the desire to remain near Anna so as to be available as her protector, a role he never completely relinquishes. Holcroft makes sure that the principle of virtue's integrity wins out, however. When it comes to Clifton's attempts on her, Anna must be her own protector. In a deliberate challenge to Richardson's *Clarissa*, whose heroine dies trying to transcend the guilt and shame attached to her rape, *Anna St. Ives* refuses to regard sexual assault as the greatest evil. So long as Anna preserves her purity of mind, she has nothing to fear and, in effect, nothing to lose. Imprisoned by Clifton — in a madhouse related to the one Wollstonecraft invents for Maria — Frank is unable to deliver his beloved Anna from the brutal rape Clifton plots. (The rape does not, finally, occur, though the reader is led endlessly to expect it.) In her review of *Anna St. Ives*, Wollstonecraft emphasises Frank's courage, a trait Holcroft polemically casts as not only class- but also gender-neutral. Facing her would-be rapist, Anna mocks Clifton's unmanly resort to stratagems and ruffians, declaring, 'But there is no such mighty difference as prejudice supposes. Courage has neither sex nor form: it is an energy of mind, of which your base proceedings shew I have infinitely the most.' Anna's fearlessness serves as a protective shield, repeatedly shaming Coke into inaction. It also enables her to escape her prison by herself, scaling a wall judged to be difficult for a man. Having pointedly effected her own liberation — Laura, her servant, is informed 'it was weakness and folly to suppose that men were better able to climb walls than women' — Anna even plays a role in delivering Frank.[4]

Anna St. Ives reinterprets the right to provide and the need to receive protection using conventional romance formulae. A related critique of white, male, aristocratic privilege is undertaken by William Godwin's *Things as They Are, or The Adventures of Caleb Williams* (1794). *Things as They Are*, however, focuses on what happens when protection is *denied* those who are most vulnerable and needy. Specifically, it reveals how legal and judicial institutions operate to protect the interests of the powerful. Falkland, the novel's upper-class antihero and former romance buff, is monomaniacally concerned with his personal 'honour'. Early on, Falkland several times rescues an 'unprotected innocent,' Emily Melvile, who falls in love with him as a result. The course of (in-) justice, not of true love, is what matters in *Things as They Are*, though. Falkland himself appears to be untouched by romantic desire, while Emily dies of shock when her vengeful cousin Mr Tyrrel suddenly has her imprisoned. When Tyrrel, in a drunken rage at his consequent ostracism, unexpectedly knocks Falkland to the ground, Falkland responds by murdering his antagonist. But he does so in secret, thereby managing to preserve his reputation as a man of impeccable virtue. From the moment the murder is committed, Falkland's exquisite sensibility is lavished solely upon his now seriously compromised honour. He devotes himself with ruthless singlemindedness to maintaining the fiction of his innocence, which requires, the successful frame-up of the liberty-loving labourer Hawkins and his son, both of whom have already been victimised by Tyrrel's abuse of the law. As a result of Falkland's machinations, the upright, hardworking Hawkins and his son are tried, condemned and executed for a murder they did not commit.

Long before this outcome could even be imagined, Hawkins's opinion of the law is that 'it is better adapted for a weapon of tyranny in the hands of the rich, than for a shield to protect the humbler part of the community against their usurpations'.[5] This view is shared by virtually every one of the countless victims of and refugees from the judicial system who populate the criminal underworld Godwin's hero is forced to join. When Caleb Williams, Falkland's servant, discovers the truth of his master's criminality, Falkland engages in a second frame-up. From this point on, the narrative action is based on Williams's indefatigable efforts to elude the all-powerful persecutory machinery set in motion by the informal trial that determines his fate. In an absurd inversion of things as they ought to be, it is Williams, not Falkland, who is judged guilty (of robbery and, far worse, of trying to sully his superior's reputation). It is Williams who is repeatedly imprisoned, pursued endlessly upon escape and socially ostracised. Williams's experiences in prison give Godwin numerous opportunities to show how the state acts only as an auxiliary of despotism. The more Williams is hounded by the law and its corrupt attendants, the more radical are the views he espouses on the unjust character of all existing social institutions. Williams's radicalism is strangely compromised by the secret, idealising admiration he feels for Falkland as a knight errant of highly wrought sensibility (a topic we will return to later). The action of Godwin's novel is, however, unambiguous. Scene after scene, character after character demonstrate the utter hypocrisy of the reigning paternalist ideology of protection, the numerous ways in which it is internalised by low and high alike, the corruption of officials associated with the law, and the penalties and indignities suffered by those who resist injustice, as Williams does. Godwin casts his two main aristocratic characters — first the brutish Tyrrel and then the refined Falkland — as tyrants whose unregulated passions lead to the arbitrary use of power. Both use the law as an instrument of revenge, despotically perverting institutions of social justice to purely personal ends. Falkland, we learn towards the end of the novel, owns a plantation in the West Indies.

Wollstonecraft's critique of chivalry and its abuses in both the *Rights of Woman* and *Wrongs of Woman* needs to be situated in the context of these and other radical texts. Though this is gradually changing, biographical readings have predominated for too long, perpetuating a view of Wollstonecraft as a solitary genius, forever troubled and forever romantically enmeshed.[6] By insisting on literary and political affiliations, however, I do not wish to suggest that biographical materials are irrelevant. On the contrary, Wollstonecraft's own experiences would have made her keenly sensitive to the ideological character of patriarchal 'protection'. As a child, Wollstonecraft not only witnessed her father physically assaulting her mother but, apparently, tried herself to intervene: her mother needed protection *from* her natural, lawful protector. In liberating her sister from a husband believed to be abusive, Wollstonecraft once again herself assumed the responsibility of providing protection *vis à vis* a socially legitimate patriarch. With Gilbert Imlay, Wollstonecraft voluntarily forwent the social protection traditionally offered by marriage. Yet with his abandonment of her, she was placed in the position of desiring protection, which she was painfully, humiliatingly denied. She was, further, expected to become the sole, natural protector for the child she had with him in a society that viewed her as an *illegitimate* mother. The ironies of this were not lost on Wollstonecraft, who comments in a letter that, though the male bird protects the female of its species, 'it is sufficient for a man to condescend to get a child, in order to claim it'. 'A man,' she concludes, 'is a tyrant.'[7]

Wollstonecraft's comments in the *Rights of Woman* on the discourse of patriarchal protection are consistently, scathingly critical. Male supremacy so effectively aestheticises female weakness, whether physical, moral or intellectual, that women themselves are seduced into desiring the artificial, more alluring goods offered by patriarchy. The benefit of male protection is one of the most patently false of these, in Wollstonecraft's view. In an especially sarcastic sally, she attacks the need for protection that women are conditioned to feel:

> Fragile in every sense of the word, they are obliged to look up to man for every comfort. In the most trifling danger they cling to their support, with parasitical tenacity, piteously demanding succour; and their *natural* protector extends his arm, or lifts up his voice, to guard the lovely trembler — from what? Perhaps the frown of an old cow, or the jump of a mouse; a rat would be a serious danger.[8]

Genuine virtue cannot possibly flourish under such conditions. Even gentleness is perverted when it becomes

> the submissive demeanour of dependence, the support of weakness that loves, because it wants [i.e. lacks] protection; and is forbearing, because it must silently endure injuries; smiling under the lash at which it dare not snarl. Abject as this picture appears, it is the portrait of an accomplished woman, according to the received opinion of female excellence, separated by specious reasoners from human excellence. Or, they kindly restore the rib, and make one moral being of a man and woman.[9]

Women who are forced to depend on their 'natural' protectors are involved in what is essentially a sado-masochistic dynamic. Its moral, religious and legal supports are playfully conveyed by the kindly restoring of Adam's rib that Wollstonecraft introduces as a metaphor for coverture, the legal term for woman's loss of personhood in marital union with her husband. Women will remain oppressed, she argues in the *Rights of Woman*, until they achieve civil existence, meaning both legal personhood and protection: 'But to render her really virtuous and useful, she must not, if she discharge her civil duties, *want individually the protection of civil laws* [my italics]; she must not be dependent on her husband's bounty for her subsistence during his life, or support after his death; for how can a being be generous who has nothing of its own? or virtuous who is not free?'[10]

As these passages indicate, the *Rights of Woman* initiates an analysis of the systemic character of woman's need for protection. It is *Wrongs of Woman*, however, that reveals the full significance of wanting — in the sense of lacking —protection. Like Godwin's *Things as They Are*, it is dedicated to revealing how protection is systematically withheld from those who most truly require it — those women, that is. Jemima, the novel's central lower-class character, is denied protection by nearly everyone with whom she comes into contact. As an illegitimate child, she sustains physical, emotional and sexual abuse within the various families that take her in. Social prejudices or condescending hypocrisy inform virtually every character's responses to her increasingly marginalised existence. The institutions she comes into contact with — the hospital, the prison, the workforce, the workhouse — flagrantly serve the interests of the privileged. As a prostitute, Jemima experiences the tyranny of the watchmen, who feel free to assault her sister sex-trade workers and who act as pimps, 'considering themselves as the instruments of the very laws they violate, the pretext which steels their conscience, hardens their heart'. In *Wrongs of Woman*, numerous inset narratives of domestic abuse convey the same message: women, without the means of supporting themselves, utterly dependent on the goodwill of others, are without recourse when subject to abuse. As one woman says to the bourgeois Maria when refusing her refuge, 'you must not be angry if I am afraid to run any risk, when I know so well, that women have always the worst of it, when law is to decide.'[11]

Domestic tyranny is the form of tyranny most aggressively taken on in *Wrongs of Woman*, whose heroine actively challenges existing marriage laws. Opening with Maria imprisoned in a madhouse by her husband, *Wrongs of Woman* dramatically reveals the discrepancy between the rhetoric of marital protection and legally permissible abuses of patriarchal power. Far from offering her protection, Venables, Maria's loutish, spendthrift spouse, wheedles money out of her and then secretly proposes to grant a business acquaintance sexual access to her in exchange for a tidy sum. The instant Maria discovers this plot, she resolves to leave him. Much more radically, she unilaterally dissolves the marital bond, refusing to consider herself married from this moment on. This resolution — a 'decision of judgement, not to be compared with a mere spurt of resentment' — places Maria in direct confrontation with both her husband and the law, in whose view she is, of course, still wife.[12] Venables, accompanied by an attorney, pursues his lawful, pregnant wife from one hiding place to another. (Wollstonecraft's attorneys and solicitors are all sleazy, unscrupulous jerks.) A maternal Caleb Williams, Maria is relentlessly hounded, harassed, threatened, and, once her daughter is born, drugged, abducted and imprisoned, all with full sanction of the law. Most sensationally outrageous, given the rhetoric of patriarchal protection, is the scene of abduction: Maria's baby is torn from her as she is being suckled. Further, Venables takes Maria's daughter in order to obtain her inheritance, thus exposing another painful contradiction in the ideology of 'natural protection': though the mother is primarily responsible for providing parental protection, both her property and her person are under her husband's control.

Like Caleb Williams, or like her prison keeper, Jemima, Maria clearly *wants*, that is *lacks*, civil protection. But what distinguishes Maria is that she also *wants* protection in the sense of *desiring* it (a meaning that stabilises later, historically). Oppressed by the laws of the land, Maria has internalised a desire for romantic love that is shown to be almost equally oppressive. In *Wrongs of Woman*, Wollstonecraft explores the dynamics of romantic desire in a heroine of acute sensibility as her friend Mary Hays had just done in *Memoirs of Emma Courtney* (1796). On its title page, Mary Hays's novel displays a passage by Rousseau on the disturbing effects that solitude has on the imagination. Hays's heroine frequently declaims against her isolation and purposelessness (like Maria, she holds radical views). But she cannot arrest the debilitating momentum of an unrequited attachment to Augustus Harley, son of a virtuous friend who has provided Emma with maternal protection. In spite of Harley's pointed, though ambiguous, rejection of her, Emma repeatedly re-engages her own frustrated desire, fuelled by a compulsive curiosity she is unable to curb. Enslaved by this curiosity, Emma is recognisably a romantic, female Caleb Williams (whose 'ruling passion' is mentioned in Hays's 'Preface'). Driven to discover the truth about Falkland, and willing to transgress any boundaries that are in the way, Williams develops a strongly charged, sado-masochistic relationship with his social superior, the intensity of which only increases once he himself takes on the task of concealing the truth. Emma expends even more intellectual energy trying to wrest Augustus Harley's secret from him, and suffers the torments of the damned in the process. Even after learning he has secretly married, she continues to protect Harley's reputation. In this way, the *Memoirs*, like *Things as They Are*, explores the psychic mechanisms by means of which oppression becomes internalised. In Hays's novel, unlike Godwin's, however, the relationship between (as it were) 'master' and 'slave' appears to conform to the ideal, heterosexual romantic relationship ending in marriage (an end Emma herself proposes). In *Memoirs* what has been internalized is precisely the romantic sensibility meant to be the hallmark of white, middle-class femininity. Incapable of constituting herself *other* than as a subject of romantic love, Emma announces at one point, 'I feel, that I am neither a philosopher, nor a heroine — but a *woman, to whom education has given a sexual character*'.[13]

Wollstonecraft's Maria, too, has clearly been *given* a sexual character by her society. Maria, however, falls in love not once, compulsively, but twice, self-deludingly (first, when a teenager, with Venables, then, in the madhouse, with Darnford). Maria's history unfolds in the memoirs she addresses to her abducted infant daughter while incarcerated. In this retrospective narrative, the reader learns that Maria's involvement with Venables originated in conditions conducive to romantic self-delusion, just as her later involvement with Darnford does. What initially seems the utter uniqueness of Maria's situation in the madhouse thus turns out to be in some ways surprisingly conventional. The discovery that Maria has twice rushed headlong into romantic love serves the same function as does Emma's repeated resurrection of her irrational desire. In each case, repetition reveals how romantic desire helps to constitute an intensely individualised female subjectivity; it shows just how deeply rooted, how impervious to rational critique it can be, and how very capable of providing its subjects with momentary pleasure and purpose. As in the *Memoirs*, romance blossoms in *Wrongs of Woman* under the conditions of enforced idleness and solitude explicitly said to foster a romantic sensibility in women. For the white, middle-class woman with time on her hands — ironically, the very situation that imprisonment creates for Maria — romantic love fulfils the want of occupation, the want, even, of self-identity.

That this desirous female subjectivity is both race- and class-specific is suggested in the *Memoirs* by a man of fashion who takes offense at Emma's intellectuality:

> Knowledge and learning, are insufferably masculine in a woman — born only for the soft solace of man! The mind of a young lady should be *clear and unsullied, like a sheet of white paper, or her own fairer face* [my italics]: lines of thinking destroy the dimples of beauty; aping the reason of man, they lose the exquisite, *fascinating* charm, in which consists their true empire; — Then strongest, when most weak — Loveliest in their fears —
> And by this silent adulation, soft,
> To their protection more engaging man.

Objecting that imbecilic fantasies of female frailty belong, with giants and ravishers, to 'the age of chivalry', Emma's father contends that a young woman should need no 'protection' other than her 'own sense of spirit'.[14] The very same pro-feminist position is taken by Emma's radical mentor, Mr Frances (modelled on Godwin). When the orphaned, nearly destitute Emma represents herself as 'a friendless and unprotected being', Mr Frances expostulates that he had not expected from *her* 'so plaintive, so feminine a complaint', and counsels her, 'You have talents, cultivate them, and learn to rest on your own powers.' When she persists in viewing herself as unprotected, he teases her about her impetuous admirer Mr Montague, 'a gallant knight, a pattern of chivalry'. Much as she respects her mentor's wisdom, Emma is convinced he cannot appreciate the psychic effects of economic dependency or how integrated into the self are the 'artificial' attributes of a woman's sexual character. Ingenious at finding reasons for persisting in her pursuit of Harley, Emma, as Hays indicates in her 'Preface' loves virtue but is 'enslaved by passion'.[15] Her self-paralysing sense of herself as someone who *wants protection* is an integral part of her experience of desire. It is also central to the tragic narrative action, for she accepts Mr Montague's offer of marriage only when she believes she has no other alternative. This feature of the *Memoirs* is thrown into relief by Hays's next novel, *The Victim of Prejudice*, whose heroine — truly a *heroine* — repeatedly rejects the protection represented by marriage with the odious Sir Peter Osborne — who has sexually assaulted her — as well as that offered by a liaison with her beloved William Pelham. Though her renunciations bring shame, poverty and illness, Mary refuses to barter personal integrity for patriarchal protection.

For Hays and Wollstonecraft, both heroinism and femininity are expressed by a superabundance of sensibility. Associated, at moments, with the progressive momentum of revolutionary genius, the passionate sensibility of their central female characters also makes them especially vulnerable, precipitating regression towards the *status quo*. In both novels, the threat of regression is signalled by a reading of Rousseau's *Julie, ou La Nouvelle Héloïse* (1761). In the *Memoirs*, the tragic trajectory of the entire action is traced to Emma's reading of 'this dangerous, enchanting, work'. Long before she is introduced to Harley, Emma invests a portrait of him with all the virtuous qualities his mother attributes to him, making him, in her words, 'the St. Preux, the Emilius, of my sleeping and waking reveries'.[16] Maria's fellow prisoner Darnford similarly becomes the St Preux of her madhouse reveries after she has had only a brief glimpse of him. Darnford lends Maria a copy of *Héloïse*, into which Maria throws herself as if entering another world. Reading *Héloïse*, Maria pictures St Preux ('or the demi-god of her fancy') as Darnford, also attributing to Darnford 'St Preux's sentiments and feelings, culled to gratify her own'. Like Emma's, Maria's desire for a chivalrous, adoring lover extravagantly pre-exists the particular man who comes to incarnate it; or, as the narrator puts it, contrasting Maria and Pygmalion, 'Pygmalion formed an ivory maid, and longed for an informing soul. She, on the contrary, combined all the qualities of a hero's mind, and fate presented a statue in which she might enshrine them.'[17]

As a genre, the novel is well used to representing this form of romantic desire. Aware that they may be expected to represent exemplary heroines, both Hays and Wollstonecraft insist on the realist dimension of their representations of female wanting. In her 'Preface,' Hays sets up a contrast between fiction that portrays characters of 'ideal perfection' and her portrait of the fallible Emma Courtney. Wollstonecraft's 'Preface' more polemically attacks the double standard that lets heroes develop while expecting heroines 'to be born immaculate; and to act like goddesses of wisdom, just come forth highly finished Minervas from the head of Jove'.[18] Wollstonecraft wants her readers to *understand* Maria's susceptibility to romance as a product of the association of ideas her experience has forged. A commitment to explaining the genesis and progress of romantic desire is inscribed in almost every paragraph of the narrative relating to Maria, whose early experience of sexism, youth, credulity and idealising tendencies (the effect, in part, of identification with a love-embittered uncle, her only protector) become the experiential conditions for her feminine fantasy-life. More indirectly, Maria's romantic desire is on both occasions linked with a longing for liberation. Painstakingly representing the psychological operations of romantic desire, Wollstonecraft exposes its contradictory relationship with the absence of real, material forms of protection. The very narrative discourse of the *Wrongs of Woman* — its dramatic opening *in medias res*, with imprisonment preceding romance — is polemically ordered with this end in view. Outrageously thwarted, woman's need for civil protection is, from the outset, the not-to-be-forgotten context for *Maria*'s two narratives of romantic desire. Thus situated, romantic desire — or, rather, the desire for romance — is to be read critically but also compassionately: it is desire for protection that is wanting.

And Darnford seems to know exactly what is wanted. The first words he addresses to Maria (in a letter delivered by Jemima) are, 'Whoever you are, who partake of my fate, accept my sincere commiseration — I would have said protection; but the privilege of man is denied me.'[19] The narrative indicates that Darnford has already exercised this patriarchal privilege *vis à vis* his heroine, who thinks of him as 'her former protector.' Revisions Wollstonecraft began before her death suggest that Darnford's role as prior deliverer was to have been fleshed out in greater detail. The purpose, I believe, was to make even more striking the romantic eroticisation of chivalric promises of protection. The hero who gallantly rescues his lover from disaster is, as we have seen, a stock feature of romantic fiction. Ordinarily, however, the hero's ability to provide protection is expressive of his eminent virtue (if not also his superior social status). Whatever a novel's politics, a truly gallant act is not supposed to draw attention to itself. Moreover, as we have seen, in radical novels the 'privilege' of offering protection is open to interrogation. Darnford's charming proclamation of his desire to play this chivalric role is therefore — at the very least — provocatively presumptuous.

Maria's response to imprisonment is equally suspect or, at least, peculiarly feminine. Caleb Williams, for example, goes to work devising mechanical methods of escape almost as soon as he is put in prison. By dint of ingenious strategising and hard, physical labour, Godwin's hero is able to liberate himself on more than one occasion. It has already been mentioned that Anna St Ives — exemplary, gender-defying heroine — also manages to free herself when imprisoned. Maria, by contrast, rests her hope of liberation completely with Jemima and Darnford. From the beginning, Maria's attraction to Darnford is inseparably a part of her desire for liberation. Anticipating their first meeting, 'she expected with trembling impatience, inspired by a vague hope that he might again prove her deliverer, to see a man who had before rescued her from oppression'.[20] Maria anticipates rescue by actively desiring it — a form of wanting protection that would seem to spell nothing but trouble. In the *Rights of Woman*, where the critique of male chivalry is overt, a woman who longs for gallantry is said to be vulnerable to seduction — vulnerable, specifically, to seduction by rakes. Alluding to *Clarissa*, Wollstonecraft works this out very clearly:

> Half the sex, in its present infantile state, would pine for a Lovelace; a man so witty, so graceful, and so valiant; and can they *deserve* blame for acting according to principles so constantly inculcated? *They want a lover, and protector* [my italics] and behold him kneeling before them — bravery prostrate to beauty! The virtues of a husband are thus thrown by love into the background [21]

In *Wrongs of Woman*, when Darnford persuades Maria to make love with him, he implores her 'to put it out of the power of fate to separate them'. The narrative continues:

> As her husband she now received him, and he solemnly pledged himself as her protector — and eternal friend. —
>
> There was one peculiarity in Maria's mind: she was more anxious not

> to deceive, than to guard against deception; and had rather trust without sufficient reason, than be for ever the prey of doubt....We see what we wish, and make a world of our own — and, though reality may sometimes open a door to misery, yet the moments of happiness procured by the imagination, may, without a paradox, be reckoned among the solid comforts of life. Maria now, imagining that she had found a being of celestial mould — was happy, — nor was she deceived. — He was then plastic in her impassioned hand — and reflected all the sentiments which animated and warmed her.[22]

It is not only at the moment of sexual surrender, though, that the reader is put on guard, or, rather, prepared for Darnford's abandonment of Maria, which is how this romance was to have ended. Signs of libertinism are there from the start in Wollstonecraft's presentation of her radically minded 'protector,' whose womanising, restlessness, political changeability, persistence as a lover, and strategic expressions of concern (signalled by a heavy dose of 'seems') are conventional attributes of the rake. No goddess of wisdom or self-suppressed Minerva, Maria is oblivious to such signs, however, acting precisely according to principles inculcated in her sex.

Wollstonecraft's novel is not simply a cautionary tale, however. Nor is Maria a victim of a predatory male sexuality. Like Hays, Wollstonecraft creates a heroine whose 'errors,' however tragic their consequences, are to be regarded sympathetically as the 'offspring of sensibility'.[23] In a sense, though, excessive 'sensibility' becomes a codeword for transgressive female sexuality in Hays's novel, whose heroine positions herself as a masculine subject in her pursuit of her lover. The *Wrongs of Woman* unites sensibility and sexuality even more directly than the *Memoirs*. In the passage just cited, Wollstonecraft vindicates Maria's sexual autonomy by eulogizing her sensibility's creative power and by rejecting moralistic discourse. A distinction between kinds of deception is implied. Though Maria may be deceived about Darnford's character — he is definitely not an angel — she is *not* deceived about her experience of sexual happiness. Re-invoking the figure of Pygmalion, Wollstonecraft quite vividly conveys a sense of the autonomy — even, again, the priority — of female desire, desire that is clearly both psychological and physical. Maria's right to sexual self-determination is not simply gestured at, however: it is the very mainspring of the narrative action. As we have seen, Maria dissolves her marriage when learning she is to become an item of exchange. Her husband's reduction of her to a piece of sexual property is, she believes, an absolute violation not only of the marital bond but (in radicalism's universalising language) of 'every moral obligation which binds man to man'. Maria herself undertakes her lover's defence when Venables has Darnford charged with adultery and seduction, thereby positioning herself, in relation to the judicial system, as a rational, civil subject. The document she prepares proclaims her freedom to dispose of herself sexually on the dissolution of her marriage, and states, unequivocally, that she 'voluntarily gave [her]self' to Darnford.[24]

In advocating female sexual autonomy, *Wrongs of Woman* greatly complicates its attitude towards feminine sensibility, or the sexual character society gives woman. Though sensibility can still enslave, *Wrongs of Woman* takes a much more positive view of its progressive potential than does the *Rights of Woman*. In a letter now appended to the 'Preface', Wollstonecraft describes Maria's plight as a woman of sensibility, 'obliged to renounce all the humanising affections, and to avoid cultivating her taste, lest her perception of grace and refinement of sentiment, should sharpen to agony the pangs of disappointment'. In the debauched Venables, Wollstonecraft has created a character who offends against every notion of the 'delicacy' essential to love. Wollstonecraft's frank portrayal of Maria's physical revulsion against her husband's reeking, dissolute body is one of the most remarkable features of *Wrongs of Woman*. Even more iconoclastic is the way in which Maria's reflections on injustice — along with her determination to resist it — arise out of her experience of revulsion. Indignantly attacking her society's sexual double standard, Maria remarks that no man would be expected to be attracted to a wife 'rendered odious by habitual intoxication', nor would anyone blame him if he became involved with someone else: 'whilst woman, weak in reason, impotent in will, is required to moralize, sentimentalise herself to stone, and pine her life away, labouring to reform her embruted mate'.[25] *Wrongs of Woman* is centrally interested in exploring the legal and economic sanctions of this double standard, together with the double bind in which women are caught up so long as it is in place. Articulating her post-Revolution, post-Imlay and post-Godwin views of female sexuality, Wollstonecraft has Maria declaim against the sexist system of 'false refinement', protest that for women as for men desire arises 'in some respects involuntarily', associate desire with both reason and nature, and associate sexual self-expression with 'that fire of the imagination, which produces *active* sensibility, and *positive* virtue'.[26]

At such moments, in her advocacy of female desire, Wollstonecraft seems most contemporary, and *Wrongs of Woman*, fragmented, incomplete, with its multiple, choric voices, a form of *l'écriture féminine*. The feelings Maria so eloquently gives voice to, however, are only questionably — what she claims they are — the 'foundation of her principles'.[27] For 'true' sensibility, as *Wrongs of Woman* and other texts repeatedly insist, occupies itself with others; sensibility is able to inform and be informed by reason in its principled search for justice precisely because it is empathic. The republicanist dimension of Wollstonecraft's work is committed to stressing the public, other-directed nature of enlightened human behaviour. But can individual, involuntary attraction and revulsion possibly be conscripted to the cause of progressive justice for all (even — to guard against the charge of transient sentiment — the 'hourly aversion' to which Maria was subject while living with Venables)? This conflict — between high-minded, other-oriented fellow feeling and irrational, individual desire — is risked when the explosive topic of female sexual autonomy is engaged. But it is also a conflict endemic to the bourgeois individualism that republicanist discourse often simultaneously advances and masks. Awareness of this conflict has, I think, motivated Wollstonecraft's efforts to make Maria's representation of her feelings as public as it can be. Maria's memoirs, made available to Darnford and Jemima, are written out of concern for her daughter's fate as a woman, while both the documents Maria produces — the memoirs for her daughter and her statement for the court — regularly generalise from her own individual situation to that of women as a group. By these means, Wollstonecraft systematically frames her celebration of female sensibility in scenes of education for liberation. Harnessed to rational, radical female speech, even sexualised female sensibility is to become a force of political resistance.

Equally problematic is Wollstonecraft's reliance on chivalric codes. When pleading her lover's legal defence, Maria explains, 'Mr Darnford found me a forlorn and oppressed woman, and promised the protection women in the present state of society want.' Here, *Wrongs of Woman* makes overt the connection between the civil and romantic forms of *wanting protection* that I have been exploring. The qualifier, 'in the present state of society', suggests that Maria invokes the ideology of patriarchal protection for rhetorical purposes, to stress women's need for civil protection and as a means of vindicating Darnford. Earlier, patriarchal 'protection' has come under direct discursive attack when Maria's uncle discusses society's double standard with regard to marital separation.

A man who leaves his partner may be admired, he claims, continuing in language reminiscent of the *Rights of Woman*: 'Such is the respect paid to the master-key of property! A woman, on the contrary, resigning what is termed her natural protector (though he never was so, but in name) is despised and shunned, for asserting the independence of mind distinctive of a rational being, and spurning at slavery.' As the tone here suggests, *Wrongs of Woman* is committed to debunking the notion that female 'honour' resides in chastity; not, however, consistently. For the shock value of Venables's attempt to profit from his wife's infidelity — the dramatic catalyst to Maria's principled resistance to existing laws — depends on a completely conventional view of white, middle-class female chastity. Repeatedly contrasting her husband's libertinism with her own sexual fidelity, Maria exclaims at the moment she formally dissolves the marriage:

> Neglected by you, I have resolutely stifled the enticing emotions, and respected the plighted faith you outraged. And you dare now to insult me, by selling me to prostitution! — Yes — equally lost to delicacy and principle — you dared sacrilegiously to barter the honour of the mother of your child.

Here 'honour' is used unironically, though in Maria's legal submission it is 'what is termed the fair fame of woman', 'what is termed my honour'. Yet, even then, Maria invokes chivalric discourse when referring to the climactic act of attempted prostitution: 'Neglected by my husband, I never encouraged a lover; and preserved with scrupulous care, what is termed my honour...till *he, who should have been its guardian*[my italics] laid traps to ensnare me'.[28] Clearly, Maria is willing to appeal rhetorically to the very ideology she contests. Or are we to understand that she has internalised it? Of Wollstonecraft, her author, we can also ask, is she self-consciously using patriarchal discourse against itself? Are these instances of strategic paternalism, on the model of the strategic gender essentialism and strategic racialism that contemporary radical discourse sometimes deploys? Or is there a deeper level of complicity with the chivalrous discourse on chastity?[29] In *Wrongs of Woman*, Wollstonecraft pushes against the very limits of paternalist ideology. What her text reveals, I think, is the difficulty of going entirely outside the ideology of patriarchal protection for a white, middle-class woman who has been *given* a sexual character. To have gone further than Maria goes — for example, to have left Venables on the grounds of unadulterated aversion, or because she had become involved with someone else — would have been to risk being left out in the cold, to risk the loss of valued protection, including that imaginative protection provided by her contemporary, progressive readers.

Related questions come up with regard to class differences as they are represented in *Wrongs of Woman*. Had Maria been unable to defend her own 'fair fame', she would have been one of the 'amiable women', unfaithful wives victimised by the sexual double standard, for whom she expresses compassion — the '*out-laws*' of the world'. But even these sketchily drawn *out-laws* have a comfortable, middle-class existence that Jemima cannot enjoy. Never having had the protection, however dubious, of marriage, Jemima, like her mother, has not had the opportunity of being an out-law in this sense. Nor is she 'amiable', that is lovingly, romantically disposed, as befits proper bourgeois femininity. Raped by an employer when young and forced to undergo a painful abortion, she is early on a social outcast, reduced to beggary and prostitution. She herself contrasts her sexual experience with that represented in romantic fiction when speaking of her revulsion against both her 'brutal master' and the 'brutes' whose needs she serviced: 'I have since read in novels of the blandishments of seduction, but I had not even the pleasure of being enticed into vice.'[30] Wollstonecraft clearly wants her readers to respond sympathetically to Jemima's narrative of violation and exploitation. By having Venables try to benefit from his wife's sexuality, *Wrongs of Woman* also establishes a connection between marriage and prostitution as institutions that deny women protection. Any commonality of experience between Jemima and Maria is *not*, however, what is emphasised. As Wollstonecraft often insists, differences in class position and therefore in education create differences in sensibility. And Maria's narrative — the dominant, controlling narrative in *Wrongs of Woman* — uncritically privileges white, bourgeois experience. Classism informs almost every feature of the following passage, in which Maria writes of her own sexual disgust:

> For personal intimacy without affection, seemed, to me the most degrading...state in which a woman of any taste, not to speak of the peculiar delicacy of fostered sensibility, could be placed. But my husband's fondness for women was of the grossest kind, and imagination was so wholly out of the question, as to render his indulgences of this sort entirely promiscuous, and of the most brutal nature. My health suffered, before my heart was entirely estranged by the loath-

some information; could I then have returned to his sullied arms, but as a victim to the prejudices of mankind, who have made women the property of their husbands? I discovered even, by his conversation, when intoxicated, that his favourites were wantons of the lowest class, who could by their vulgar, indecent mirth...rouse his sluggish spirits. Meretricious ornaments and manners were necessary to attract his attention.[31]

The various signifiers of downward mobility here — from 'promiscuous' to 'vulgar' to 'meretricious' — have the effect of conflating sexual and class defilement. Contaminated by his contact with 'wantons of the lowest class', Venables's arms are 'sullied' not only by infidelity *per se* but also by his sexual slumming. Lacking the delicacy afforded by an educated sensibility, these lower-class 'wantons' — in effect, the prostitutes represented sympathetically when Jemima was among them — are both an appropriate match for the coarse Venables and a pernicious pollutant.

Rhetorically, this passage is crucial to Wollstonecraft's agenda. It serves to legitimise Maria's revolt against domestic tyranny: to return to Venables's 'sullied' arms would be to risk sullying her own bourgeois identity as a fair lady. The same strategy, deploying an even more vicious classism, appears in the analogy Maria uses to convey her outrage when Venables, in a desperate bid to rationalise his behaviour, proposes an open marriage. These 'sophisticated sentiments', Maria states, 'had excited sensations similar to those I have felt, in viewing the squalid inhabitants of some of the lanes and back streets of the metropolis, mortified at being compelled to consider them as my fellow-creatures, as if an ape had claimed kindred with me.'[32] Here, the instinct to preserve her own integrity takes the form of disavowing relationship — literally with Venables but symbolically with members of the underclass to which his libertinism threatens to introduce her. This violently classist denial of common humanity, this shame-propelled rejection of her fellow creatures, who fall, momentarily, into the category of the fully sub-human, reinforces the class-specific, melodramatic character of Maria's self-vindication. In its absolute privileging of the delicate, educated female sensibility, this passage also shares something with the aggressively racist contrast Mary Ann Radcliffe draws in *The Female Advocate* (1799) between the sensibility of an enslaved African and that of an unprotected British gentlewoman who falls on hard times:

The slave is little acquainted with the severe pangs a virtuous mind labours under, when driven to the extreme necessity of forfeiting their virtue for bread. The slave cannot feel pain at the loss of reputation, a term of which he never heard, and much less knows the meaning. What are the untutored, wild imaginations of a slave, when put in the balance with the distressing sensations of a British female, who has received a refined, if not a classical, education, and is capable of the finest feelings the human heart is susceptible of? A slave, through want of education, has little more refinement than cattle in the field; nor can they know the want of what they never enjoyed, or were taught to expect; but a poor female, who has received the best instruction, and is endowed with a good understanding, what must not she feel in mind, independent of her corporeal wants, after the adversity of fate has set her up as a mark, for the ridicule, the censure, and contempt of the world? Her feelings cannot be described, nor her sufferings sufficiently lamented.[33]

For anyone who still imagines that feminist discourse is by definition liberatory, this passage will be awfully sobering. I reproduce it here in part because it so exactly inverts the terms Wollstonecraft uses to satirise the natural virtues of sensibility in the *Rights of Men*, as quoted at the beginning of this chapter. For Radcliffe, only the suffering of fair ladies counts. Set against the exquisitely honed sensibilities of British gentlewomen, the feelings of the ungendered, acultural, generic 'slave' barely register as feelings. Though Wollstonecraft does not engage in overt, aggressive racism of this kind, she definitely shares Radcliffe's belief in the superior qualities of a white, educated, bourgeois sensibility. There is little to chose, finally, between the savagely classist othering of Wollstonecraft's 'ape' and Radcliffe's racist 'cattle'. Ever racism's next of kin, classism haunts the *Wrongs of Woman*, whose overt commitment is to justice for all. (Just a little later, for example, a progressive Maria describes herself as being free of class-bound fastidiousness, as being 'ever glad to perceive in others the humane feelings I delighted to exercise'.)[34]

In *Wrongs of Woman*, the heroine's 'fostered sensibility' is definitely far from being only a liability. Maria's sensibility both grounds her advocacy of sexual autonomy and prompts her heroic challenges to oppressive double standards. Maria's sensibility also makes her a heroine in the more technical sense of being the novel's central protagonist. What needs further examining is how class privilege structures this position. As Wollstonecraft presents it, the relationship between Maria and Jemima is forged by sensibility. Her feelings numbed by a history of unremitting abuse, Jemima is on her way to becoming a prototype of Frankenstein's monster when Wollstonecraft's novel opens. Her relationship with Maria saves her from this fate; Jemima's sensibility — formed, significantly, by contact with an upper-class gentleman — is re-awakened. Just as significantly, Jemima's sensibility is rekindled by her vicarious participation in the romantic relationship between Maria and Darnford. Witnessing their tenderness, Jemima finds 'a tear of pleasure trickling down her rugged cheeks' — the first time social enjoyment has ever so moved her, we are told. Indeed, being involved, however indirectly, in this romance effects a kind of conversion: 'She seemed indeed to breathe more freely; the cloud of suspicion cleared away from her brow; she felt herself, for once in her life, treated like a fellow-creature.' Immediately afterwards, in a passage extolling the power of the imagination, the narrator heightens the sense of intimacy said to be enjoyed by all three of them. Jemima is no doubt included in Maria and Darnford's bourgeois heterosexual relationship for the solid, republicanist reasons already mentioned: as the basis for a new, equitable order, sensibility must be empathic, other-directed and inclusive.

Ultimately, however, Jemima's token membership in Maria's romantic relationship only underlines her marginalised status in the novel as a whole. For Jemima is not in any way a heroine. It is the title character, Maria, whose romantic experience opens Jemima's heart to humanitarian impulses. Likewise, it is Maria's resistance to oppression to which Jemima commits herself, not her own. The luxury of longing for a gallant male protector is one that Jemima has never been able to afford. As a result, no intensely focused analyses of subjective states are given over to her. In the passage on Venables's slumming cited above, for example, the same sexual brutality that casts Jemima into an economic underclass is what exacerbates Maria's subjective alienation, prompting her to resist her own marital oppression. Not being the subject of romantic entanglement, Jemima is displaced from the novel's central feminist plot. Her displacement has a certain impeccable logic, however. Without romantic interest to give it shape, Jemima's narrative is effectively not a single, coherent narrative at all. Reflecting the multiple ways in which society denies women of her class protection, Jemima's story becomes one of a series of ever-inset case studies, each dramatising the wrongs of woman as a class. Each also, however, illustrates 'difference' — a burden Wollstonecraft lays on lower-class shoulders when describing the novel's purpose. '[T]he delineation of finer sensations, which, in my opinion, constitutes the merit of our best novels' is what she has attempted in portraying the 'matrimonial despotism of heart and conduct' affecting Maria; in her final statement she adds that the novel intends 'to show the wrongs of different classes of women, equally oppressive, though, from the difference of education, necessarily various'.[35]

This conception of difference — as (implicitly) difference from a white, bourgeois norm — has been a divisive, oppressive feature of mainstream Euro-American feminism for at least two hundred years. *Wrongs of Woman* opens a window onto the genealogy of this conception. In self-advertised reference to the *Rights of Woman*, the polemical tract that precedes it, *Wrongs of Woman* illustrates how the novel, even when critiquing two of its favourite institutions, romantic love and marriage, can enable a broadly based feminist discourse and yet simultaneously encode race- and class-determined privileges. For the context-specific reasons that both Hays and Wollstonecraft expose, their central female characters become heroines through their passionate, resistant responses to romantic love and marriage as institutions oppressive to women. Unacknowledged, however, is the way in which both institutions tend to benefit members of the dominant classes. Colonial slaves, for example, were not allowed to marry, not having any civil status. Male slaves — together, in various ways, with their descendants — were systematically denied the 'right' or privilege of offering protection, while female slaves were in no position to benefit from protection in any form. Though this clearly deserves a separate study, it is important to recognise that for good, material, socio-economic reasons, it is white, middle-class women who are most able to articulate their experience of *wanting protection*, that is actively desiring both the chivalric and the civil protection that capitalist-patriarchal society seductively promises yet arbitrarily withholds.

Uneasiness with at least some of the difficult issues I have been raising seems to be expressed in the final pages of *Wrongs of Woman*. In the most detailed version of the novel's ending, Wollstonecraft has Jemima bring about the romantic reunion of Maria and her daughter. Jemima becomes Maria's housekeeper, a position on which she insists: it provides the protection she had despaired of obtaining and which Maria had promised her were she to become an active ally. Though presented as mutually beneficial, the relationship obviously reinforces existing modes of class stratification. But at least it continues, where Maria's relationship with Darnford does not. Further, in spite of — or rather because of — her class identity (Hays, too, has a servant come to the heroine's rescue in *The Victim of Prejudice*), Jemima plays a heroic role in the concluding action. Though Darnford apparently does the necessary behind-the-scenes wheeling and dealing, it is Jemima who effects Maria's actual, physical liberation, engineering their joint exit through the madhouse garden gate. Not coincidentally, the garden gate is the site of transgressive female refusal of patriarchal protection, i.e. control, in numerous novels from *Clarissa* on. Just before reaching it, Maria and Jemima are accosted by a terrifying, barely human figure. When he seizes Maria's hand, she throws herself on Jemima, crying 'Save me!'[36] Though he mutters curses and, a latter-day Cyclops, hurls a stone after them, the two women do escape. *Wrongs of Woman* can hardly be accused of sentimentalising female-female relations. Throughout, numerous women are portrayed as abusing their power over other women. By having Jemima liberate Maria from the madhouse, however, *Wrongs of Woman* strategically has *her* provide the protection Maria has been awaiting and that Darnford has gallantly promised. It is also Jemima who makes sure they both actually get through the garden gate, ghastly Gothic apparition notwithstanding. I like to think that Wollstonecraft's innovative scene of rescue drives a cross-class nail in the coffin of the ideology of patriarchal protection. Judging from the responses of the countless students I have asked to read this novel, the relationship between Jemima and Maria — based on inequalities, out of focus and undeveloped — can perhaps inspire us to carry on the struggle for social justice, marching, for want of any other protection, through the garden gate.

Feminism and Race

5. Mary Wollstonecraft and the Problematic of Slavery
Moira Ferguson

> A traffic that outrages every suggestion of reason and religion...[an] inhuman custom.
> *A Vindication of the Rights of Woman*

> I love most people best when they are in adversity, for pity is one of my prevailing passions.
> *Collected Letters of Mary Wollstonecraft*

History and Texts before A Vindication of the Rights of Woman

From 1790 onwards, Mary Wollstonecraft became a major participant in contemporary political debate for the first time, due to the evolution of both her political analysis and her social milieu. In contrast to *A Vindication of the Rights of Men* (1790), which drew primarily on the language of natural rights for its political argument, *A Vindication of the Rights of Woman* (1792) favoured a discourse on female subjugation in terms of slavery. Whereas the *Rights of Men*, refers to slavery in a variety of contexts only four or five times, the *Rights of Woman* contains over 80 references; the constituency Wollstonecraft champions — white, middle-class women — are constantly characterised as slaves. For her major polemic, that is, Mary Wollstonecraft decided to adopt and adapt the terms of contemporary political debate. Over a two-year period, the terms of this debate had gradually been reformulated, as the French Revolution in 1789, that highlighted aristocratic hegemony and bourgeois rights, was followed by the San Domingan revolution that focused primarily on colonial relations.

Wollstonecraft's evolving commentaries on the status of European women in relation to slavery were made in response to four interconnected events: first, the intensifying agitation over the question of slavery in England, that included the case of the slave James Somerset in 1772 and Phillis Wheatley's visit in 1773; second, the French Revolution in 1789; third, the publication of Catherine Macaulay's *Letters on Education* (1790) that argued forthrightly against sexual difference; and, fourth, the successful revolution by slaves in the French colony of San Domingo in 1791.

The discourse on slavery employed by Wollstonecraft was nothing new for women writers, although it was now distinctly recontextualised in terms of colonial slavery. Formerly, in all forms of discourse throughout the eighteenth century, conservative and radical women alike railed against marriage, love and education as forms of slavery perpetrated upon women by men and by the conventions of society at large.

Prior to the French Revolution, Mary Wollstonecraft had utilised the language of slavery in texts from various genres. In *Thoughts on the Education of Daughters* (1787), Wollstonecraft talked conventionally of women subjugated by their husbands who in turn tyrannise their servants, 'for slavish fear and tyranny go together'.[1] One year later, in *Mary, A Fiction* (1788), her first novel written in Ireland during a trying period spent as a governess, the heroine decides she will not live with her husband and exclaims to her family: 'I will work..., do anything rather than be a slave.'[2] Here, as a case in point, Wollstonecraft uses an orthodox conception of slavery that had populated women's texts for over a century: marriage was a form of slavery, and wives were slaves to husbands.

Wollstonecraft's early conventional usage, however, in which the word 'slave' stands for a subjugated daughter or wife, was soon to complicate its meaning. From the early 1770s onwards, a number of events, including James Somerset's court case, Quaker petitions to Parliament and reports of abuses had injected the discourse of colonial slavery into popular public debate.

The Abolition Committee, for example, was formed on 22 May 1787, with a view to mounting a national campaign against the slave trade and securing the passage of an Abolition Bill through Parliament.[3] Following the establishment of the committee, the abolitionist Thomas Clarkson wrote and distributed two thousand copies of a pamphlet entitled *A Summary View of the Slave-Trade, and of the Probable Consequences of Its Abolition*.[4] Wollstonecraft's friend William Roscoe offered the profits from his poem 'The Wrongs of Africa' to the committee. The political campaign was launched on the public with full force.⁵ Less than a year after the Abolition Committee was formed, Wollstonecraft's publisher, Joseph Johnson, co-founded a radical periodical entitled the *Analytical Review* and invited Wollstonecraft to become a reviewer. Wollstonecraft's reviews soon reflected the new influence of the abolition debate.⁶ One of the earliest books she reviewed in April 1789, was written by Britain's most renowned African, a former slave; Wollstonecraft was analysing a text based on specific experiences of colonial slavery for the first time. Its title was *The Interesting Narrative of The Life of Olaudah Equiano, or Gustavus Vassa the African, Written by Himself*, in which Equiano graphically chronicles being kidnapped from Africa, launched on the notorious Middle Passage, and living out as a slave the consequences of these events.⁷

While the *Analytical Review* acquainted the public with old and new texts on the current debate, Wollstonecraft was composing an anthology for educating young women that also reflected her growing concerns. Published by Joseph Johnson and entitled *The Female Reader, or Miscellaneous Pieces for the Improvement of Young Women*, the textbook-cum-anthology included substantial extracts promoting abolition. It included Sir Richard Steele's rendition from the *Spectator* of the legend of Inkle and Yarico, Anna Laetitia Barbauld's hymn in prose, 'Negro-woman', about a grieving mother forcibly separated from her child, and a poignant passage from William Cowper's poem 'The Task'.⁸

A series of events then followed one another in rapid succession that continued to have a bearing on the reconstitution of the discourse on slavery. In July 1789, the French Revolution erupted, as the Bastille jail was symbolically stormed and opened. Coinciding with the French Revolution came Richard Price's polemic, Edmund Burke's response and then Wollstonecraft's response to Burke and her review of Catherine Macaulay's *Letters on Education*. Meanwhile, in September and the following months, Wollstonecraft reviewed in sections the anti-slavery novel *Zeluco: Various Views of Human Nature, Taken from Life and Manners, Foreign and Domestic*, by John Moore.⁹ Let me now backtrack and briefly elaborate on how all this attentiveness to colonial slavery affected public debate and Mary Wollstonecraft's usage of the term.

On 4 November 1789, Wollstonecraft's friend the Reverend Richard Price, Dissenting minister and leading liberal philosopher, delivered the annual sermon commemorating the 'Glorious Revolution' of 1688 to the Revolution Society in London. The society cherished the ideals of the seventeenth-century revolution and advocated Dissenters' rights. This particular year there was much for Dissenters to celebrate. Basically, Price applauded the French Revolution as the start of a liberal epoch. The written text of Price's sermon, *Discourse on the Love of Our Country*, was reviewed by Wollstonecraft in the *Analytical Review*'s December issue. A year later, on 1 November 1790, Edmund Burke's *Reflections on the Revolution in France*, attacking both Price and his sermon, was published virtually on the anniversary of Price's address.[10] It soon became a topic of public debate, and several responses quickly followed.

As the first writer to challenge Burke's reactionary polemic, Wollstonecraft foregrounded the cultural issue of human rights in her title: *A Vindication of the Rights of Men*.[11] The first edition immediately sold out. It was not coincidental that Wollstonecraft composed this reply while evidence about the slave trade was being presented to the Privy Council during the year following the first extensive parliamentary debate on Abolition in May 1789. The *Rights of Men* applauded human rights and justice, excoriated abusive social, church and state practices, and attacked Burke for hypocrisy and prejudice. Wollstonecraft argued vehemently for a more equitable distribution of wealth and parliamentary representation. By 4 December of the same year, Wollstonecraft had revised the first edition, and Johnson rapidly turned out a second one in January 1791.[12]

In the *Rights of Men*, Wollstonecraft also frontally condemns institutionalised slavery:

> On what principle Mr Burke could defend American independence, I cannot conceive; for the whole tenor of his plausible arguments settles slavery on an everlasting foundation. Allowing his servile reverence for antiquity, and prudent attention to self-interest, to have the force which he insists on, the slave trade ought never to be abolished; and, because our ignorant forefathers, not understanding the native dignity of man, sanctioned a traffic that outrages every suggestion of reason and religion, we are to submit to the inhuman custom, and term an atrocious insult to humanity the love of our country, and a proper submission to the laws by which our property is secured.[13]

In the *Rights of Men*, Wollstonecraft explicitly argues for the first time that no slavery is natural and that all forms of slavery, regardless of context, are human constructions. Her scorching words to Burke about his situating slavery 'on an everlasting foundation' (in the past and the future) sharply distinguish her discourse from her more orthodox invocations of slavery in *Thoughts* and *Mary*. Contemporary events have begun to mark her thinking on slavery in a specific and concrete way.

In particular, Wollstonecraft challenges the legal situation. In the *Rights of Men*, she graphically represents slavery as 'authorised by law to fasten her fangs on human flesh and...eat into the very soul'.[14] Nonetheless, although she supports abolition unequivocally, she considers 'reason' an even more important attribute to possess than physical freedom. 'Virtuous men', she comments, can endure 'poverty, shame, and even slavery' but not the 'loss of reason'.[15]

In the same month in which Wollstonecraft replied to Burke, she favourably reviewed Catherine Macaulay Graham's *Letters on Education*. Macaulay's argument against the accepted notion that males and females had distinct sexual characteristics was part of the evolving discourse on human rights that connected class relations to women's rights. Macaulay, too, expropriated the language of physical bondage and wove it into her political argument. Denouncing discrimination against women throughout society, the *Letters* also rail against 'the savage barbarism which is now displayed on the sultry shores of Africa'.[16] Macaulay takes pains to censure the condition of women 'in the east' — in harems, for example — and scorns the fact that men used differences in 'corporal strength...in the barbarous ages to reduce [women] to a state of abject slavery'.[17] Macaulay's historical timing separates her from earlier writers who used this language; by 1790, slavery had assumed multiple meanings that included the recognition, implied or explicit, of connections between colonial slavery and constant sexual abuse.

In the *Rights of Men*, Wollstonecraft had not exhibited any substantial attention to the question of gender. After she read Macaulay, however, her views on gender and rights shifted. Notably, too, as one edition after another of *A Vindication of the Rights of Men* hit the presses, Johnson was concurrently publishing Wollstonecraft's translation of Christian Gotthilf Salzmann's *Elements of Morality for the Use of Children*.[18] In the preface to this educational treatise, Wollstonecraft pointedly inserted a passage of her own, enjoining the fair treatment of Native Americans. In terms of democratic colonial relations as they were then perceived, Wollstonecraft rendered Salzmann more up to date. There was, however, still more to come before Wollstonecraft settled into writing her second *Vindication* in 1792.

First of all, information about slavery continued to flow unabated in the press. According to Michael Craton, 'William Wilberforce was able to initiate the series of pioneer inquiries before the Privy Council and select committees of Commons and Lords, which brought something like the truth of slave trade and plantation slavery out into the open between 1789 and 1791.'[19] Nonetheless, in April 1791, the Abolition Bill was defeated in the House of Commons by a vote of 163 to 88, a massive blow to the anti-slavery campaign.

Just as much, if not perhaps much more to the point, in August of that year slaves in the French colony of San Domingo (now Haiti) successfully revolted, another crucial historical turning point. The French Caribbean had been 'an integral part of the economic life of the age, the greatest colony in the world, the pride of France, and the envy of every other imperialist nation'.[20]

The conjunction of these events deeply polarised British society. This triumphant uprising of the San Domingan slaves forced another angle of vision on the French Revolution and compounded the anxiety that affairs across the Channel had generated. Horrified at the threat to their investments and fearful of copycat insurrections by the domestic working class as well as by African Caribbeans, many panic-stricken whites denounced the San Domingan revolution.[21] King George III switched to the pro-slavery side, enabling faint-hearted abolitionists to change sides with him. Meanwhile, radicals celebrated.

Although no one spoke of pessimism outright, abolition was temporarily doomed. When campaigners remobilised in 1792, they were confident of winning a new parliamentary vote and refused to face the implications of the dual revolutions in France and San Domingo. Supporters of slavery, now quite sanguine, capitalised on the intense conflicts and instigated a successful policy of delay. A motion for gradual abolition — effectively a plantocratic victory — carried in the Commons by a vote of 238 to 85.

A Vindication of the Rights of Woman

The composition of *A Vindication of the Rights of Woman* was begun in the midst of these tumultuous events, its political ingredients indicating Wollstonecraft's involvement in all these issues. Indeed, Mary Wollstonecraft seems to have been the first writer to raise issues of colonial and gender relations so tellingly in tandem.

More than any previous text, the *Rights of Woman* invokes the language of colonial slavery to impugn female subjugation and to call for the restoration of inherent rights. Wollstonecraft's 80-plus references to slavery divide into several categories and subsets. The language of slavery — unspecified — is attached to sensation, pleasure, fashion, marriage and patriarchal subjugation. It is also occasionally attached to the specific condition of colonised slaves.

Wollstonecraft starts from the premise that all men enslave all women and that sexual desire is a primary motivation: 'I view, with indignation, the mistaken notions that enslave my sex.... For I will venture to assert, that all the causes of female weakness, as well as depravity, which I have already enlarged on, branch out of one grand cause — want of chastity in men'.[22]

Men dominate women as plantocrats dominate slaves: 'As blind obedience is ever sought for by power, tyrants and sensualists are in the right when they endeavour to keep women in the dark, because the former only want slaves and the latter a play-thing.... All the sacred rights of humanity are violated by insisting on blind obedience; or, the most sacred rights belong *only* to man.'[23] In permeating the text with the idea that women are oppressed by all men, Wollstonecraft accords all women, including herself, a group identity, a political position from which they can start organising and agitating.

Wollstonecraft contends that this age-old subjugation enables men's desire to transform women into tools for sexual lust. These beaten-down women with bent necks resemble the brute creation, 'brute' being a synonym in contemporary vocabulary for 'slave'. Thus, white women, slaves and oxen become part of a metonymic chain of the tyrannised. This association of colonial slavery with female subjugation opens up new political possibilities: the yoke, for example, suggesting excessive maltreatment, also suggests insecurity on the part of the oppressor, a combination that precipitates insurrection. The question that permeates the image is: who will eternally bear a brute-like status? Remember, too, that the San Domingan revolution was at this point less than a year old, so Wollstonecraft's words imply a threat of resistance: 'History brings forward a fearful catalogue of the crimes which their cunning has produced, when the weak slaves have had sufficient address to overreach their masters.'[24]

Moreover, Wollstonecraft deliberately uses the language of slavery to define women's status: 'When, therefore, I call women slaves, I mean in a political and civil sense; for, indirectly they obtain too much power, and are debased by their exertions to obtain illicit sway.'[25] This imposed status, this condition of subjugation provokes women into the flirtatious behavior she dislikes, but also provokes duplicitous strategies of gain-ing power. In the history of slave insurrections, the ear of the master — necessary for finding things out and for facilitating the timing of rebellions — was frequently obtained through such 'illicit sway'. While decrying the domestic sabotage of coquetry, she affirms a time-honoured slave strategy and the need for resistance. Perhaps most importantly, Wollstonecraft is suggesting collective opposition, but can do so only through positing the resistance of slaves and the London mob. Put bluntly, to suggest that women politically resist — although she herself does — seems possible for Wollstonecraft only at an oblique level, given her social construction.

Wollstonecraft also re-emphasises that the historical subjugation of women is linked to male desire for sexual as well as political and social power. In doing so, she fuses the oppression of white women and black female slaves, as well as that of slaves in general. A striking passage from the *Rights of Woman*, based on the trope of sexual abuse, exemplifies the point. It includes one of the few specific references to contemporary African slaves in the *Rights of Woman*, or in any of Wollstonecraft's texts for that matter.

> Why subject [women] to propriety — blind propriety, if she be capable of acting from a nobler spring, if she be an heir of immortality? Is sugar always to be produced by vital blood? Is one half of the human species, like the poor African slaves, to be subject to prejudices that brutalise them, when principles would be a sure guard, only to sweeten the cup of man?[26]

The passage announces that slaves and white women are subjected to tyrannical practices that have no purpose beyond the paltry one of 'sweeten[ing] the cup of man'. On the one hand, slaves should not be expected to give 'vital blood' to produce sugar and cater to white British colonial-patriarchal whim and profiteering. On the other hand, the 'cup of man' symbolically intimates that a female (opponent) is doing the filling. This sexual innuendo is consistent with Wollstonecraft's complex socio-sexual discourse throughout the *Rights of Woman*. Her awareness of the generic use of *man* further problematises her provocative phraseology and the relationship she hints at between sweetening men's cup and 'poor African slaves'. If only as faint shadows, black female slaves and the specific kind of sexual persecution they endure are ushered into view. Aware of both political and personal levels, Wollstonecraft subtly denotes sexuality as one of the 'prejudices' that brutalise white and black women alike. As Cora Kaplan suggests, 'We must remember to read *A Vindication [of the Rights of Woman]* as its author has instructed us, as a discourse addressed mainly to women of the middle class. Most deeply class-bound is its emphasis on sexuality in its ideological expression, as a mental formation, as the source of woman's oppression.'[27]

Sex and resistance interact. A coquette's cunning, which can overpower (manipulate) men, links to subterfuges and plots by slaves, especially by black female slaves who double as objects of desire. Or at least Wollstonecraft might unconsciously recognise that undue attentiveness to one's person means that desire is suppressed and life is lived on almost self-destructive, self-contradictory planes; excess vanity is not as foolish as she superficially thinks. Thus sexuality becomes the site of black female and, by implication, white female resistance. Women use the very object of desire — themselves, their bodies — to thwart those who desire.

Wollstonecraft knows, too, that external forces caused sexual and racial difference. She articulates this understanding in a positive review of Samuel Stanhope Smith's *An Essay on the Causes of the Variety of Complexion and Figure in the Human Species* (1787). She agrees with Smith that climate and social conditions are the principal causes of difference between men and women throughout the world, but that, above and beyond these differences, human beings constitute a unity.[28] She again pinpoints superior male physical strength as the reason for this ongoing situation.

Thus Wollstonecraft denies the conservative argument of innate difference and necessary cultural separations — that God created essentially distinct beings.[29] Such subjected people as African-Caribbean slaves and white Anglo-Saxon women are *prevented* from developing and exercising their reason; certain environments have precipitated their alleged propensity for passion. Once again, Wollstonecraft is arguing opposing sides of a question. Whereas attention to dress proves that Africans, conceived in an homogenised way, are an unmeditative people, in this reading they become people historically cut off from intellectual pursuit. With a change in circumstances, she argues, reason can replace alleged naiveté and infantilism.[30]

Wollstonecraft's intervention regarding sexually abused female slaves is not surprising. Through reviews and personal reading, she was well attuned to this phenomenon. In 1789, a review of Equiano's *Travels* emphasised her horror at 'the treatment of male and female slaves, on the voyage, and in the West Indies, which make the blood turn its course'.³¹ Equiano categorically indicts 'our clerks and many others at the same time [who] have committed acts of violence on the poor, wretched, and helpless females'.³² In chronicling his feelings on finally leaving Montserrat, Equiano harrows readers by highlighting his despondency, disgust and (silently) his sense of impotence: 'I bade adieu to the sound of the cruel whip and all other dreadful instruments of torture; adieu to the offensive sight of the violated chastity of the sable females, which has too often accosted my eyes.'³³

Besides her intimacy with Equiano's first-hand experiences, Wollstonecraft had presented a paradigm of slavery in an extract on Inkle and Yarico in *The Female Reader*. Shipwrecked British merchant Inkle is rescued and nursed back to health by islander Yarico. After they fall in love, Inkle promises to take Yarico to London and treat her royally; a rescue ship appears, but Inkle cavalierly sells her to slave traders when their ship docks in Barbados. To top off his inhumanity, after Yarico pleads for mercy on account of her pregnancy, Inkle 'only made use of that information to rise in his demands upon the purchaser'.³⁴

Since Wollstonecraft's discourse as a white woman was already shockingly untraditional, to speak of sex, and of all things to speak openly of black women's sexuality and hint at abuse suffered at the hands of white planters, would have been an untenable flouting of social propriety. She had to maintain a semblance of conventional gender expectations; hence, her subtle approach to the sexual abuse of black women in the 'vital blood' passage, in reviewing Equiano and in spotlighting that last look at a pregnant Yarico in an anthology for adolescent girls.

On the site of the body and sex, then, Wollstonecraft foregrounds the relationship between black and white women and their common point of rebellion. At one point she refers to women as 'brown and fair', meaning dark- and fair-haired white women, most likely: slippage and connection between black and white women reopens a fissure of sorts for comparing overlapping oppressions. Slave auctions and the marriage market, for example, are represented as related activities that are life-threatening to African-Caribbean and Anglo-Saxon women respectively.³⁵ Nonetheless, Wollstonecraft acknowledges by her loaded silences that the representation of others' sexuality, like sexual self-representation, is a tricky business.³⁶ Thus, in one sense, equal rights and a self-denying sexuality go hand in hand, because for Wollstonecraft sexuality (dictated at large by men) imperils any chances of female autonomy. And yet Wollstonecraft recognises dissimilar codings for white female and bondswomen's bodies, differences in degrees of complicity and coercion. In keeping with her sense of singularity, she is much harder on middle-class white women, in part because she is closer to them. She does not feel affected by or implicated in female social conditioning. Unlike Catherine Macaulay, who argues that women will wake up only if they understand their oppression, Wollstonecraft implicitly recommends imitation of her own bold behaviour as the 'wakening up' device. To recap briefly: all women have the same choices available as she did and should forego vanity and self-indulgence; they should break their 'silken fetters'. If she can short-circuit subjugation, her brief goes, so can anyone.

Thus, beyond a rhetorical appeal to women to effect a revolution in female manners, Wollstonecraft tends to eschew a group response to the absence of female rights. This aloofness permeates — even undercuts — her sense of vindication. A buried sense of identification and solidarity expresses itself, instead, in a displaced way.

Specifically, Wollstonecraft talks about resistance only by talking about slaves. The successful revolution by slaves in San Domingo taught the British public that slaves and freed blacks could collectively overthrow systematic tyranny. In the following passage, by equating slaves with labouring-class 'mobs' and using highly inflated diction for the rebels, Wollstonecraft censures the slaves' reaction. 'For the same reason,' states Wollstonecraft, quoting from Jean-Jacques Rousseau, 'women have, or ought to have but little liberty; they are apt to indulge themselves excessively in what is allowed them. Addicted in every thing to extremes, they are even more transported at their diversions than boys.' She continues with this response to Rousseau: 'The answer to this is very simple. Slaves and mobs have always indulged themselves in the same excesses, when once they broke loose from authority. — The bent bow recoils with violence, when the hand is suddenly relaxed that forcibly held it.'[37]

Yet, since Wollstonecraft disdains passivity and servitude, she may be expressing an unconscious desire for female resistance that corresponds to her own. She could be hinting that women should emulate the San Domingan insurgents and fight back. That nuance is further stressed by the sexual overtones of female compliance in the image of the 'bent bow'. Just as importantly, the image echoes the previous textual image of women from earliest times having their necks bent under a yoke.

Put succinctly, what slaves can do, white women can do; or, as Wollstonecraft asserts in the *Rights of Woman*, authority and the reaction to it push the 'crowd of subalterns forward'.[38] Sooner or later, tyranny incites retaliation. San Domingo instructs women about the importance of connecting physical and moral agency. Struggle creates a potential bridge from ignorance to consciousness and self-determination. In the most hard-hitting sense, the San Domingan revolutionaries, by their bold example, loudly voice — to anyone ready to listen — that challenge to oppression is not an option but a responsibility. The social and political *status quo* is anything but fixed.

Wollstonecraft's metaphor of the bent bow also decrees a stern warning to men. It reminds readers that male tyrants and predators incite their own opposition; at some point those who are 'bowed' may uncoil themselves and assault the 'bender'. This image recalls Wollstonecraft's own situation in the previous decade. Undeterred by an emotionally unnerving home life, she had tried her hand at most of the humdrum occupations open to women, refusing to be moulded or deterred by social prescription. Befriending and being befriended by Dissenters such as Richard Price only fortified Wollstonecraft's already firm opposition to women's lot. Her subtle, analogous and multiply-voiced threats address at least two major audiences. She overtly advises women to educate themselves and warns men that vengeance can strike from several directions. The fierce conservative reaction to *A Vindication of the Rights of Woman* was a response to the covert as well as the overt text.

In that sense, the wheel comes almost full circle. Wollstonecraft recognises that all women are opposed by all men in a general group identity. However, because she privileges personal and political singularity and takes pride in independent thought and action, she identifies her own resistance to gendered tyranny as the means by which women should subvert domination. She projects outwards from her personal response to female domination, oblivious to more devious practices on the part of other females to assert themselves and gain at least some personal, if not political, power. In one sense, her bourgeois individualism prevents that insight, since she sees herself outside customary female assimilation. Faced with oppression, she believes, women have simply made wrong choices. Consequently, she can posit collective rebellion by white women to prescribed subordination only by analogy.

With this displaced reaction in mind, certain re-views of Wollstonecraft's diatribe against female reactions to males — their flirtatious behavior — can be more sympathetically read. Just as Wollstonecraft can indict Africans for being neither intellectual nor reflective while portraying a carefully executed and successful revolution, so, too, does she exhibit an ambivalent stance towards women. Since slaves resist masters and since all men oppress all women, women will, by implication, resist their male masters. Thus, indirectly, Wollstonecraft registers that a woman's resistance could be enacted through coquettish manipulation, however feebly or distortedly.[39]

This argument about slaves and mobs creates a fissure in the text. If we doubled back, say, on salient passages where Wollstonecraft condemns Rousseau — 'Women should be governed by fear,' he says, 'to exercise her natural cunning and made a coquettish slave'[40] — Wollstonecraft's view of slaves' and mobs' resistance become open to reinterpretation. Even though she assaults self-trivialising behaviours and deplores their forms, at some level she may recognise them as tropes of insurrection; she uses female reaction to male domination in a variety of ways. Deploring how women try to please men through sexual manoeuvring, she rhetorically conflates 'coquettish' with 'cunning' and makes sexual manipulation double as a form of resistance to tyranny. Women 'play at' blind obedience not only to get some of what they want, but unconsciously to ridicule their 'masters', to cancel out tyranny with emotional excess, with a mirror-image perversion of power. Frivolous giggling is also a signal act of mimicry whereby women seem to conform to expectations. Ironically, the artificiality of forced laughing marks male desire and orthodox prescriptions for female behaviour.

If Wollstonecraft is (unconsciously or not) subtly mocking the idea that fear works as a governing principle to produce obedience, she foregrounds the idea that forced obedience linked to sex is a practice that can turn into its opposite: women will mimic the master's desire with design, they will use conformist ideas about womanhood to gain power. At times, Wollstonecraft recognises these strategies more openly. The state of warfare which subsists between the sexes (races), makes the tyrannised group employ those ruses or 'illicit sway' that often frustrate more open strategies of force.

The aim of the *Rights of Woman*, then, is to vindicate women's rights. Starting from the premise that all women are oppressed by all men, Wollstonecraft subscribes to a concept of overall group identity. This is undercut, however, when she probes particulars because her sense of a personally wrought self-determination causes her to find women culpable for their vanity, their acceptance of an inferior education, their emphasis on feeling. She locates herself outside what she deems self-demeaning behaviour.

So, in the end, she posits a group response indirectly, by looking at oppressed communities who have actively resisted — in particular slaves, and sometimes, 'mobs'. Her suppressed sense of solidarity and identification with other women expresses itself through her discussion of the rebellion of slaves, whose bow (back) has been bent too far. This analogy also constitutes a threat against masters: conflict is there from the beginning since all men are in opposition — within Wollstonecraft's political framework — to all women.

Put another way, Mary Wollstonecraft's personal development within specific social and cultural boundaries, that she then resists, produces a covert text. Her sense of personal singularity occludes her vision so that she cannot always imagine or conceptualise flirtation as a tool of resistance. Despite a radical outlook, moreover, she still subscribes to a sense of class hierarchy that contradicts her demands for greater distribution of wealth and legal representation and for female independence and colonial emancipation. In that sense, her text brilliantly illuminates the bourgeois project of liberation. She embodies the liberal ideal of progress in demanding freedom for certain individuals, but the shortcomings inherent in that ideal undercut it. The conditions that produced the text, then, end up subverting the text itself, and highlighting its gaps and its long series of tensions between bourgeois values and issues of class, race, gender and desire. So deeply estranged from its internal conflicts is the *Rights of Woman* that it cannot ideologically fulfil itself; an authentic, workable solution to female subjugation is impossible. The text trips over itself, its variant vindications ideologically incompatible. As a result, contradiction emerges as a major element of textual coherence.

Additionally, because the text invokes the French and San Domingan revolutions, the complexity of sexual difference, inequities perpetrated against Dissenters and the abolition movement, textual implosions inevitably occur. Even while the text appears to dampen inflammatory ideas and to underwrite the current system, liberating ideas erupt to refute the self-contradictory discourse of bourgeois feminism.

Thus the issues that Wollstonecraft avoids or bypasses end up hollowing and shaping the text into a new direction. She talks about disaffection, yet often blames women's alienation on their own behaviour; she poses the problem as one for which women bear responsibility. Her socio-cultural myopia leads her to misread resistance. Concurrently, she undermines her own argument through parallels between white women and black slaves. Yet her illumination of the condition of women pinpoints an important area of sexual difference and pushes the frontiers of this debate forward. Put baldly, the text ironically subverts the very bourgeois ideology it asserts (which creates alienation), and demands liberation despite the restrictive system it promotes.

Furthermore, Wollstonecraft's usage of colonial slavery as a reference point for female subjugation launches a new element into the discourse on women's liberation. It is no coincidence, then, that Charlotte Smith in *Desmond* (1792) and Mary Hays in *The Memoirs of Emma Courtney* (1796) criticise colonial slavery alongside discussions of women's rights; exploring popular controversies, they allude to Wollstonecraft's innovative investigations and connections. First of all, their inscription of colonial slavery presupposes the presence of women of colour and assumes a white, patriarchal class system as a common enemy. Second, it suggests unity between the colonised and their allies. Third, it highlights the question of sexuality in gender relations and stresses the ubiquity of sexual abuse in qualitatively different environments.

By theorising about women's rights using old attributions of harem-based slavery in conjunction with denotations of colonial slavery, Wollstonecraft was a political pioneer, fundamentally altering the definition of rights and paving the way for a much wider cultural dialogue.

6. It Ain't all Black and White
Delia Jarrett-Macauley

I chose the title for my talk to the Wollstonecraft 200 Conference long before I knew what I was going to say. I had decided one thing, however: I was going to be optimistic in spite of the fact — or perhaps, conversely, because of the fact — that in Britain the debate on 'feminism and race' seems to have calcified. Some activists, scholars and writers have done commendable work in this area, and yet today the discussion seems to have been reduced to, and sometimes dismissed as, a question of strife between oppositional groups: black against white, 'First' world against 'Third' world, privileged against underprivileged, powerful against voiceless.

Let me give you an example of this: the South African writer Lauretta Ngcobo's *Let it be Told* opens with this sentence:

> In the mainstream of life in Britain today, Blackwomen [one word] are caught between white prejudice, class prejudice, male power and the burden of history.[1]

Here we are, seemingly reduced to the status of social victims, the 'mules of the world'.[2]

I would not wish to discard this analysis, for there is certainly a need for more books, articles, conferences and courses which correct imbalances and alert the growing body of scholars and thinkers to previously unacknowledged works by black women. The tone and quality of those unacknowledged works interests me. The African-American novelist Toni Morrison has written about the need to recognise 'discredited knowledge', discredited because it is known only or almost exclusively by black people. This kind of knowledge blends an acceptance of the supernatural with a 'profound rootedness' in reality. Morrison writes:

> We are very practical people, very down to earth, even shrewd people.

But within that practicality we also accepted what I suppose could be called superstition and magic, which is another way of knowing things.[3]

If black feminist writings are to flourish, they must be rooted deeply in the real world and at the same time propel flights into 'discredited knowledge'.

It is amazing and disgraceful that there are so few writings about black women's experiences here in Britain. Rarely does one find an in-depth study on black women and education, their relations with the law, their participation in the democratic process or their representation within the media. During the 1970s white radical and socialist feminists, while attacking the male-dominated social system, failed to understand black women's experience of the family, the labour market, the health service or immigration law, and produced a biased, inherently racist, feminist agenda.

Today many white feminists accept that they were misguided in creating a hierarchy of oppression and shelving debates on 'race' and racism, classism and homophobia. And yet many white feminists still (seem to) regard black feminist theory as an intrusion on their exclusive domain — 'Theory' — a field which they have taken for granted for over twenty years. Fortunately a growing minority of white feminist writers now observe that diverse feminist, post-colonial and (following Alice Walker's inventive approach), womanist viewpoints all provide vital, though incomplete visions.

In attempting to enhance the overall growth of non-racist feminist thought, black writers have had to debunk myths about black female identity, to analyse the nexus between racial and sexual oppression, and to produce knowledge which is a corrective of standard feminist theory. In the field of literary theory, some black feminists have produced methodologies which analyse and contextualise the work of black women writers. The writer Lauretta Ngcobo plays a part in a vast project — the celebration of previously ignored black women — but this is just one element of the work which needs to be done in advancing our discussion of 'Feminism and Race'. It is not my main concern here. This chapter is about the cultivation of roots of infinite variety: it is a personal, optimistic view on the alternatives to marginalisation and separatism. It arises from my belief that we do not always need to acknowledge a history of polarisation more firmly and more tenaciously than our shared history and present troubles.

England, whose England?

> No store she set by the epaulette,
> Be it worsted or gold-lace;
> for KCB or plain private Smith,
> She had one still pleasant face.
>
> But not alone was her kindness shown
> To the hale and hungry lot,
> Who drank her grog and ate her prog,
> and paid their honest shot.[4]

In 1857, a fair-skinned Jamaican woman, Mary Seacole, published her autobiography, in which she revealed how, although the British authorities had attempted to exclude her from serving as a nurse during the Crimean war, she set up as a doctress there and helped many servicemen. For over a century after her death in 1881, Mary Seacole's story remained buried in the archives, and it was not generally known until Audrey Dewjee and Ziggi Alexander edited it for modern readers. Since then, Mary Seacole's life story has been cherished by nursing organisations, black teachers, historians and community leaders. They have recognised how effectively such a text can bestow a sense of authority and ownership on a minority group which is socially and culturally disenfranchised.[5]

But this is only a start, and feminist historians have no reason to feel complacent about questions of 'race' and the presence of black British women in nineteenth- and early twentieth-century women's history. The traditional absence of the Black perspective from British history has denied us an appreciation of black women's role in this society, and continues to skew our understanding of life here today. However, multiple sources affirm that during the last century black women made an impact on the cultural and political life here. From the ex-slave Ellen Craft's arrival in Britain in December 1850 on an anti-slavery tour, she impressed audiences more than her husband, William. Befriended by Harriet Martineau, the political economist who helped them to settle in Ockham, on the outskirts of London, the couple broadened their education and continued their political work while raising a family.[6] There were also in nineteenth-century England black classical musicians, such as the daughters of the Shakespearean actor Ira Aldridge, entertainers in theatre, musical comedy and in the music halls and concert singers. African-American anti-slavery campaigners such as Sarah Remond and anti-lynchers such as Amanda Smith visited Britain and also left records of their experiences here. Issues of class and gender have always structured divisions in black communities, and, unsurprisingly, we know even less about the nursery maids, launderesses, domestic servants and factory workers who inhabited Britain's multiracial cities, such as Liverpool, Bristol and Cardiff.[7]

The search for primary source material in the form of letters, diaries, testimonies and visual sources has been occasional and spasmodic, and indubitably much of value has been lost through this unsystematic approach. How has this been allowed by academics and feminist historians? Much lip service has been given to the importance of 'race' considerations within women's studies — nationality, ethnicity and nationhood are tagged onto discussions — but the concrete evidence that such concepts have been grasped is still lacking. (It is still the case that black women are assumed to specialise in 'race' and black women's experience — subjects which are seen as marginal, limited and purely 'autobiographical' — while white feminists might specialise in postmodernism, theoretical developments in poststructuralism and *all* women's lives — subjects which are viewed as mainstream, serious and progressive.) Today, those tokenistic moves towards acknowledging the centrality of 'race' and ethnicity still have to be turned into genuine scholarship and new work. What might that new work look like?

It would involve me in yet another reorganisation of my small, untidy study. The ordering of things would be different. There would no longer be occasional, compensatory texts, struggling single-handedly to take on huge debates, as in a row of the issues of the journal *Feminist Review* with a special issue on black women at the end. At present, I have a few books and papers on 'Women and the Wars', that is on white women and the wars. Next to these is another entitled *West Indian Women at War*, by two black men, non-academic historians, who felt that:

> too frequently black history is projected as black male history. Such an interpretation is not only sexist, but also displays a complete misunderstanding of black history. It fails to recognise that in the African diaspora black women have always played a powerful role in the history of their race.[8]

So here, from *West Indian Women at War*, is Connie Mark, a remarkable woman, who believes passionately in the value of black history, talking about her good memories of being an ATS member in Kingston, Jamaica:

> My first experiences were good — I enjoyed it. You came and got your uniform and then you got your training. Also, when you're young you don't have any hang-ups. My first salary was £3 6s 8d a week and I was rich! I'll never forget it until the day I die. I remember giving my brother-in-law a pound a week for the new furniture, and then a pound a week for material (for a new dress each week), and I gave my mother another pound and the rest of it could do for everything else.
>
> People always ask me about the difficulties I experienced, and I think they're always surprised when I say I didn't have any difficulties. You see, what was on my side is that I have got a strong personality and I think they [the English officers] had more difficulties with me that I had with them.[9]

There is nothing very inaccessible here! But there are some insights. As a black colonial subject, the youthful Connie Mark began by fighting Hitler's xenophobia, but in the process she quickly came to see how wider power relationships were also being challenged and transformed — how women workers were subordinated to men, and how the personal inequalities between white men and black women were played out. Through the words of black women, important questions emerge as to whose history and images have been recorded, the nature of the historical archive, the different perspectives and aims of feminist/womanist historians, and the relevance of these for feminist praxis. Without analysing the whole picture, only segments of life can ever be transformed.

Much white feminist writing is partial and 'separatist'. As the American poet and critic Adrienne Rich has said: 'it has not always been able (yet) to free itself from guilt feelings and false consciousness, self-blame and embarrassment.'[10] Rich also talked about how white women's writing has sometimes laboured under the feeling of ignorance of the realities of black women's lives and has therefore suffered from an inadequacy in dealing with them:

> Even where racism is acknowledged in feminist writings, courses, conferences, it is too often out of a desire to 'grasp' it as an intellec-

tual or theoretical concept; ... in the effort to stay on top of a painful and bewildering condition, and so we lose touch with the feelings black women are trying to describe to us, their lived experience as women.[11]

Nevertheless these real and serious difficulties are not beyond redemption. I should like to think about how this redemption can be envisaged: what do we need to do to respond to the space that is now termed 'difference'. I shall consider three issues: anti-racist female tradition, the question of invisibility, and the use of terminology. The idea is to see the segments as a whole. Later, I shall locate my own research within this field.

Anti-racist Female Tradition

It is clearly inadequate for white women to claim that they were duped by the patriarchal ideologies of the white male hegemonic force, and that they share little or no responsibility for the construction and perpetuation of inequality. It is also clearly inadequate for white women to claim that they are embarrassed and guilty, but still too fearful to act. There is an anti-racist female tradition, to which Rich's ground-breaking essay marking an important moment in contemporary feminist politics, belongs. This tradition opens a way to re-examining relations between black and white women. The primary purpose of such a re-examination is not to criticise whiteness and femininity, but to provide an opportunity to learn about the theorists, activists and leaders who have established this tradition, in order to extend the search for a more radical and more inclusive feminist politics. For example, we might draw an anti-racist continuum which would include the radical theorist C.L.R. James, the Trinidadian historian and political scientist, who, although author of the great slave resistance history, *The Black Jacobins*, also reminded us that some whites would always stand beside black radicals. The likes of James, together with the British women who defended black American soldiers from white men's hatred in dance halls and in cafes during the Second World War, and those who campaigned to end slavery, would all be a part of the line-up.

Throughout history, there have been activists willing to defend the rights of the 'Other', such as Annie Besant, who went to India in 1893 and a few years later, in 1916, founded the India Home rule League, denouncing British Rule in her paper *New India*. The government of

India regarded her as a threat to British rule, and she was ordered to leave the country, but she refused and was subsequently imprisoned. Indians rallied to her support and she was released. At the Congress session in 1917, Annie Besant was elected president of the Indian National Congress. From the late 1930s onwards, the former suffragette Sylvia Pankhurst worked tirelessly for the Ethiopian cause and in support of H.I.M. Haile Selassie, whose country had fallen to the Italian fascists in 1936. This was not Sylvia's first political association with black activism. In 1919, the Jamaican poet Claude McKay arrived in London, where he had a terrible time with some of the white men of the Labour Party. McKay also secured an audience with his fellow writer George Bernard Shaw, the eminent Fabian, whom he, McKay, regarded as 'the wisest and most penetrating individual alive'. Shaw, in his wisdom, advised the young black man not to bother with poetry suggesting boxing instead. But Pankhurst was better than either the Labour Party chaps or Shaw in her attitude towards the Jamaican writer. This is how McKay describes their first encounter:

> And then I became acquainted with Sylvia Pankhurst. It happened thus. The *Daily Herald*, the organ of British organised labour and of the Christian radicals, had created a national sensation by starting a campaign against the French employment of black troops in the subjection of Germany.
> The headlines were harrowing: 'Black Scourge in Europe', 'Black Peril on the Rhine', 'Brutes in French Uniform',...'Appeal to the Women of Europe'....
> The instigator of the campaign was the muckraker E.D. Morel, whose pen had been more honourably employed in the exposure of Belgian atrocities in the Congo. Associated with him was a male 'expert' who produced certain facts about the physiological peculiarities of African sex, which only a prurient minded white man could find.
> Behind the smoke screen of the *Daily Herald* campaign there were a few significant facts. There was great labour unrest in the industrial region of the Rhineland. The Communists had seized important plants.
> The Junkers were opposing the Communists. The Social Democratic government was impotent. The French marched in an army. The horror of the German air raids and submarine warfare was still fresh in the mind of the British public. And it was not easy to work

and arouse moral righteousness of the English in favour of the Germans and against the French. Searching for a propaganda issue, the Christian radicals found the coloured troops in the Rhineland. Poor black billy goat.[12]

Indignant, McKay sent off a letter of protest to George Lansbury, editor of the *Daily Herald*, pointing out that such headlines would stir up more racial hatred. Lansbury did not print the letter, but wrote McKay, a private note saying he was not personally prejudiced against black people. McKay who was not interested in personal issues, then decided to try Pankhurst, who was immediately and politically concerned; she printed his letter in the *Workers' Dreadnought* and arranged a meeting:

> Sylvia Pankhurst must have liked the style of my letter for she wrote asking me to call at her printing office in Fleet Street. I found a plain little Queen-Victoria sized woman with plenty of long unruly bronze-like hair. There was no distinction about her clothes, and on the whole she was very undistinguished, but her eyes were fiery, even a little fanatic, with a glint of shrewdness.[13]

Sylvia Pankhurst was quick to recognise McKay's journalistic talents and offered him work, including the opportunity to interview both black and white seamen at the docks and to cover news from the British Empire. Willing to challenge both patriarchy and imperialism, Sylvia Pankhurst addressed both sexual and racial oppression and made an ally of an able black male writer in the process. Today, black women activists are obliged to take the lead in combining racial and sexual solidarity; it does not have to be so.

The Question of Invisibility

The invisibility of black people has been noted in many areas. In 1984, the Asian artist Rasheed Araeen published a stylish monograph about his work and the cultural politics of the day entitled *Making Myself Visible*, challenging mainstream arts institutions to recognise the cultural diversity in their midst and the status of black (political) artists. Araeen discusses 'Eurocentrism — Racism and Domination' as well as 'The Art Britain Really Ignores'.[14] In the same vein, it is worth noting that Liverpool, a city with a black community dating back four hundred years, has ignored its black citizens and failed to promote them to positions of power — in the press, in politics or in the professions.

But what particularly concerns me here is our visibility: where is the black woman visible and how has she reached that place? For instance, at the Wollstonecraft 200 Conference, I spoke before an audience of five hundred, and yet there was only a handful of black women present. I was not sorry to be there, but I was forced to ask myself, as I now ask you what this situation means. At the moment of the conference all was well, but what happened after the moment of visibility? What remained of me after I left the lecture hall?

The black feminist Pratibha Parmar once submitted an article on 'Racism and the Women's Movement' to *Spare Rib*, in which she and co-author Kum-Kum Bhavnani argued that the movement had never taken racism seriously and pointed out the anomalous relationship of black women to feminism. The article was rejected by the collective on the grounds that it could not 'form a basis for discussion inside the feminist community as it betrays so many misconceptions about the movement's history'.[15]

Is visibility acceptable only when we deny our knowledge? Amryl Johnson, a Trindidian poet who now lives in Coventry, had this to say about an early experience with a publisher.[16] (This is another piece from Lauretta Ngcobo's *Let it be Told*, quoted before, which has many such interesting quotes in it.) A publisher read some of Amryl Johnson's work and said 'I would like to take on your work but how do I market it? IT is like a scream of rage? How do I market a scream of rage?'[17]

When I hear this, I agree with Amryl's judgement that such screams are not uncommon in writing by black people; but, even more than this, I think such screams are common to much feminist writing. Did not Simone de Beauvoir scream with rage? Did not Virginia Woolf or Emma Goldman? What is so very different or difficult about the black female scream?

Is visibility acceptable only when the screams are silent?

Terminology

The ideas and words of black women may be repeated and appropriated, but that does not mean they are fully understood and valued. In 1851, the activist and former slave Sojourner Truth, who is now famous for her question 'Ain't I a woman?' addressed to the Akron, Ohio, women's rights convention, analysed the construction 'woman'. Today we have anthologies, books and essays entitled *'Ain't I a Woman?'* and everyone knows about the breast being revealed, but what of the intellectual history to which Sojourner Truth belongs?

Patricia Hill Collins asserts, in her recent work *Black Feminist Thought*, the need to reclaim a black feminist intellectual tradition, and illustrates the way in which it has been neglected by citing the case of Sojourner Truth:

> Her actions demonstrate the process of deconstruction — namely, exposing a concept as ideological or culturally constructed rather than as a natural or simple reflection of reality. By deconstructing the concept woman, Truth proved herself to be a formidable intellectual, though she was a former slave who had never learnt to read and write.[18]

It is extremely rare, even today, to hear of a black woman being described as an intellectual. The first time I heard the term 'genius' applied to a black woman writer was when Alice Walker spoke of Zora Neale Hurston, an African-American foremother who was equally celebrated by Toni Morrison, Gloria Naylor and other (male) writers. Such acknowledgement is rare indeed.

With the insight of hindsight, black writers know that without the genius and intellect of their mothers, 'othermothers' and grandmothers, they would not be published today. Those who truly respect the words of Neale Hurston, Sojourner Truth, Maria Stewart and other pioneers will refrain from intellectualising racism and believing that an obligatory mention of it means that real differences among women have been taken into account. Intellectual correctness is not an adequate response to social and political injustice.

During the last five years, I have been researching the history of black women in twentieth-century Britain and Jamaica, partly as a means of learning about gender and imperialism and partly in order to understand the black woman's strand in contemporary feminist politics. Little has been published about black women's lives in any part of the Caribbean before the abolition of slavery, although Caribbean women's creative writing has started to flourish and a handful of anthologies on gender issues within the region has been published during the last ten years.[19] Black West Indian women have been consistently relegated to the footnotes of history except in a minority of texts, so devoting a whole book to one has felt both ambitious and exciting. In my biography of Una Marson, a Jamaican writer resident in London during the 1930s and 1940s, I am attempting to dispel some of the myths of black women's political passivity and deculturization. To put the work in a wider cultural context, this is a Pan-African project especially because Una Marson's cultural politics were informed by thinkers such as Jamaican leader Marcus Garvey and honed by African-American writers such as James Weldon Johnson and Langston Hughes. Una Marson is an important writer in early black feminist thought, not least because of her association with white feminists of the 1930s and the interventions she made within the women's movement in Britain. She lamented the sex role conditioning meted out to black middle-class women and urged them to enter higher education, rewarding careers and politics. In her creative writing she also focused in particular on images of black women, observing how black female identity is distorted and denigrated.[20]

Una Marson, like me, wanted to restitch those precious fragments of black history and culture, some of which had been deluged by the Middle Passage. Her creative writings, especially her last play, *Pocomania*, were the high point of the Pan-African project, giving back to Africa what is her due and pulling together the scattered threads of her full, disrupted past. This work returns 'discredited knowledge' to a dignified place and, as is usually the case with such texts, speaks to black peoples the world over.

Within my work, I have another major concern: to explore cultural identities as changing, unfixed, renewable possibilities. This is also very exciting, particularly in the context of the Caribbean — a region of fusions and diversity *par excellence*. Yes, there are orientations, but these are frequently overlapping orientations, from several ethnic bases, if you like. The Barbadian poet and cultural historian Kamau Brathwaite has discussed how 'in the Caribbean there has emerged a more truly creole norm: not white but black/white: mulatto; the 'white' and 'black' still locked in competition for ascendancy'. Caribbean cultural theorists are obliged to recognise that social and cultural movements have no single point of origin, but are born in a diversity of places. Indeed the black/white duality has had to respond to new waves of cultural incursion from the Chinese and East Indians introduced into the plantation system to fill the gap left by the African slaves after emancipation.[21]

In Jamaica during the period of slavery, many white creole ladies were using the kind of head ties worn by African slave women and cleaned their teeth with 'chaw-sticks' (not toothbrushes). Lady Nugent, wife of the governor (from 1801 to 1805), recorded in her journal the cultural norms of her day, including the crossing of boundaries in language, style and manners:

> The Creole language is not confined to the negroes. Many of the ladies, who have not been educated in England, speak a sort of broken English, with an indolent drawling out of their words, that is very tiresome, if not disgusting. I stood next to a lady one night, near a window and, by way of saying something, remarked that the air was much cooler than usual; to which she answered 'Yes, ma'am, him railly too fraish.'

Plantocratic racism, forged in the eighteenth century by such men as John Locke, David Hume and Edward Long, asserted that black people belonged at the bottom of a 'racial hierarchy' which justified their enslavement.[22] For white people to fraternise with and/or marry black people was deemed hazardous by the defenders of racial purity. Here in Britain there was and is plenty of evidence of this crossing of boundaries and of the mutability of identities.

During my research in Cardiff, Wales, three years ago, I visited the home of a woman in late middle age whose father came from Sierra Leone, West Africa and whose mother had been a white, Welsh woman. Our conversation that spring afternoon was full of references to West African retentions along that Welsh coast, such as burial services in which a pretence is made of tottering to the point of falling over with the coffin. But what struck me most was this: on the mantlepiece stood a doll, dressed in Welsh national costume complete with steeple hat, carrying the Welsh flag — but this doll was different. She had a black face. Such are the contradictions of British ethnicities.

The evidence of cultural plurality should lead us not to sentimentality, but to recognise our common values and the specifics of shared history, so that feminists and historians may change their vision to think in terms of an interculturation of feminist thought. It is up to us what type of vision we have for the future, and in what kind of practical action we are prepared to engage together.

I should like to end with a dedication, or in fact two, to two women, two black women who have done almighty works for women: Audre Lorde, the African-American writer...and Anna...

In September 1992, I attended a small pan-European workshop for women of colour in Berlin where I met a number of Afro-German women including Anna. She was wonderful. I remember her chairing very long and difficult meetings, and thinking how remarkable it was to see a young woman — a mere 23 or 24 — functioning with the aplomb of a skilled stateswoman. What impressed me most was her handling of the debate between Jewish women and black women, in which, after identifying the correspondences between our different histories, we struggled to find ways of working together in the face of contemporary racism. It was a complex dialogue between feminists of different diasporas, who shared a sense of political legitimacy born of suffering, abuse and ethnic degradation. It was also a tortuous exchange, because no one wanted to fall into the trap of asserting that group had suffered the most, nor could we grapple easily with some of the wider issues which affected our discussion: a lack of knowledge about Zionism, the psychological impact of European eugenics on black peoples today, the relationship between nationality and ethnicity for Afro-German women. We were, however, excited about coalition, because the climate of militant fascism which was affecting German minorities, especially Turkish refugees, impelled us to work together. Many of the women present had been called out at night to defend the homes and comfort the children of Turkish families who had been attacked. During my short stay in Berlin, white Jewish women provided transport and other 'services' to the workshop, so that black women were free to concentrate on organising the sessions and welcoming their African sisters. We knew that coalition was the way forward, not simply for Jewish and black women in Germany, but for the intellectual and political development of the international women's movement. At the close of the debate, Anna concluded: 'I want the coalition, I want to work with these white Jewish women, but deep down in my heart I am still an old-fashioned African woman.'

It is only through setting aside our cultural nationalism that we gain special redemptive powers.

I would also ask that you remember Audre Lorde, the African-American lesbian writer and cultural activitist whose prose and poetry has strengthened many women over the years. Her writing was frequently autobiographical, visionary and brave, especially *The Cancer Journals*, which document in meticulous detail her battle with the terminal disease and with the medical profession. The following piece is from *A Burst of Light*, a collection of essays published in 1988. Here, Audre Lorde writes about attending the Feminist Book Fair in London, where, on finding no local black women in the audience, she challenged the white women organisers to rethink their views of 'race' and sisterhood and to confront the hostility inherent in their exclusions:

> Feminism must be on the cutting edge of real social change if it is to survive as a movement in any particular country. Whatever the core problems are for the people of that country must also be the core problems addressed by women, for we do not exist in a vacuum. We are anchored in our own place and time, looking out beyond to the future we are creating, and we are part of communities that interact. To pretend otherwise is ridiculous. While we fortify ourselves with visions of the future, we must arm ourselves with accurate perceptions of the barriers between us and that future.[23]

What I think we need is not so much better writing about feminism and race, though that helps us, but a better practical and caring approach to feminism and race. We are witnessing the evolution of feminist thought into a highly sophisticated academic and frequently elitist business. The media has granted huge critical attention to the notion that the backlash against women is the fault of guilty feminists; 'victimhood' is a dirty word; fragmentation within the women's movement is a sign of its inherent weakness. We still need our feminism to provide a profound transformation of world society and of human relationships.

Feminism and Class

7. Some Contradictions of Social Motherhood
Eileen Janes Yeo

Women who tried to break through 'mind-forg'd manacles', as several chapters of this book have shown, often did so by reworking, rather than junking, dominant constructions of gender. Over the last two hundred years, motherhood has provided one of the most powerful models of femininity. Mary Wollstonecraft herself argued for women's rights on the basis of both sexual equality and sexual difference, and equated the latter with maternity. She demanded that women be admitted into the Rights of Man on the grounds that both sexes possessed equal rational and moral capacity. Yet at the same time when detailing the social roles of men and women, she saw their citizenship as distinctly gender-divided, prescribing public duty for men and maternal citizenship for women whose primary task would be raising and educating the future citizenry. Women's 'first duty', she insisted, 'is to themselves as rational creatures, and the next,...as citizens, is that which includes so many, of a mother'.[1]

Some historians have viewed this tension between equality and difference as an opposition between incompatible strands in the feminist tradition. But it is more useful to see both as options available for women to employ at specific historical moments, depending upon which offers the most hopeful avenue of advance.[2] This chapter will look more closely at a 'difference' strategy often chosen in the West, that of maternal feminism. A large literature[3] has recently spotlighted 'social maternalism' and shown how women reformers from the late-nineteenth century onwards, all over the Western world, concentrated on the needy situation of the mother-child couplet as a way to press for the development of some kind of welfare state, and as a way to expand their own role in social and political work. It is also important to notice how these activists not only made mothers and children their special focus, but often structured their own identity around a variety of social motherhood that could especially, although not exclusively, embrace single women who were not biological mothers. Taking into account experience in Britain, Germany and the United States, this chapter will explore how social motherhood opened opportunities for publicly active women, albeit in historically limited ways.[4]

As importantly, social motherhood provided a women's language of power, and needs to be carefully analysed from this point of view. It is easy to be seduced by sweet murmurings about love in feminist rhetoric. In the early days of the second-wave women's liberation movement, when relationships among women were being proposed as intrinsically nurturing and supportive, when sisterhood was being explored and celebrated, and when mother-and-daughter relations were being positively revalued, it was harder to explore the dark side of the moon. Since then, more space has opened to articulate experiences of relations with mothers and siblings which are full of rivalry, hostility and ambivalence.[5] Tensions also exist within the family language used in women's movements, where fractures along class, race and ethnic lines and power relations between groups of women can sharply undercut the possibilities of supportive sisterhood.

The Attraction of Maternal Feminism

By the mid nineteenth century, both in Europe and America, the dominant bourgeois ideal of femininity was that of the married mother located in the conjugal home. This model created difficulties for some married women, who wanted regular work, even voluntary and unpaid work, in the public sphere. It proved far more problematic for single women who by choice or chance did not marry or bear biological children. (Single mothers, in the modern sense of unmarried biological mothers, were largely dismissed as prostitutes.) In Britain, Germany and the United States, powerful cultural voices engaged in anxious official discussions about what they perceived as anomalous single women.

In Britain, still suffering post-1848 revolutionary jitters, the discussion centred on the censuses of 1851 and 1861, which showed more women than men in the population and suggested a pool of single women over the age of 30. The British statistics, like the German, are not very alarming to a modern eye, but nonetheless became the subject of debate, and in Britain led to the offensive labelling of such women as 'surplus' and 'redundant'.⁶ In America, single women were also called 'superfluous', as when Wisconsin Justice Ryan ruled in 1875 against the admission of Lavinia Goodell to the bar, arguing that 'it is public policy to provide for the sex, not for its superfluous members'.⁷ The 'problem' of 'surplus' women in America related partly to the decrease in the number of potential husbands due to deaths in the Civil War. Perhaps the most insulting solutions to the 'problem' were proposed by W.R. Greg in Britain, who recommended in 1862 that surplus women be shipped off to the colonies or else model themselves on successful courtesans at home in order to make themselves more feminine and attractive to men!⁸

This kind of offensive prompted feminist retaliation. The women's movement in each country subverted these negative messages and turned them to its own advantage. Rather than abandon motherhood as the central element of femininity, feminists developed a concept of motherhood which could also fit the single woman. Side by side with the image of the married mother, they placed an icon of a virgin, moral, spiritual or social mother, who used her mothering capacities in the public sphere and thereby introduced a family and home influence into it. In mid-century Britain, Mary Carpenter, the daughter of a Unitarian minister, who pioneered the study and treatment of juvenile delinquency, started an article on 'Women's Work in the Reformatory Movement' (1858) by referring to a sermon on the 'glory of the virgin mother'. She went on to try to recruit women 'who are mothers in heart, though not by God's gift on earth', who 'would be able to bestow their maternal love [on] those most wretched moral orphans whose natural sweetness of filial love has been mingled with deadly poison'.⁹

Similarly, in Germany, a concept of spiritual motherhood (*geistige Mütterlichkeit*), separating motherhood from physical maternity, was created in the 1850s and linked to the new profession of nursery-school teacher. In 1928, Agnes von Zahn-Harnack was still stressing that

> It is not simply a paean to physical motherhood that the women's movement sings. It is only where physical motherhood purifies itself and breaks through into spiritual motherhood that we can speak of the highest fulfilment of life, which does not at all consist in the fact that a newborn child is lying in a cradle.¹⁰

In the context of German unification, the concept of social mothering was also extended to cover married women, as a means of asserting women's contribution to nation-building. Leaders of the bourgeois

Allgemeiner Deutscher Frauenverein (German Women's Association), such as rabbi's wife Henriette Goldschmidt, argued analogically in 1877 that 'just as the moral strength of women, is essential to the development of family life, in the same way, women must make a wider commitment to fulfil their mission to the national family'.[11] Like British women, they suggested that their intervention would heal the social fractures of class conflict by binding everyone into an organic national family. Octavia Hill, the pioneer of housing management as a woman's profession and an exemplary social mother, insisted in 1877 that women could think 'of the poor primarily as husbands, wives, sons and daughters, members of households, as we are ourselves, instead of contemplating them as a different class'.[12]

This idea of the social mother was not only a central construct in the platforms of women's movements seeking new opportunities for education and dignified work, but also supplied a structuring principle for women's philanthropy and, in time, for much of women's professionalisation. In America, in the networks of white women reformers, as in the professions that women entered after their college training, single women predominated and with them a concept of the social mother.[13] In the words of Fannia Cohn of the Women's Trade Union League, 'A Woman is the mother: whether she has children or not her mission is to work for the good of the race'.[14] Eugenic panics in all three countries in the first decades of the twentieth century gave new impetus to the expansion of training and professions for social mothers, who would help less well-off mothers.

Contradictions in Women's Professionalisation

The social mother concept certainly opened new vistas of possibility for women, but at the same time it fenced in these very avenues of advance. Two kinds of limitations operated in the professionalisation of women, the first as the result of the gender division of professions into masculine and feminine, and the second by a further gendering within professions to which women had won entry. Like others in England or Germany, Barbara Bodichon and the influential Swede Ellen Key linked social mothering to nurturing and peace-making activities. This resulted in certain professions sometimes being declared inappropriate because they involved dispute and conflict, not to say aggression and violence. Thus Bodichon, considered one of the more radical mid-century bourgeois feminists, thought it 'unlikely' that women would consider 'being in the army, mixing in political life, going to sea, or being barristers'.[15]

In all three countries, the professions which expanded most rapidly for women at the turn of the twentieth century, setting a pattern which has continued ever since, involved an element of 'caring' especially for children and other women. Health professions, especially those concerned with childbirth and child-rearing, such as midwifery, nursing of all varieties and health visiting, grew rapidly. In Britain, state licensing and municipal takeover characterised the trend in the first decade of the twentieth century, in the context of the panic over the unfitness of the race following revelations of the poor physical condition of British Army recruits during the Boer War. In Germany, volunteers at health centres (increasingly being run by municipalities) were being joined by trained and paid health workers. In the United States, not only did the British and German patterns exist, but women also gained entry into high-status educated male professions such as medicine.[16]

Teaching, too, from early on a predominantly female occupation, increased its numbers. In the United States, the post-Civil War period witnessed a rapid expansion in Western state universities, which provided opportunities for women to train as teachers. Indeed, by the 1890s, there was widespread anxiety that American college education stood in real danger of being feminised as men tended to aspire to business careers which they felt required no higher educational qualifications.[17] In Germany, the first respectable profession for women was that of kindergarten teacher, which also became popular in the United States with the spread of the Froebel movement.

Where women gained access to the more traditional 'educated' professions, the social mothering role, even if they did not want to play it, tended to constrain what they were permitted to do. Thus in the British civil service, despite a Sexual Disqualification (Removal) Act of 1919, women could enter the higher grades only in a supervisory role over other women workers, such as clerical staff and telephonists.[18] In America, women reached positions of government influence through a maternalist politics, most spectacularly in the United States Children's Bureau. The German bureaucracy was virtually closed to women and even traditional philanthropic home visiting on the Elberfield pattern (established in 1853) was reserved for male citizens.

In all three countries, medicine was the learned profession which was, comparatively, the most open to women (the British Medical Association even insisted on equal pay for equal work). However, women doctors tended mainly to treat women and child patients, or to work in school clinics. In the United States, women entered the legal profession in 1870 earlier than elsewhere, but protracted resistance inhibited their ambition unless their male relatives supported and funded their careers. In 1890, one third of women lawyers were lawyers' wives, while single women were placed, usually as backroom girls, into family law firms, where they concerned themselves with divorce cases and, following Clarence Darrow's advice, with 'the free defense of criminals'.[19]

Educational programmes used for training social mothers often had great success in the short run, but tended to be consigned to a lower place in academic hierarchies in the long run. Thus in Britain, from 1899 onwards, women enthusiastically took advantage of training in Schools of Sociology, Social Economics or Social Science, which offered ambitious theoretical and practical content; by contrast, men stayed away in large numbers. These schools were often set up with the help of voluntary associations in which women took an active role and occupied positions of command, like the women's social settlements, the Charity Organisation Society and the National Union of Women Workers, a proto-professional association for social mothers. The pioneering London School of Economics Ratan Tata Department of Social Science was nicknamed 'Urwick's Harem' after its Director, even by women in more masculine programmes such as economics. Yet, like the Household Science Department at King's College for Women in London, it was more dynamic than other academic departments, including sociology or the natural sciences, before the First World War. In the same period, in Germany, where social mothers were expected to operate with a distinctive ethos, *Soziale Frauenschulen* (Women's Social Schools) were founded for the training of social workers.[20] These schools aimed to be as demanding as universities, but to offer a feminine alternative that would safeguard women's approach to understanding, especially their practicality and affinity with emotional reality.

'Separate but equal' has always been a problematic formula. Separateness certainly did not result in equality after the First World War in Germany, when universities not only maintained their higher status but began to admit women students, thus marginalising and demoting the *Soziale Frauenschulen*.[21] In Britain, as in America, social science remained within universities, but came to occupy a lower-status position in relation to sociology, just as home economics became the less-esteemed counterpart to economics and domestic science the Cinderella sister to pure science. In America, this position was engineered in some institutions by means of deliberate divorce. Faced with the prospect of the feminisation of academic life and with the accusation of being a hotbed of socialism because it provided action-oriented study, institutions such as the University of Chicago decanted the applied studies from Sociology into new departments, such as Household Administration and a School of Social Work, aiming specifically to sop up the women students.[22] Thus, partly as a consequence of the social mother identity which enlarged women's educational and occupational opportunity, a kind of gendered hierarchy came into being in education as well as in the world of professional work.

Contradictions in Social Mother-Love

More problematic still has been the issue of mother love when directed towards women of other, less powerful, social groups. Social motherhood has not been a unitary practice or idea. I have been playing for some time with a typology of three facets of motherhood — a disciplining or punishing facet, a protective and an empowering facet, two of which, like Janus faces, are quite contradictory.[23] Although I am concerned with developing a tool for social rather than for individual analysis, my thinking has been helped by the psychoanalytic theory developed by Carl Gustav Jung and by Melanie Klein, who clearly theorise the irreducible ambivalence towards the mother and thus rupture a seductively benign conception.

While Melanie Klein makes her ritual bow to the importance of Freud's staging of the Oedipal drama, in fact she lays enormous emphasis on the first six months of life, when the mother or mother-substitute is the key player, as being decisive for shaping the basic contours of the personality. Klein envisages the infant as being born with contradictory and eradicable inner feelings of love and aggression. The hostile feelings are not only very powerful but very frightening, and need to be managed and made ostensibly less threatening. A characteristic infantile defence mechanism, according to Klein, is to split the feelings off, projecting them outside and investing them into some other object. The usual receptacle for these feelings is the breast, which is fantasised in pre-verbal understanding as the good breast that feeds and creates happiness and the bad breast which withholds nourishment and inflicts suffering and death.[24] Thus, to extrapolate from Klein, embedded in all humans, in an early layer of personality, is the dual perception of the good nourishing mother and the bad mother who has the capacity to kill.

Moving away from individual history, Jung is concerned with suprapersonal, cross-cultural archetypes which exist in the collective unconscious, a layer of personality present in all human beings and accessible from myths and dreams. In brief, Jung condenses the ambivalent attributes of the mother archetype into 'the loving and the terrible mother'. At greater length, he lists as important features, on the positive side,

> maternal solicitude and sympathy; the magic authority of the female; the wisdom and spiritual exaltation that transcend reason; any helpful instinct or impulse; all that is benign, all that cherishes and sustains, that fosters growth and fertility. The place of magic transformation and rebirth, together with the underworld and its inhabitants, are presided over by the mother. On the negative side the mother archetype may connote anything secret, hidden, dark; the abyss, the world of the dead, anything that devours, seduces and poisons, that is terrifying and inescapable like fate.[25]

These psychoanalytic ideas fracture any unitary view and can sensitise social analysts to the possibilities of highly ambivalent tendencies in the area of motherhood, including the area of social motherhood.

The rest of this chapter will explore the extremes of the disciplining and empowering types of motherhood in the relationships between social mothers and the social groups they adopt or position as putative children. Although it is unusual to find only one variety of motherhood in any one woman s consciousness and behaviour, nonetheless to separate the types for analytical purposes can bring into bolder relief the tensions and contradictions which can too easily be concealed under the comforting blanket term of mother love. Some types of motherhood need to be seen as a woman's discourse of power: both the disciplining and the protecting motherhood preserved femininity by talking of motherhood and safeguarded hierarchy by positioning women (or children) as defective or defenceless and in ongoing need of guidance from maternal authority figures. The disciplining, supervising or punishing type of motherhood, which is the least attractive both to modern historians and to the past objects of such efforts, has usually stemmed from an inability or refusal to respect cultural difference. This attitude often informs genuinely well-intentioned attempts to improve or reform other people, and operates by trying to assimilate these others into the esteemed cultural pattern. However, the intention often falls wide of the mark, because the efforts look so different from below. As a British journalist, Stephen Reynolds, who lived with Devon fishermen, remarked, 'what seems reform to the giver may be reformatory to the recipient'.[26]

A discourse of disciplinary social motherhood was conspicuous in some of the social work starting to professionalise at the turn of the twentieth century in all three countries. The eugenic panic and the accompanying concern about deficient or defective social groups both shaped the thinking of women activists and was interpreted in maternal ways by them. A political agenda which prioritises population issues usually spotlights mothers, and this type of concern also tends to benefit social mothers, who present themselves as strategic to the creation of good biological mothers. In the United States, white reformers often identified themselves as the key Americanisers of immigrant mothers, according to Eileen Boris, by proposing a version of motherhood 'as understood by white protestant middle-class women to working-class ethnic women as a goal towards which to strive'.[27] The General Federation of Women's Clubs, aimed to 'carry the English language and American ways of caring for babies, ventilating the house, preparing American vegetables, instead of the inevitable cabbage, right into the new homes'.[28]

In Britain, class differences were more pressing than those of ethnicity or race, although in places like London these all blurred together where Irish or Jewish immigrants were concerned. British social workers tended to be more concerned with the supposed inability of the poor to provide an adequate disciplinary framework for their children, which resulted in feckless or delinquent character. Even where professionals such as the nurse M.E. Loane were sensitive to a profound difference in cultural values, they could not relate to this as social diversity but only as cultural deficiency. Loane recognised that poor people prioritised a giving, obliging and flexible personality over a highly disciplined character trained in postponed gratification in the service of a higher principle. Speaking of the difference of attitude in moral values, Nurse Loane observed that the poor

> range the list of human virtues in a different order from that commonly adopted by the more educated classes. Generosity ranks far above justice, sympathy before truth, love before chastity, a pliant and obliging disposition before a rigidly honest one.[29]

But then she concluded 'the less admixture of intellect required for the practice of any virtue, the higher it stands in popular estimation', scarcely a verdict that dignified the culture of the poor.

Several recent works on British mothering and on growing up in poor families at the turn of the century have underlined the discrepancy between the maternal practices of the poor, which often suited their material circumstances, and the child-rearing practices being urged by social workers at the time.[30] In America, the dissonance became sharply apparent in the campaigns for the protection of women workers. White women activists and social workers not surprisingly subscribed to an ideal of mothers as home-based dependants, while also recognising the material necessity for some mothers to work for wages. They preferred these women to be located in public workshops where conditions could be regulated by legislation and where premises could remain highly visible for purposes of inspection.

Yet in immigrant communities, especially those with Sicilian connections, it was precisely the conditions of industrial home work which enabled women to live out their own idea of a good mother, relative and neighbour. Working at home enabled them to keep an eye on children and attend to household duties, to conform to cultural norms of seclusion for women and to share (needle)work with relatives and neighbours when it was available.[31] Boris describes attempts to foil inspectors, even women inspectors, which were replicated in Britain, and points to a considerable accumulation of mutual misunderstanding on both sides. Nurse Loane, who was particularly aware of the British allergy to inspectors, also described how

> any working man's wife, would more readily confide her private affairs to a neighbour with whom she has had bitter, year-long quarrels, than she would to the kindest and most discreet of nurses or district visitors.[32]

To modern eyes, and also to the poor at the time, the most punitive form of social work was epitomised, in both Britain and America, by the Charity Organisation Society. This organisation felt that giving nothing was better than giving doles that produced no permanent results, consigned 'unhelpable' cases to the hated Poor Law, was constantly on the lookout for imposters and had no reluctance to prosecute them. To the COS, this kind of robust, scientific charity, although it might feel unpleasant to the giver as well as to the (non-) recipient, signified the social worker's ability to take the womanly or motherly road of renunciation, 'to renounce, in fact, the easy paths of charity and take the hard ones'.[33] Sadly, in the United States, these kind of attitudes continued into the 1940s, according to Linda Gordon, with white women reformers supporting 'welfare programs that were not only means-tested but also "morals-tested" and believing that aid should always be accompanied by supervision from experts'.[34]

By contrast, the most striking examples of empowering social motherhood made room for putative daughters to begin to stand on their own two feet, by giving them the skills for public citizenship and by ratifying their capacity to manage their own family and domestic affairs. The Women's Co-operative Guild, under the inspiration of its general secretary, Margaret Llewelyn Davies (discussed in the next chapter), was exemplary in this regard. Davies was well connected in ways typical of social workers of that era. But she was also very different in her attitude to poorer women, and the setting of the working-class co-operative movement also provided a good environment for the development of her democratic tendencies.

This is not to argue that a mixed-sex working-class movement necessarily provided the most favourable setting for working women's development. Guildswomen disagreed with male co-operators about affirmative action over people's stores in poor areas and, as the next chapter shows, broke with Catholic male members over the issue of divorce. In other British labour movements of the period, women grew frustrated over the men's insensitivity to gender issues, to the point of channelling their main energies into women's suffrage campaigns.[35] In the German Social Democratic Party, however much Clara Zetkin and Lily Braun pressed for practical ways to enable women to be both mothers and workers, their male comrades were more sympathetic to women's domestic role.[36] Nonetheless a *sine qua non* of British labour movements, of the SDP in Germany and of American socialist movements at the turn of the century was the belief in the full human capacity of working people and the commitment to providing them with the skills for taking an active role in all areas of social life — although, again, the theory did not always extend into practice with regard to women.

In the Women's Co-operative Guild, not only did women learn to speak in public, to write papers, to chair meetings, to frame resolutions, to participate in voting and so on, but Llewelyn Davies took every opportunity to develop a style of social investigation and a practice of politics based on self-representation for the members. Even when asked by government for her views, she invariably solicited and submitted the views of members instead, as was the case with the evidence to the Royal Commission on Divorce and Matrimonial Causes, as well as with the material that was published as *Maternity: Letters from Working Women* (1915). The maternity material makes it clear that she was very open to the analysis which her members made and incorporated their ideas into her own interpretations, for example adopting their argument that low wages were the main cause of their difficulties, which were in turn eased or exacerbated by the degree of companionability of their marriages.

Reciprocal listening and learning is a necessary part of any practice of empowering social motherhood. As part of such listening, sympathy and support, which can be acknowledged as helpful within the cultural terms of the recipient are also important. The US Children's Bureau (created in 1912) was regarded by many rural women, such as Mrs W.M. of Wisconsin, as a kind of distant surrogate mother: 'I couldn't tell this to anyone else but you, as I have no mother, & no one else cares'.[37] Under the leadership of Julia Lathrop, herself a single woman, staff replied personally to the hundreds of letters received, and often gave material help from their own pockets, as well as sympathy. One woman wrote bitterly about how poverty and an abusive husband were the reasons why her mothering had failed. After Lathrop replied acknowledging 'the importance of all you say' and asked for a 'non-institutional' visitor from Hull House to call, the woman wrote again to apologise for her earlier letter and to express thanks for sending such a 'loveable person — so different from the other people I have met'. Molly Ladd-Taylor speculates that it may have been because contact with the Bureau was largely by mail and intermittent rather than via a regular case worker, and because assistance could not be withdrawn as a punishment that women felt their relationship with the Bureau was one of gain. Perhaps, too, for some women, the fact that the Bureau also related well to local women's clubs might have been a factor. Certainly, in Britain, a version of welfare was being proposed by working-class movements such as friendly societies which left the administration of government monies to known local and sociable voluntary associations like themselves.

Evidence from below indicates that the respectful, responsive, empowering social mother was the preferred type. Guildswomen made clear that they disliked being treated as children at the mothers' meetings run by health and church workers:

> I did not feel to have the patience to listen to the simple childish tales

that were read at the former, and did not like to feel we had no voice in its control. There is such a different feeling in speaking of trials and troubles to Guilders (where they are real) than speak to the ladies of the Mothers' Meeting. You know that they [Guildswomen] have a fellow feeling being all on an equality.[38]

When Guildswomen, such as Eleanor Hood of Enfield, expressed their love for Llewelyn Davies, they evoked her as the perfect empowering mother: 'you have found out our capabilities and drawn them out without us knowing it'.[39] Such historical lessons in mothercraft are still relevant today.

8. Working-Class Feminism?
The Women's Co-operative Guild, 1880s-1914
Gillian Scott

Feminism 'has not spoken with a single voice'[1] in the two hundred years since *A Vindication of the Rights of Woman* appeared, nor have feminist ideas found organised expression in the form of a single women's movement. During the nineteenth century, Wollstonecraft's basic claim that women are not the natural inferiors of men but have an equal entitlement to opportunities for self-development was advanced in a variety of social and political contexts. This chapter looks at its elaboration in the context of a working-class women's organisation, the English Women's Co-operative Guild (WCG), at the turn of the twentieth century. From 1889 to 1921, the Guild was shaped by an outstanding general secretary, Margaret Llewelyn Davies (1861-1944), who saw women's rights as an integral part of the democratic socialism which she espoused. Under her leadership, the Guild worked at the intersection of the labour movement and the women's movement, evolving a distinctive working-class feminism that sought to hold in equilibrium the politics of class and gender.

During these years, the WCG grew to be the largest and most secure of the working-class women's organisations. Its membership expanded from under 5,000 in 1890 to about 50,000 in 1921, and by the eve of the First World War it had established a national reputation as a 'sort of trade union for married women'.[2] For one admiring journalist who visited the 1913 annual Congress, the Guild was 'a microcosm of a women's democracy, and a mirror of the politics of the millions of disenfranchised working women'.[3] The Russian Social Democrat Alexandra Kollontai, a guest speaker at a regional Guild conference in the same year, was also struck by the unusual social composition of the Guild. In her experience, she told the delegates, 'factory women could be politicised but housewives, never — they could never get outside their homes.'

Yet now the Guild, with its hundreds of branches and thousands of members, was proving her wrong and she wanted the organisation to join 'the International Socialist Congress to show what women had done'.[4]

It is evident from Davies's earliest contributions in the WCG that she was the moving force behind these achievements. When she first joined the organisation, its leaders were at best ambivalent towards feminism. Founded in 1883 to enable co-operative women to do more than 'just come and buy', the Guild conformed for several years to the socially conservative values that dominated the Co-operative movement. Its founder, Mrs Acland, wife of a prominent Liberal, insisted that there was no intention of raising the 'vex'd question of women's rights', 'departing from our own sphere', or undertaking work which could be 'better done by men'.[5] The domestic arts provided the main focus of branch activity during the 1880s, and in 1889 the president, Mrs Ben Jones, made it plain to members that she

> would not advise anyone to take up co-operative work and neglect household duties....They had a duty to their husbands and children; and though they should try to help one another, still they had to remember in the first place home duties.[6]

Davies's first recorded interventions in the Guild contrast sharply with these cautious injunctions. Her paper on Guild organisation at the 1888 national meeting contained the novel suggestion that branches might discuss such questions as 'Women's Trade Unions' and 'Women's Suffrage'; in her first speech as general secretary she warned members that Guild meetings 'must not descend into being mere mother's meetings'.[7] Her agenda for the Guild was neatly summed up in an 1896 pamphlet, *How to Start and Work a Branch*. 'Working women', it declared,

> are beginning to find out, as men have done, that the means for improving their conditions and redressing their wrongs lie largely in their own hands....Some privileges have belonged too exclusively to one sex; other privileges too exclusively to one class. It is high time that, as far as possible, all that makes a life most happy and fruitful should be brought within the reach of all.[8]

Yet it would be wrong to conceive of the Guild's successes during her term of office as the project of a 'great woman' who projected onto the organisation a vision of a working women's democracy. At a leave-taking ceremony in 1922, Davies accepted a tribute for her Guild work only 'because it identified her with that host of other women without whom she would have been nothing'.[9] Setting aside the self-effacement for which she was renowned, this statement was true in the sense that her qualities as a leader included the capacity to learn from the women with whom she worked in the Guild. This dynamic and collaborative relationship meant that the social ideals which she brought to the organisation were tested out and adapted in the light of the new ideas and realities that she found there, and it was this two-way process that was responsible for the progress that followed.

Generically, Davies might be described as one of the late nineteenth-century 'second generation feminists': educated middle-class women who, as the socialist feminist Enid Stacey wrote in 1897, were in a position to enjoy 'the fruits' of the labours of the pioneers earlier in the century, but who brought a wider vision of social justice to their own public work.[10] Her upbringing, Davies later wrote, had been, for the time, 'one of advanced social and religious thought',[11] with active support for women's emancipation on both sides. Her mother, Mary Crompton, came from a progressive Unitarian family which was closely connected with early moves to win female suffrage, and Mary's sister married George Croom Robertson, an associate of John Stuart Mill. Margaret's father, the Christian Socialist John Llewelyn Davies, was a pioneer of female education and worked for several years as the principal of Queen's College, Harley Street. His sister, Emily, was the founder of Girton College, Cambridge. In raising their children, the Llewelyn Davieses practised as they preached: Margaret's education, at Queen's and Girton, was treated as seriously as that of her six brothers, as was her quest for useful employment rather than a suitable marriage, while the financial independence provided by the family freed her to search for a worthwhile occupation untrammelled by the need to earn a living.[12]

In Davies, the various socialist and feminist causes upheld by her relatives melded to produce a primary allegiance to the cause of working-class women. While she respected her Aunt Emily's role as 'an opener-of-doors and a breaker-down of barriers', she recognised that the kind of equality for which she aimed could serve the interests of only a limited group of women; Margaret would probably have shared Enid Stacey's assessment of that kind of feminist agitation as exclusively 'middle and upper class' in composition and preoccupied with 'individual rights'.[13] Emily Davies, her niece drily commented, wanted the vote 'more because she thought it *infra dig* for an employing lady not to have a Vote when her gardener did, than because the Vote was a protection from injustice and a weapon for reform'.[14]

She might well have added that her own priority would have been to secure the vote as a means of ending injustice for the gardener's wife and all women of that class. In the 1880s, however, the most effective means of pursuing this objective was not immediately apparent to her. As a young woman, interested in social work and motivated by 'a passionate desire to promote the freedom and education of working women',[15] Davies was briefly involved in attempts to establish 'profit-sharing workshops' for female workers, but she soon moved on from the precarious realm of producers' co-operation to the sturdier consumers' Co-operative movement. She became convinced not only that co-operation represented the seeds of a future good society but that its network of stores in working-class communities and its ready access to women shoppers qualified its fledgling women's organisation, the WCG, as 'an ideal instrument for carrying to the working-class housewife the message of the movement for the emancipation of women'.[16] Davies had found her vocation: the Guild, she later wrote, soon became 'the pivot of my work', and for more than 30 years she was to be the main instigator of its many achievements.[17]

Yet, despite her *a priori* commitment to the cause of working women, the young general secretary knew very little about the circumstances of their lives. Like any middle-class girl, Margaret Llewelyn Davies grew up in a protected, albeit progressive and enlightened, environment. The work of general secretary, she later wrote, 'opened up to me a new world, practically unknown to the well-to-do classes'.[18] One important discovery that she soon made was that, far from constituting an homogenous social block, the working-class was riven by sexual divisions. Travelling around the country on speaking tours, and staying in the homes of members gave her privileged access to the inner workings of family life and opened her eyes to the price that many women were paying for its maintenance. Frequently, she found

> hard battles being waged against heavy odds, or the marks which such fights have left behind them...struggles with daily want, concealed under thick coverings of pride; daily work done under the weight of constant ill health; unselfish devotion rewarded by lack of consideration.[19]

As well as realising that 'the need for reforms in the lives of the married women themselves was urgent',[20] Davies began to appreciate that these women possessed a previously unrecognised potential for political activity. The overall picture, therefore, was one of agency rather than of victimisation. 'Personally,' she wrote in 1899,

> I seldom return from a co-operative tour without feeling impressed by the lives of unconscious heroism I see; impressed, too, by the great capacity — the practical wisdom and public spirit — which the guild is bringing out and turning to valuable account.[21]

These two discoveries conjoined to furnish the Guild with its distinctive identity as the only organisation through which married working women could become active in tackling the social and industrial problems of the day, and whose 'interests were specially those of married working women'.[22]

The Guild's work involved an inflexion of mid nineteenth-century feminism towards the needs of a constituency of women whose class and marital status differentiated them from the mainstream of the women's movement. Previously, the pursuit of equality had involved campaigning for the right of middle-class women to have roughly the same things as middle-class men: an education worth the name, decent employment, property, the vote. Translated into a working-class context, such goals immediately lost their resonance. The vote was worth having, but equal access to a working-class education, to an exploited labour market, to marginal wealth, all suggested a very limited conception of equality, unless linked into a wider struggle for social justice.

A further problem concerned the sexual division of labour in the family. Outside the Utopian traditions, the practical possibility of equal roles for men and women in productive and reproductive work has emerged in the twentieth century only with the growing availability of such facilities as contraception, labour-saving devices, and maternity leave, alongside structural changes in the labour market itself.[23] Nineteenth-century feminism was cautious in regard to married women's employment, and such pronouncements as did emerge (such as Harriet Taylor Mill's claim that maternity should not disqualify a woman from professional practice or a seat in Parliament, and John Stuart Mill's advocacy of the need for a married woman to have the power to earn — even if he did find the prospect of her having to exercise that power undesirable) took for granted a ready supply of domestic servants.[24] For married women who performed their own domestic labour, whose homes were 'workshops of many trades, where overtime abounds, and where an eight hours' day would be a very welcome reform',[25] paid work outside the home was often viewed as an act of desperation rather than of emancipation.[26]

From the Guild's perspective, any effective strategy to improve the position of the majority of women, who were working-class wives, had to deal with their rights in the private sphere as well as in the public sphere, and to take account of circumstances arising from sexual difference as well as those that reflected sexual inequality. Thus as the Guild's 'citizenship' work for women's rights developed, the subjects of women's trade unions and suffrage that Davies first proposed, were supplemented and at times eclipsed by campaigns for divorce law reform and maternity care. These significantly extended the concerns of organised feminism and involved the translation of knowledge that had previously been private and atomised into the stuff of collective action and public debate. The 'isolation of women in married life', Davies wrote, had previously 'prevented any common expression of their needs. They have been hidden behind the curtain which falls after marriage, the curtain which women are now themselves raising.'[27]

The 131 case summaries submitted as part of the Guild's evidence to the 1910 Divorce Law Commission[28] and the letters describing members' experiences of pregnancy and childbirth collected as part of the Guild's campaign to secure state maternity care,[29] yielded evidence which graphically illustrated the 'hidden suffering'[30] of many women, and thoroughly substantiated Davies's early impressions of sexual oppression within working-class marriage. Instances of beatings, the withholding of housekeeping money, infidelity, post-natal and other forms of rape, and attempts by husbands to induce miscarriages all supported Davies's observation that, in a failed marriage, 'the suffering is evidently much more on the side of women than on the side of men....No woman could inflict on a man the amount of degradation that a man may force on a woman.'[31]

Such insights strengthened Davies's conviction that, while working men and women were both at the sharp end of class exploitation and had a common cause in the fight for social equality, not all the hardships that the women experienced could be rectified through that struggle alone. Labour demands for union rights, and co-operative and socialist strategies to secure a more equitable distribution of wealth could ameliorate and even abolish poverty, and free working women from relentless toil, but such reforms would not necessarily eradicate the oppressive relations that often existed between man and wife. 'In plain language and in popular morality,' Davies explained in her introduction to *Maternity*,

> the wife is still the inferior in the family to the husband. She is first without economic independence, and the law therefore gives the man, whether he be good or bad, a terrible power over her. Partly for this reason, and partly because all sorts of old, half-civilised beliefs still cling to the flimsy skirts of our civilisation, the beginning and end of the working woman's life and duty is still regarded by many as the care of the household, the satisfaction of man's desires, and the bearing of children.[32]

These layers of subalternity meant that if women were simply recruited into the male-dominated institutions of working-class politics they would never be able to set their own agenda for change. Firstly, women who were politically inexperienced and unconfident in public would remain at a disadvantage in a mixed grouping: 'if men took part in the work,' Davies asked, 'would the great mass of the members overcome their shyness of speaking in public, or take their full part in organising the work?'[33] Secondly, it seemed that those questions that related to their sexual oppression and mattered greatly to the women, were likely to be perceived by the men as in some way unsuitable for public debate, or simply a reflection of natural difference. As a WCG leaflet pointed out: 'Our experience is that a body practically composed of men, does not understand or give due consideration to the views of women', and it was therefore 'most undesirable that the Guild's freedom of action should be limited by such a body'.[34]

The tenacity with which the women upheld the need for self-government was the product of friction arising from the Guild's 'citizenship' work; suffrage and maternity both conflicted with various masculine interests in the labour movement[35] but the importance of organisational autonomy was posed most explicitly by the controversial subject of divorce law reform. Following its submission of evidence to the Royal Commission in 1910, the Guild supported the Majority Report's recommendations for a lowering of the costs and an equalisation of the grounds for divorce between men and women (under the terms of the 1857 Act, men were able to divorce their wives for adultery, while women had to prove desertion or cruelty in addition to adultery), but it went much further in proposing, more than half a century ahead of the law-makers, that the grounds for divorce should include mutual consent after two years' separation.[36]

In 1913, this attracted complaints from the Manchester and Salford Catholic Federation that Co-operative funds were being used 'to propagate a purpose' that was 'alien' to Catholic and to many non-Catholic Co-operators.[37] When the Guild Central Committee replied that it was not prepared to drop what it considered to be 'one of the most important moral and social reforms which affect Co-operative women',[38] the Federation appealed to the movement's executive body, the United Board of the Co-operative Union, thus precipitating a major dispute not simply about divorce but about democratic principles.

While few Board members admitted to moral or religious objections to divorce as such, the majority believed that here was another instance of the women taking up questions that did not belong in a trading movement. As one Board member put it, they were not antagonistic to divorce law reform but 'to its advocacy on co-operative platforms'.[39] He did not find any subject too sacred to be discussed,

> he was only objecting to it being brought into the co-operative movement. Miss Davies said it was a social problem; another person would say it was a religious question, or a sex question; but he would say it was a boundaries question.[40]

On the grounds that if 'the Board had to pay the piper, they should be able to call the tune',[41] the Guild was presented with an ultimatum: abandon divorce law reform and any other matter not approved by the Board or forfeit the £400 annual grant from the Co-operative Union.

Miss Davies's private opinion was that here was a classic illustration of the despotic tendencies characteristic of bureaucracies, and of traditional masculinity. 'The official men of the Bd.' she wrote to Leonard Woolf, 'cant (*sic*) stand our acting independently. It is just the same feeling as between husband and wife.' They believed that

> there must be a controlling head in a democracy....The idea of rank and file independence, and experimenting in democracy, makes no appeal....They would like us well inside the movt (*sic*) — a position really fatal to us of course.[42]

She was not alone in this view. Far from curbing the scope of the Guild, the Board succeeded only in strengthening the commitment of its members to divorce law reform in particular and to the principle of self-government in general. At Guild Congress in 1914, delegates expressed their outrage at the men's interference. One woman protested at 'the ignorance of the Union. Did they think that they were the only ones who knew what was good for the women? Then they forgot that the women could think for themselves. (Applause)' Guildswomen, another delegate explained,

> wanted to work with the men side by side, not as subordinates with restrictions, for they possessed the powers and abilities of adult women. (Hear, hear, and applause.) They were open to criticism; but they did not take any action without having first carefully considered the question. (Hear, hear.)....This subject of Divorce Law they had been considering for the past four years; but for how many years had women been suffering?[43]

More than two decades of organisation and education had generated a considerable level of self-confidence among these Guildswomen, and both their determination to fight their own battles over the matters that affected them most closely and their contempt for the masculine assumption that the women of the movement might sit back and allow male officials to take control of their destiny were very pronounced. When the principle of democratic control was debated at the Co-operative Union Congress in 1915, a Guild delegate pointed out that all the women wanted was the same degree of agency that the men claimed for themselves. A previous speaker, she noted, had stated that:

> the salvation of the workers depended upon the workers taking their destiny in their own hands. Would he refuse to the women the same right of salvation? She believed that the women should work out their own salvation, and if they did not agree with them, the men should leave them alone.

There was no doubt in this speech about the gender of the category 'workers', or about the balance of power between the men and the women of the movement. 'In all sweet reasonableness,' she complained, 'the lion and the lamb were asked to lie down together; without discussing which was the lion and which the lamb.' Of course, she added, taking a swipe at the Catholic Federation, they might have sorted out their differences had it not been for 'the interference of the wolf'.[44]

The Guild's refusal to abandon either divorce law reform or the principle of self-government involved it in a protracted dispute with the Co-operative Union. The Union withheld the £400 grant for four years, until the coincidence of the enfranchisement of women over 30 and the foundation of the Co-operative Party shifted the balance of power in the Guild's favour. 'Guildswomen will find,' wrote the general secretary in 1918, 'that they have suddenly become much more important, and that their views and actions will receive far greater consideration.'[45] Keen to secure the Guild's energies in building up the women's vote, the Board of the Co-operative Union agreed to a settlement that did not violate the principle of self determination.[46]

The divorce conflict underlined the Guild's need to be able to defend its feminist politics within the context of the working-class movement. Yet, in other settings, it was necessary to emphasise a basic working-class solidarity. Thus, in an interview for the suffrage journal *The Englishwoman* in 1914, Davies explained that while membership of the Guild was open to all,

> those who join...be they ladies of leisure or women working hard for their living, have to take their place on an equality with all, standing for election with the rest and winning their way only if the other members wish it. Women of leisure must identify themselves with working-class interests, and come as interpreters of the needs and wishes of the workers.

In a similar vein, Davies's introduction to *Maternity* showed that even those aspects of women's experience that might be taken as essential, such as childbearing, were mediated by material circumstances. From the beginning of a pregnancy, she pointed out, a middle-class woman received proper medical care: 'she is not called upon to work; she is well fed; she is able to take the necessary rest and exercise.' During the labour, a doctor or nurse would be in attendance, and afterwards the woman could stay in bed until she was fully recovered.

> For a woman of the middle class to be deprived of any one of these things would be considered an outrage. Now, a working-class woman is habitually deprived of them all. She is lucky if her husband hands her over regularly each week 25s with which to provide a house, food, and clothing. It has to be remembered that the ordinary family wage

leaves nothing over for the additional outlay upon maternity.⁴⁸

Of course, there were points of convergence between working-class and middle-class women which made alliances desirable, for example in the struggle for the vote, but there was always a need to be aware of the potential tensions and contradictions arising from women's different material positions. As Davies pointed out, the problem with many women's organisations which claimed to represent all women was that for political and ideological reasons they actually operated a middle-class bias that preserved the *status quo*. The Women's Institute movement, which emerged during the First World War, she noted, was a form of association in which 'all classes are supposed to work together', but in reality 'the lead is usually taken by the richer people in the district. It is natural that the privileged classes and those with vested interests should not see eye to eye with the disinherited.'⁴⁹

Margaret Llewelyn Davies believed that working women could no more afford to give up their class solidarity in pursuit of women's rights than they could sacrifice their feminist principles to the imperatives of a male-dominated labour movement. This determination to defend the specific interests of working-class women found expression in Davies's most strongly held conviction about the politics of women's organisation. 'From my general experience,' she wrote, after her retirement from the Guild, 'I have found that, so long as there is class and sex inequality, it is necessary that working women should have their own separate and affiliated organisations.'⁵⁰

For two or three decades, her adherence to this principle combined with the exceptional opportunities presented by the Co-operative movement at the turn of the century to produce a democratic movement of working women which significantly broadened the social base of feminism and focused important new questions about the nature of women's oppression. It remains an outstanding achievement.

Inconvenient Feminists

9. Ernestine Rose (1810-92) and her Multiple Identities

Françoise Basch

From the pages of *The History of Woman Suffrage*, Ernestine Louise Potovsky Rose looks at us with piercing black eyes under her dark tidy ringlets.[1] Stiff and alert, her face expresses personality and intelligence. Contemporaries used flowery metaphors to highlight her cosmopolitan side: 'She was the morning glory of Poland, she was the lily of England, and she is the rose of America.'[2] They also underlined her fragmented identity: 'Polish by birth, Jewish by race, German by education, American by adoption, English by affection'.[3] Ernestine Rose, the Polish Jewish expatriate, brought to the *antebellum* American women's rights movement an outlook inspired by Mary Wollstonecraft, the Enlightenment and Utopian socialism. She challenged her contemporaries on the issues of identity, marginality and integration.[4]

Before settling down in the United States for 33 years from 1836, the 'wandering Jew' had lived in Poland, Germany, France and England, fighting against political and sexual oppression. She was born in 1810 in a ghetto in Poland and rebelled early on against the misogyny of orthodox Judaism. Her mother had died when she was a child, and her rabbi father hoped to marry her off to a suitor of his choice to appropriate his wife's dowry. But Ernestine Potovsky was determined to avoid forced marriage. She drove through a snowstorm to the town of Kalish to contest the will in court, won the case, returned home to find her father remarried to a wife of her own age and left for Berlin. Alice Blackwell Stone reports a slightly different story: Ernestine prepared her flight while confined in her room by her father.[5] She sewed precious stones (her mother's dowry) into her clothes, and on her way to the synagogue, she fled into another carriage that took her away to Berlin. She was 17.

She seems to have spent the year 1827 there, occupying herself politically and professionally — she invented a deodorant against cooking smells — and also travelled around Europe, observing the struggles between absolutist tyrants and liberals. Later, in England, she met Robert Owen (1771-1858), self-made factory owner, enlightened employer, philanthropist and advocate of Utopian socialism. With him, Ernestine Rose participated in the birth of trade unions and communities, an experience that marked her for life and inspired her social and political struggles. Among Owen's followers she probably heard echoes of Mary Wollstonecraft's demands for women's emancipation.[6]

When Ernestine and her husband William Rose, an Owenite cabinet-maker, arrived in America in 1836, they found the *antebellum* 'reform movement' going strong. Rose involved herself in various anti-institutional ventures, including 'anti-Bible' groups, revolutionary circles (such as the 'Friends of Thomas Paine'), communities and abolitionism — she was nearly tarred and feathered — and committed herself to women's rights. Her active and coherent involvement in American culture and politics continued her European commitment to Enlightenment, freedom and socialism.

Within the context of the *antebellum* reform movement, women's rights partisans asserted equality between the sexes in the social and political spheres. Ernestine Rose's contribution was that of a theoretician as well as of a tireless militant; she spoke and organised all over the country, and took part in the major campaigns about married women's property, suffrage and divorce.[7] Even from the other side of the Atlantic, Joseph Barker, an English opponent of Rose, paid her homage:

> She has travelled alone for months together, along the rivers and lakes, through the towns and cities, the woods and swamps, of that vast continent, under a burning sun, amid winter storms, exposed to the deadly vapors of unhealthy regions, lecturing in Legislative halls and rude log huts, to the highest and lowest, the richest and the poorest....Her eloquence...shakes, it awes, it thrills, it melts, — it fills you with horror, it drowns you in tears.[8]

Unlike her WASP co-workers, Rose came from a Jewish, Utopian socialist environment, which had taught her to believe in progress and human goodness. Shaped by their environment, she claimed, men and women bore no moral responsibility for the evil in the world: a perspective which highlighted the potentialities of education. She constantly denounced the warped socialisation of boys and girls and its key role in the oppression of women.[9]

The early women's rights discourse bore the evangelical imprint of its origins: belief in sin and salvation and in the essential difference between man and woman. Rose's analysis of gender socialisation denied the so-called 'natural' difference, which she viewed largely as a cultural construct designed to keep women within a subordinate sphere.[10] She demystified the high-flown rhetoric of female purity and influence that put women on a pedestal. Rose's rationalist approach set her somewhat apart from the temperance discourse, which had established the paradigm of the male brute trampling the helpless female victim. She acknowledged the victimisation of women, but looked for its causes elsewhere.

When Rose arrived in America, communities were blossoming, inspired by millenarian fervour and also by Owen and Fourier. In 1843, we find her involved in an Owenite community in upstate New York. As reported by the local and community newspapers, Rose held forth on the 'association principle' and invested energy in propaganda and fundraising in this community where members were free to marry and divorce without the sanction of judges or priests.[11]

Other episodes in her life confirm her interest in marriage reform. She attended the 'Free Convention of the Friends of Human Progress' in Rutland, Vermont, in 1858, where her name was linked with that of Julia Branch, who had made a fiery speech against marriage and the family.[12] She was also acquainted with Stephen Pearl Andrews and his free love communities.

For all women's rights advocates, marriage was the paradigm of woman's oppression. Rose had long learned to deconstruct and demystify Christian dogma. In 1860, when she supported Elizabeth Stanton in her struggle to liberalise divorce, her anti-clerical perspective clashed strongly with that of Antoinette Brown and Lucy Stone, believers in the sanctity of the bond of marriage. However, Rose never advocated its abolition. She believed in the adjustment and reform of marriage and the desirability of terminating a bad match, but firmly dissociated herself from the label of 'free love' used to discredit reformers.

Rose had known Europe as a battlefield where patriots and partisans of national independence defied tyrants. The members of the Women's Rights Association welcomed Rose's revolutionary internationalism, at least publicly. At the convention in Worcester in 1851, she was asked to respond to letters written from jail in 1848 by two French Saint-Simonian feminists, Jeanne Deroin and Pauline Roland, and made an eloquent speech on tyranny and the rights of man.[13]

Rose had always found her arch-enemies to be religion, the church and priests: all of them she saw as the perpetrators of slavery and tyranny. She coined a new commandment, 'Love MAN', and held these views until the very end of her life.[14] Nearing death, she worried that 'she would be invaded by religious persons who might make her unsay the convictions of her whole life when her brain was weakened by illness' and gave strict instructions not to be buried in chapel.[15]

How did society treat this remarkable outsider, and how did Ernestine Rose cope in this position? Despite her partial assimilation in the United States, Ernestine Rose experienced hostility as a foreigner, as an atheist, as a rebel and as a woman: xenophobia merged into misogyny, religious fanaticism and anti-Semitism. When Rose exhorted her audience 'to trample the church, the priests and the Bible under their feet', she unleashed conservative anger against anti-conformism.[16] 'We know of no object more deserving of contempt, loathing and abhorrence than a Female Atheist.'[17] The conjunction of those two categories, female and atheist, appeared a violation of the laws of God.

Antebellum America was not immune to xenophobia.[18] Attacks against Ernestine Rose, the foreigner and the Jew, though devious, were frequent. A journalist, for example, pointed to her foreign accent and physical appearance. On 5 August 1853, an article discussed

> Mrs. Rose, the Polish female advocate of women's rights....She had the same corkscrew ringlets on each side of her face, the same white teeth and the same disposition to show them. Time deals gently with Mrs. Rose, and it would be gratifying if she would do so with the English language.

In the same way, the *Albany Register* singled out 'such foreign propagandists as the ringleted, gloved exotic, Ernestine L. Rose'.[19]

In 1854, Susan B. Anthony reported an exchange between her and Rose which shows rampant xenophobia even among reformers. When Rose complained, Anthony pretended to ignore the reasons of her distress.[20] In later years, she mentioned resisting various pressures exerted on her and on Stanton to keep Rose out of the limelight. The accusation of atheism came to the fore more often than issues of nationality or 'race', yet racial hatred underlay the anger, confusing Rose's sex, ethnic origins, race and godlessness.

How did Ernestine Rose react to such attacks and assert her identity? Sometimes she opened her speeches with an apology about her inadequate command of English. Sometimes she presented herself as 'a daughter of poor, crushed Poland and the downtrodden and persecuted people called the "Jews", a child of Israel'.[21] On the other hand, she rarely identified with Jewish religion and culture. Her frame of reference was rather a universal, humanist model derived from the Enlightenment and Owenism.

Only on one occasion did she identify strongly as a Jew. The editor of the *Boston Investigator*, George Seaver, had accused Jews of being 'bigoted and narrow'. Feeling personally attacked — and by a friend — Rose responded with a sermon on universalist tolerance in a tone of rage and revulsion against bigotry and racism.[22]

Historians today do not doubt the unique contribution of her European heritage to the cause of women's rights: her acute sense of social justice, woman's bondage, and racial and national oppression set her in a place apart and also enriched the causes she embraced. 'This noble Polish woman' enjoyed remarkable recognition during her life and after her death, as an orator and a fighter. Yet she did not emerge as one of the great leaders. We are indeed struck by a sense of isolation and loneliness in the woman who 'had the fire of Judith in her'.[23] Reserved and shy, she left few personal traces. One of many unanswered questions concerns her retreat to Britain after 33 years of activity in the United States. She sounded burnt out and disillusioned when she left New York in 1869.

Fifty-nine years old when she returned to London, she severely restricted her activities. Some account for this withdrawal by the unpopularity of atheism with English suffragists; others, like Stanton and Anthony when they visited London in the 1880s, explain it by Rose's state of chronic exhaustion and depression.

So, for all her intense involvement in a major social movement, Ernestine Rose did not feel integrated in the United States. Neither had the wandering Jew found a resting place in England. The scene of her youthful apprenticeship was a place of isolation in old age. To the end she remained an exile.

10. Ignota, the Unknown Woman
Elizabeth Clarke Wolstenholme Elmy, 1833-1918
Muriel Fielding

Many articles published in journals from the 1890s onwards were attributed to Ignota, the apt pen name adopted by Elizabeth Wolstenholme Elmy, a relatively unknown feminist. For over 50 years she worked for reform in education, employment, the law — emphasising its unfairness to married women — the franchise and double standards of sexual behaviour, believing that all the campaigns were interrelated. 'Women suffer as women, as wives, and as mothers from evil laws,' and ask to have a direct voice in so reforming these laws' she argued.[1] Gender bias in education, marital rape and the role of a wife as an unpaid servant were issues about which she argued fiercely. Yet Elizabeth's writing and actions in support of the emancipation of women and in particular her concern with sexuality, exposed tensions within the women's movement. Defiant in her refusal to adopt a lower profile, she became an irritant to many of her sister feminists, who subsequently wrote her out of the history of the suffrage movement.

Born in 1833, Elizabeth lived just long enough to hear that the parliamentary vote had been granted to a select group of women; at least, I like to believe she was aware of this momentous occasion. She died in March 1918; her obituary in the *Manchester Guardian* paid tribute to her tireless devotion to the women's cause and to her advanced thinking. Elizabeth pursued her ideas with dogged determination, driven by her belief in the right of women to have equality with men and fired by the example of Mary Wollstonecraft, her role model. She suffered gender discrimination in education at first hand, being denied the academic opportunities offered to her brother and then pressurised, at the age of 19, into opening her own small boarding school for girls. In the 1860s, Elizabeth joined other activists from northern towns in working towards educational and political reform to extend women's opportunities.

Representatives of these activists founded the first suffrage committee in October 1865 in Manchester, and Elizabeth served as secretary.

Becoming increasingly enraged by the legal disabilities attached to married women, Elizabeth worked closely with Lydia Becker to reconstitute the Married Women's Property Committee in 1867. She argued:

> Foremost of all the wrongs from which women suffer and in itself creative of many of them, is the inequality and injustice of their position in the marriage relation, and the legal denial to wives of that personal freedom, which is the most sacred right of humanity.[2]

So deep was Elizabeth's commitment to this view that she entered into an informal marriage with Ben Elmy, a silk manufacturer and freethinker of Congleton. Elizabeth's protest action, although supposedly known only to close colleagues, exacerbated tensions in the women's movement. With Elizabeth's obvious pregnancy, the couple were strongly urged to legalise their relationship, as suffrage workers feared that irreparable harm would be caused to the movement if Elizabeth's free union became common knowledge. The couple capitulated to this pressure, and were married in a civil ceremony in October 1874; their son Frank was born in January 1875. Rumours circulated that Ben was unfaithful and cruel to his wife. Elizabeth was said to neglect her son because of her obsessive involvement in the women's cause.[3] Whether there is any truth in these stories is open to speculation but gossip was inevitable in view of the couple's unconventional lifestyle. Yet in letters to Harriet McIlquham, Elizabeth always referred to her husband in loving terms and worried constantly about her son's health and future.

Clashes had occurred in the movement over the insistence of the more radical northern-based activists, Elizabeth included, that the vote should be secured for all women, whether married or single. The proposal to exclude married women from a new Suffrage Bill, favoured by the London-based suffragists, together with Elizabeth's affront to Victorian morality, split the suffrage movement. In 1874, all references to Elizabeth were omitted from the pages of the *Women's Suffrage Journal*, edited by Lydia Becker, who had joined the supporters of a limited franchise.

Whilst still working to redress the rights of married women over their property, Elizabeth was strongly criticised by Millicent Fawcett about 'the circumstances connected with your marriage and what took place previous to it'. Mrs Fawcett argued that Elizabeth's irregular actions had caused 'a great injury to the cause of women' and continued 'I purposely do not touch upon the moral question: although there, too, I cannot think you were right.' She insisted that if Elizabeth resigned as secretary of the Married Women's Property Committee, scandal could be avoided.[4] Although continuing to work for the committee, Elizabeth's name disappeared from official records until the late 1870s, but with the passing of the Married Women's Property Act in 1882 she was praised for her 'intellectual power, legal knowledge, practical skill and unflagging energy'.[5]

In working for the repeal of the Contagious Diseases Acts, with their implicit double standards of sexuality, Elizabeth alienated suffrage and education workers, who were convinced that their work would be tainted by links with prostitution. Ever a strong-minded woman, Elizabeth refused to give up this work, seeing it as part of a multifaceted movement to release women from all aspects of exploitation and one which linked the campaigners with working-class women. Campaigning vigorously for many decades against the sexual abuse of women, Elizabeth sought to ensure the right of women to control their own bodies. She believed that the sexual demands of men, both in and out of marriage, put a strain on women's lives, often with disastrous consequences: her own mother gave birth to three children in less than five years of marriage, and died just days after Elizabeth was born. In the 1870s, when infant mortality became a prominent issue, Elizabeth, with others, attempted to direct attention to the irresponsibility of fathers, rather than blaming solely mothers for infant death and disease. Improved training for midwives was also on her campaign agenda. In her work for the Custody of Infants Act 1886, Elizabeth again challenged the system of male power, recognising that women's inferior legal position was linked to men's desire to control all aspects of their lives. Her pamphlet, *Woman and the Law*, detailed the inconsistencies and capriciousness of the legal system in its dealings with women. The successful appeal in the Clitheroe case Elizabeth jubilantly claimed as the greatest victory ever yet gained for the women's cause and a triumph for married women.[6] Her published letters succinctly argued the case against marital rape, but her perseverance in linking sexuality with politics did not meet with general approval.

Although brought up in a pious Christian household, Elizabeth flouted convention in her rejection of orthodox Christianity, seeing it as a recognition of man as the source of power and authority, and thus a perpetuation of women's subservient status, a view that conflicted with prevailing middle-class ideology based on evangelicalism. Ben Elmy's secularist convictions coincided with Elizabeth's changing views on religion. Their close association with the humanists Charles Bradlaugh and Annie Besant aggravated already strained relations with their fellow activists in the women's movement, many of whom were firm believers in the Christian faith.

After taking up a paid position as secretary of the newly formed Vigilance Association for the Defence of Personal Rights in 1872, Elizabeth moved from Congleton to London to act as a parliamentary agent. Economic dependence on prestigious figures in the movement, together with rumours of cohabitation, made her position in several administrative roles extremely vulnerable, but she refused to be intimidated. Relative poverty set her apart from more affluent campaigners.

Financial instability, due to the failure of Ben's mill, prompted the couple to use their literary ability to supplement the family income. Elizabeth's emphasis on female and male sexuality was further extended in articles written under the pen name Ignota, published in the *Westminster Review* until after the turn of the century. These included 'Judicial Sex Bias' and 'Privilege v. Justice to Women'.[7] Her influence was evident in sex education booklets edited by Ben under the pseudonym Ellis Ethelmer, publications no doubt unpalatable to many Victorians.

Writing to Harriet McIlquham in 1897, Elizabeth astutely summed up the delay in granting the franchise to women:

> It is the fear of men that women will cease to be no longer their sexual slaves either in or out of marriage that is at the root of the whole opposition to our just claim. No doubt their fear is justified for that is precisely what we do mean.[8]

To Elizabeth, sexual politics were inseparable from more formal politics. It was her refusal to keep silent over contentious subjects, together with her cohabitation and rejection of orthodox Christianity, which undoubtedly resulted in her exclusion from the history of the women's movement. It is ironic that it was women who consigned her to invisibility. She was indeed an inconvenient feminist!

11. Ada Nield Chew
An Uncomfortable Feminist
Gerry Holloway

Feminism has long been described and dismissed as a middle-class affair, a movement that talks in the name of women, but pursues the narrower concerns of those more privileged ones.[1]

The debate around class in the women's movement is not a new one. However, its persistence indicates that we have yet to reach any feminist alternative to patriarchal constructs of hierarchy. This means we marginalise women who could contribute greatly to the struggle against patriarchy. In this chapter, I want to examine the way in which this marginalisation affected one such woman, who was active at the beginning of this century. That woman was Ada Nield Chew. Chew is particularly important to our understanding of class relations within the Edwardian women's movement because she is one of the few working-class activists who wrote about their politics. Her writings depict the difficulties of being both a woman and working-class at a time when this meant being doubly silenced. And yet, despite being economically dependent on various women's organisations for her livelihood, she was not afraid to criticise those organisations.

Ada Nield was born on 28 January 1870 at Talke on the edge of the Potteries.[2] She was the second child and eldest daughter in a family of 13 children, nine of whom survived infancy. Her only sister was an epileptic, who was eventually institutionalised, so the burden of helping her mother fell wholly upon Ada, who hated to see the drudgery of her mother's life even more than she hated housework. The role of woman as wife and mother was to become central to Ada's feminism, but her analysis differed from that of most of her middle-class contemporaries. Her father was a small farmer whose fortunes declined during the 1880s, and eventually the family moved to Crewe. Like most parents at this time, the Nields did not concern themselves with Ada's education and work prospects. Consequently, Ada drifted from job to job, eventually finding work in a clothing factory in Crewe. Here she learned her next lesson in feminism and began her career as a political writer.

At the factory, not only were the wages low, but women received a third of the male wage for the same work. This discovery so outraged Ada that she wrote a series of anonymous letters to the *Crewe Chronicle* exposing the low wages and the injustices of factory life for women and giving a vivid account of their daily life. This was such an unusual and sensational occurrence that the editor commented patronisingly that 'Our correspondent writes a most intelligent letter; and if she is a specimen of the factory girl, then Crewe factory proprietors should be proud of their "hands".'[3] The correspondence continued from May to September 1894, until her employer discovered her identity and sacked her. The Independent Labour Party (ILP) recognised her worth, and she began her career as a peripatetic speaker.

The *Crewe Chronicle* episode was the first indication that Ada was not afraid to stand up and speak on behalf of women of her class. However, at this time she still believed that middle-class women could, and would, help working-class women. In one of the *Chronicle* letters, she wrote in support of the Minority Report of the Labour Commission, which opposed legislation regulating women's employment:

> will you allow me to urge upon your readers, upon those of my own sex who though not yet having the privilege of voting themselves, yet have influence with those who have, to use that influence intelligently, in the right direction?[4]

This faith in the 'intelligent influence' of middle-class women was to diminish over the years in which she worked for the ILP, the Clarion Van, the Women's Trade Union League (WTUL), the Fabian Society, the Women's Labour League and the National Union of Women's Suffrage Societies (NUWSS). Her first recorded clash with a middle-class feminist was with none other than Christabel Pankhurst over the debate between women's and adult suffrage in 1904. At this point Ada supported adult suffrage and she debated the question with Christabel in a series of letters in the *Clarion*. It was obvious that she no longer trusted middle-class women to represent the best interests of working women:

> Well-to-do women would by means of this Bill, [Bamford Slack's] be

enfranchised almost to a woman, and...their vote, *given naturally in their own interests*, would help swamp the Labour vote [my italics].⁵

Over the next ten years, Ada found her ideas often at variance with her middle-class paymistresses in the women's movement. The middle-class feminist press published many of her stories and articles, and she used this platform to educate middle-class women about the reality of working-class women's lives and to promote her remedies for their ills. The *Common Cause* featured her articles frequently, but eschewed association with her views on controversial issues: 'IN NO CASE does the NUWSS take responsibility for the views set forward in signed articles. Our object is to provide a platform for free discussion.'⁶

So why was there such a breach between Ada and other feminists with whom she worked? It was in the area of the married working woman and economic independence that Ada's views were at greatest variance with mainstream feminist opinion. In this area she was more in line with the Social Democratic Federation (SDF), which advocated communal childcare as part of its socialist vision; this was in contrast to the liberal readership of the *Common Cause*, who wanted to mould working-class women into an ideal they were rejecting for themselves, that of the domesticated mother dependent on her husband.⁷

This was one reason for Ada's marginalisation within the movement, but a more complex reason was the issue of class. Feminism as we know it in this country developed at the time when patriarchy fused with capitalism and imperialism. Although it challenged patriarchal assumptions about women, it did not necessarily offer a direct challenge to capitalism and imperialism. In other words, assumptions about class and race went largely unchallenged. Class was not seen as a special problem, insofar as middle- and upper-class women presumed that it was their right, if not their duty, to instruct working-class women. By regarding gender as a unifying concept, the driving principle behind much of their activity, the early women's movement masked other problems, particularly those of class and race. Feminist historians have continued this practice by arguing that class is an inappropriate category when discussing women. Philippa Levine, for instance, plays down the importance of class in the movement, arguing that gender was the unifying idea and claiming that women's relationship with class is associative because it is dependent on their relationship with men.⁸

However, class is not defined solely by occupational or economic status, as Levine suggests. It is also a question of access to opportunity.

Moreover, people in the nineteenth century were very conscious of both their social and their economic status in society, and used their status in very precise and important ways to achieve their aims. In this matter, feminists were as conventional as anyone else. It is perhaps more helpful to consider the idea of cultural capital when thinking about power relationships between groups of women. By cultural capital I mean the acquisition of certain social knowledge (accent, dress, kin and social connections, behaviour, etc.), which allows one to know how to participate in certain organisations and social situations. Like Ada, many middle-class feminists had very little money of their own and their education had been neglected. However, through their socialisation and familial and social connections they were able to take a leading position in the women's movement. Emily Davies is a well-known example of such a woman.

Ada never believed that middle-class women were better qualified to decide strategy or policy as a whole. For her, sisterhood was about equal participation.[9] Consequently, she decried suffrage societies that were organised in a way that excluded working-class women from active involvement:

> There is one point of attack which I think is too much ignored by all the suffrage societies. They are far too 'classy'....The branch of the society in my own town is probably typical of most others and of whom does it consist? The professional and 'independent' classes almost entirely. The working woman is conspicuous by her absence. Our public meetings are cold and ladylike. Yet the working woman is quite eager to come to meetings and be interested....Here lies an enormous and most promising field of work. It is much too neglected. And we neglect it at our cost.[10]

This attitude was hardly likely to endear her to women who regarded working-class women as 'our poor oppressed sisters' and saw it as their duty to patronise the working class.

Feminist networks offered comradeship and support to many activists.[11] However, networks can be exclusive as well as inclusive, and many women's organisations at this time operated in very similar ways to male networks, where positions were gained through whom you knew rather than through personal qualities.[12] This meant that a woman like Ada would not fit into the organisational hierarchies with which she worked, despite her obvious talent. For example, although the WTUL recognised her qualities as an organiser, and although by 1900 they had realised that it was more effective to send out working-class women to organise women workers than Lady Dilke or Gertrude Tuckwell, Ada was not part of the decision-making mechanism. An episode that occurred while her daughter Doris was carrying out research some time after her death illustrates Ada's marginalisation within the women's movement. Doris met Gertrude Tuckwell, the president of the WTUL, who had employed Ada and worked closely with her for several years on the Potteries Fund. Tuckwell could not remember her at all.[13] Further, as far as I know, she is not mentioned in any of the autobiographies written by suffragists after the First World War. Doris puzzles over this amnesia putting it down to the fact that Tuckwell was an elderly woman. However, Tuckwell was no ordinary elderly woman. She had collected an enormous archive on the WTUL and on issues concerning the industrial position of women at this time, including Ada's reports. I believe that class difference caused the amnesia. Tuckwell was an upper-class woman, who had made the WTUL her life's work. She would not regard Ada as a colleague with whom she was on equal terms, but as a working-class employee who reported to her employer on the conditions of workers throughout the country. She shared no experience of Ada's life beyond the reports she filed each month. Consequently, she forgot one of the most interesting, vivacious feminist thinkers of her day because she was not 'one of us'. This forgetfulness offers a salutary lesson to us all.

Engendering Politics Today

12. Leading a Normal Family?
Sexuality and Nation in the 1991 Winnie Mandela Trial

Rachel Holmes

> Comrade Nomzamo and myself contracted our marriage at a critical time in the struggle for liberation in our country. Owing to the pressures of our shared commitment to the ANC and the struggle to end apartheid we were unable to enjoy a normal family life.[1]

Nelson Mandela's public announcement of his formal separation from Nomzamo Winnie Mandela in 1992 heralded the end of a heterosexual romance which, over a period of 34 years, had acquired a symbolic importance in the iconography of resistance politics in South Africa. But the symbolic weight of this marriage was inevitably, and dangerously, abstracted from the real constraints placed upon the Mandelas' relationship from the very beginnings of their romance. Nelson Mandela's announcement of their separation bore eloquent and frank testimony to the fact that his and Winnie's functions as husband and wife, father and mother, had never unproblematically occupied the familial spaces nominally accorded to these roles, but that rather he and Winnie had performed their functions in a symbolic way. They courted sporadically and hastily in moments stolen between political meetings and trials, married without time to complete the full marriage rituals expected by African customary law, and lived together only briefly. Nelson Mandela was never able to be present at the births or in the bringing up of their children, and Winnie's own status in relation to his time and attention was always subordinate to the requirements of the struggle and inhibited by the sanctions of the state.[2]

Many commentators have made attempts to diagnose the reasons for the collapse of this marriage,[3] and some have identified the symbolic excess through which the Mandela relationship was made into public and, more importantly, political property.[4] All, however, have uncritically naturalised the heterosexual character of this iconographic coupling, and ignored the implications of the fact that Nelson and Winnie Mandela's separation was precipitated by Winnie's involvement in a state trial — in which she was charged with kidnap and assault. This trial and the debates surrounding it produced homophobic public discourses on the issues of male homosexuality and 'child' abuse. Furthermore, these alleged public statements on sexuality were marked by a *racialisation* of homophobic discourses which featured to an unprecedented degree in the juridical proceedings and in the media responses to the trial.

The public articulation of this homophobia brought Winnie Mandela's symbolic role, tied to the name of the ANC, into direct confrontation with the fledgling lesbian, gay and bisexual movement in South Africa, a movement whose sexual dimensions could never be accommodated within the image of the supposedly 'normative' national family. Equally, much has been spoken and written about the way in which the Winnie Mandela trial of 1991 became a focal point through which South African societies rearticulated and highlighted their pressing concern with the endemic culture of violence. However, in discussing the significance of this particular foregrounding of violence, it is necessary to focus far more carefully on the symbolic importance of the specific locale from which it was generated, namely a residence whose internal functions and image in the community occupied the figural space accorded to the familial household, a site which, in the resonances of the social imaginary, is imbued with the schematisations of 'the family' and 'familial'.

In January 1989, the *Weekly Mail* (Johannesburg) and the *Guardian* (London) had published a scoop story revealing that on 29 December 1988 four 'youths' had been abducted from a manse presided over by a Methodist minister, Reverend Paul Verryn, in Orlando West, Soweto, and taken to the Diepkloof Extension home of Winnie Mandela, against their will. Here they were allegedly subjected to a variety of accusations concerning both their political affiliations and their sexuality, seriously physically assaulted and then held captive. The victims of this abuse were Kenny Kgase (29), Thabiso Mono (18), Pelo Gabriel Mekgwe (19), and Stompie Moeketsi Seipei (14). These revelations sparked off media publicisation of the continuing community anxieties that had been developing over the conduct of the Mandela United Football Club (the MUFC, Winnie Mandela's personal 'team' of, ostensibly, bodyguards) and over the disappearance and alleged murder of Stompie. The controversy highlighted questions relating to the extent of Winnie Mandela's complicity and personal involvement in the events, as those abducted claimed that she had personally assaulted them. This story, and the subsequent trial, led to Jerry Richardson, former 'coach' of the MUFC, being found guilty of the kidnap and assault of Mono, Mekgwe and Kgase, and of the murder of Stompie. At Richardson's trial, Winnie Mandela argued that the 'boys' had been removed from the manse to protect them from sexual abuse by the Methodist priest in charge, Paul Verryn. The Richardson trial cleared Verryn of the allegation of sexual abuse.

On the basis of the allegations that emerged during the Richardson Trial, Mandela herself was brought to trial on 4 February 1991. In the presence of a court packed with high-profile ANC leaders, including Nelson Mandela, Winnie Mandela and three co-accused were charged with kidnapping and assault with intention to do grievous bodily harm, and a basis of common purpose was alleged. All pleaded not guilty to the charges. Key witnesses for the state prosecution were Kgase, Mono and Mekgwe, the survivors of the assault. When testifying, Winnie Mandela denied that she had assaulted anyone or that any assault had been committed in her presence, but did not deny that the complainants had been brought to her home. She claimed that in December 1988, Xoliswa Falati, who was working in Verryn's manse, had approached her and claimed that (homo)sexual abuse was occurring there, and 'that a youth Katiza Chebekhulu had, as a result of indecent assault on him by Verryn, become mentally disturbed'.[5] Mandela claimed that she had responded by suggesting to Falati that Chebekhulu be brought to her, and that on 29 December they went to the surgery of Dr Abu-Bakar Asvat, where Chebekhulu was examined. Two days later Falati told her of arrangements (made with Jerry Richardson) to bring four 'youths' from the manse in order to deter the absent Paul Verryn from frustrating investigations into the alleged sexual abuse upon his return, and to prevent the spread of such practices amongst the youths staying in Verryn's Orlando West refuge. Dr Abu-Bakar Asvat, a fellow political activist and long-time colleague of Winnie Mandela, was shot dead in his surgery on 27 January 1989; whether he found that Chebekhulu had been sexually assaulted or not is therefore only conjectural. However, his surgery notes and Winnie Mandela's testimony stated that he recommended that Verryn and Chebekhulu should seek psychiatric treatment.

Mandela's account of events stressed the need to remove the 'youths' from the danger of continued sexual assault.[6] As indicated above, it was Xoliswa Falati who was the apparent origin of the allegations of sexual misconduct. The main co-accused in the trial, Falati had been working in the manse and involved in the supervision of household arrangements at the time of these events. In her testimony, she represented herself as a house-mother figure, who cooked, washed, cleaned and urged the male residents of the manse to 'make this house a home'.[7] Whilst Falati valorised her self-styled role as house 'Mama', the testimony of Thabiso Mono and Kenneth Kgase challenged this representation with descriptions that expressed an equally gendered schematisation. These male house inmates 'described Falati as a bossy, interfering troublemaker who threatened those who didn't help with the housekeeping with discipline from Mandela United'.[8] Significantly, Mono and Kgase also stressed Falati's divisive and violent behaviour in the household, in particular the violence she directed at Stompie. Throughout the trial Falati maintained a position which focused attention on the imputed sexual behaviour of both Reverend Paul Verryn and the male inmates of the house.

In court, her testimony concerning the sexual activities at the manse seemed to combine self-righteousness with contradiction. For example, at times she stated that Chebekhulu *had* been raped by Verryn, at others that Verryn had *attempted* to rape him. Her testimony included extensive reference to the 'insertions' of genitalia into 'private parts', 'touching all over', 'buttocks', 'thigh-rubbing',[9] and 'rape'. Interestingly, the only aspect of her testimony that appears to have been consistent regarding sexual matters was that, however much she confused who exactly was doing what to whom at what particular time, effectively she created the general impression that all the 'youths' were involved in having sex with each other, and by turns with Verryn, whom she depicted as a paedophile Christian minister. A statement attributed to her by the *Daily Dispatch* typifies this approach, characterising the way in which the testimonies produced by the trial encoded alleged homosexual practices as sexual abuse and, by stressing the 'youth' of the males in the manse, created the discursive conditions for these implied practices to be understood as 'child abuse'. As Falati exclaimed, 'What should I have done about Reverend Paul Verryn raping our children?'[10]

This theme of rape, ascribed to the figure of Verryn who was depicted as abusing a position of trust, was echoed in the words of the mother figure presiding over her communal home in Diepkloof Extension. In an interview she gave to *Tribute* magazine in 1991, Winnie Mandela stated:

> I could not believe that a minister of religion entrusted with children's

lives would abuse them. Children who could not make any other choices but depend on him. What kind of beast is this? Who wears a collar on Sunday, and goes to preach to parents of these children, and preaches the word of God even to some of these children? At night he becomes something else.[11]

Through such forms of expression the key female defendants in the trial — both self-styled symbolic 'Mothers' — incited a sexualisation of the discourses produced by the trial. Mandela's defence lawyer, George Bizos, leaned on and exploited this sexualisation in order to construct his case, which was designed to exonerate Mandela from her implication in the charges of kidnap, assault and intention to do grievous bodily harm. Nursing justifiable public anxieties that the case represented yet another state (and thus implicitly white) conspiracy aimed at discrediting the figure of Winnie Mandela, Bizos mobilised his defence by sanctioning the encoding of imputed homosexuality as sexual abuse, and through the figure of the white Methodist minister Reverend Paul Verryn promulgated a public discourse of homosexual practice as a white, colonising depredation of (heterosexual) black culture. 'Homosex is not in black culture', read a placard held by one of Mandela's supporters outside the court, sloganising homosexuality as a white exploitation of black subjectivity and rendering it as a perversion of black culture produced by white colonisation.

During the progress of the trial, Winnie Mandela addressed the Toekomsrus branch of the ANC Women's League in a manner that fed into this accumulation of racialised accounts of sexual practices and historical subjectivity:

> You are called coloureds because not long after they [Europeans] landed here in 1652, these despicable people raped our grandmothers.[12]

Placed within the context of the trial, this attempt to provide a historical account of the origins of mixed-race identities in South Africa has an implicit logical congruence with the portrayal of homosexuality that emerged through the trial itself. Under this system of thinking, both homosexuality and mixed-race subjectivities (be they homo- or heterosexual) become tragic products of the same thing: white colonial rape and abuse. The narrative of the events provoking the case and of the trial itself thus intertwined the question of interracial sex (through the figure of Verryn) and homosexuality. In so doing, the defence strategy relied to a large extent upon a conflation of historical narratives of white contamination with a deliberate exploitation of public susceptibility to homophobia.[13]

The incitement of these discourses[14] was inextricable from the violence that had become almost synonymous with the name of South Africa itself.[15] The Mandela trial became another point through which to focus national anxieties about the penetration of violence into many aspects of social and political experience. As Paul Trewhela somewhat polemically argues:

> These thoughts rise to the surface with each further revelation about the crazed cycle of violence centring on Mrs Mandela's household in the late 1980s, following the defeat of the mass township revolt of 1984–6: a defeat inflicted, through hundreds of dead, by concentrated military and police violence. Given the present slaughter of scores of people every week, culminating in the massacre at Boipatong, the epic levels of homelessness and unemployment, the grim reaper of drought extending across the whole subcontinent, it might be thought that the matter of Mrs Mandela deserves merely a shrug of the shoulders, as a piece of trivia to titillate the media. *That would be to mistake its emblematic importance* [my italics]: for an understanding of the past, and for clearing a way through the present to a more sane and humane future.[16]

Situating — and, significantly, domesticating — the events that led up to the Winnie Mandela trial against a backdrop of national violence and uncertainty, Trewhela here identifies how the attention focused on the trial can be rationalised only through an understanding of its symbolic excess. This symbolism circulated around the figure of Winnie Mandela in her emblematic roles of 'Mother of the Nation': female political figurehead, militant community activist, hounded wife of the nation's most prominent resistance leader, a mother of some of his children, and by implication symbolic 'mother' of the future nation's children, social worker, and protector of disenfranchised and politically abused black youth. The development of the discourse surrounding the trial failed to resist this powerful cohesion of gendered symbolic functions, and deliberately deployed them in order to shore up the heterosexual integrity of Mandela's putative complicity in violence against black youths implicated in homosexual practices.

The defendant's insistence during the trial on the relevance of Paul

Verryn's imputed sexual behaviour was further emphasised by John Morgan's testimony. Morgan, a co-accused in the trial and driver of the vehicle that had 'collected' the 'youths' from the manse on the night in question, claimed from the witness stand that Jerry Richardson had questioned Stompie specifically about his relationship with Verryn, charged him with being an *impimpi* (informer),[17] and slapped him. The testimonies of Kgase and Mono seemed to suggest that the real location of 'abuse' and 'assault' was in fact Mandela's home, rather than the manse. Both claimed that they were questioned in a back room of the Diepkloof Extension, that Mandela herself attended, and that they were instructed to refer to her as 'Mummy' by Richardson. They maintained that Mandela stated Chebekhulu to be hysterical because he had been raped by Verryn, and that she beat them. Stompie, as indicated above, was accused of being an *impimpi*, and Mekgwe and Mono were 'accused' of sleeping with Verryn. Kgase alleged that Winnie Mandela stated that 'we were not fit to be alive', and that he was gripped by the hair and shoulders and asked why he had to protect a white person he had made friends with: 'She kept punching me saying that I was an intellectual ignoring my call to free Africa.'[18] Thus, to the imputation that homosexual practices were punishable was added the idea that a combination of whiteness and intellectualism betrayed the fight against oppression. The theme of betrayal also associated homosexual practices with untrustworthiness and informing.

At this juncture, it is worth pausing to investigate George Bizos's defence strategy, which throws light on the ways in which sexual struggles continue to be embedded within wider historical and political issues. The central issue in the Mandela trial, legally speaking, was not whether or not the violence actually occurred, but whether or not this violence was justified. It was thus positioned as a question of assessing the legality of violence. Bizos's approach situated his case within that branch of legal philosophy which, in Walter Benjamin's words, 'imposes itself in the question [of] whether violence, in a given case, is a means to a just or an unjust end'.[19] Since the formation of Umkhonto we Sizwe (MK, the liberation army of the ANC) in December 1961, and the Rivonia trials[20] — in which Bizos was involved — the ethics of a distinction between legitimate and illegitimate violence had been a key facet of the ANC's struggle with the apartheid state. Moreover, during the early 1990s the ANC and incumbent Nationalist Party had frequently clashed in negotiations at the Congress for a Democratic South Africa over the issue of the future role of MK, with F.W. De Klerk demanding its dismemberment and Nelson Mandela insisting that this could not be a consideration until national security services were sanctioned by a democratically elected state. The question of violence, and how it is sanctioned, was therefore a high-profile issue at the political level of negotiations aiming to redefine the future of South Africa, which were running concurrently with the trial.

As Benjamin points out, natural law determines violence as a product of nature, 'appropriate to all the vital ends of nature', and positive law sees violence as a product of history: 'Natural law attempts, by the justness of the ends, to "justify" the means, positive law to "guarantee" the justness of the ends through the justification of the means.'[21] The discursive formations generated by the Winnie Mandela trial equivocated between this 'natural' and 'positive' casting of violence. On the one hand, the roles of those concerned were implicitly gendered through being linked to a symbolic status (black heterosexual mother, white homosexual mission preacher, vulnerable black male 'youths') that codified the events into a 'familial affair' threatening the 'laws of nature' pertaining to the notion of 'the family', whereby the symbolism of consanguinity became the vehicle for representing the notion of a political family. On the other hand, the violent response putatively occasioned by the perceived threat to heterosexual 'laws of nature' was justified as a response to the colonial history that had produced the perceived sexual deviancy.

> [A]partheid is simply one form of the division into compartments of the colonial world. The first thing which the native learns is to stay in his place, and not to go beyond certain limits.[22]

Franz Fanon here describes colonialism as being effected through the organisation of space, and it is the history of colonialism as a contaminating and limiting production of space that formed the background to the trial. By ignoring this history, Bizos's line of defence, augmented by Winnie Mandela's public statements, effectively misused historically determined economic material conditions to produce a dehistoricised version of 'unnatural' sexuality. In doing so, the defence case and public discourse surrounding the trial denied the pre- and post-colonial history of homosexual practices in black South African cultures. To read homosexuality as a by-product of colonialism is not only historically inaccurate, but fatally seals the homosexual subject within the inescapable boundaries of oppression and suggests that the dismantling of colonial space necessarily carries with it the 'destruction' of homosexual practices; homosexuality hereby becomes a waste product of colonialism which has no right to expression in the new emancipatory social order. The issue, therefore, is that there is no legitimate historical space for the homosexual practices of the colonised. As Fanon reminds us, the subject of colonisation lives in, 'a world without spaciousness'.[23] This question of the relationship between space and sexuality was — quite literally — 'embedded' in the defence of violence against imputed homosexual behaviour in the Winnie Mandela trial. Crucially, it is the relationship in which the distinction between sexual consent and sexual abuse is grounded.

From March 1991 onwards, George Bizos shifted the emphasis of the defence case from concentration on the alleged kidnapping and assault by Winnie Mandela and her co-accused to the imputed sexually abusive conduct of Paul Verryn. Bizos's line became clear: if it could be proven that Mandela and Falati believed Verryn had been sexually abusing the inmates of his manse, then the removal of these inmates from the manse could be justified, as presumably could verbal abuse, sjambokking, slapping, beating, repeatedly dropping victims to the ground from a height,[24] and holding them against their will. Bizos's suggestion that the 'young boys' were removed to protect them from a damaging environment was effected by linking homosexuality with child abuse in a manner that deliberately did not attempt to distinguish between them. Connecting homosexual practice with abuse in terms of it being an exploitation of the vulnerability of disadvantaged and dependent people, Bizos relentlessly pursued details concerning the alleged sexual relationships in which Verryn had engaged with those under his supervisory care. The approach was a powerful one which fed off both historical inaccuracy and social homophobia, as demonstrated in the 'Homosex is not in black culture' slogan, and in the dramatising moralism of press language:

> Is Methodist Minister Paul Verryn a sex abuser who corrupts black youths or is he a dedicated Christian martyr who has made many sacrifices in the struggle? And was the Orlando West Methodist Manse a refuge for the unfortunate, or a den of iniquity?[25]

These rhetorical forms, placed in the context of the allegations against Verryn, immediately suggested that putative homosexuality, by then hopelessly conflated with images of sexual abuse and colonial contamination, was incompatible with dedication to the struggle and resistance against oppression. This division between, at a basic level, 'appropriate politics' and 'appropriate sex' characterised those located at the manse as politically evacuated homosexuals and/or abusers who were simultaneously disadvantaged victims of abuse, and those in Mandela's household as dedicated supporters of the struggle endeavouring to maintain the heterosexual moral values of the community.

This conflation of homosexuality and abuse was fabricated in a narrative of bed-sharing arrangements. Bizos drew the witnesses out regarding a pattern whereby new arrivals at the manse would spend their first night in the bed of Verryn's two-bedroomed manse, accompanied by one or two other residents. Mono and Kgase confirmed this as having been their experience, producing such media headlines as: 'Pastor slept with boys, court told',[26] 'The men in the Reverend's bed',[27] and 'I slept in priest's bed, says witness'.[28] In the context of this kind of sensationalising language, the testimony of Peter Storey, Methodist Bishop of Johannesburg, becomes relevant. Storey claimed that in mid October 1988 it was reported to him that rumours regarding homosexual practices at the manse were being circulated in the local Sowetan community. Verryn himself reported these rumours to the Bishop, who set up a pastoral commission to investigate the charges; Verryn was cleared when no-one provided the commission with evidence in support of the rumours. Knowing that due to shortage of space in the manse Verryn was at times obliged to share a double bed with its residents, Storey advised him to make his bedroom out of bounds. Verryn apparently agreed, but pointed out that it would take time to arrange this due to shortage of space. Mono had confirmed in his testimony that there were insufficient beds to house all those staying in the manse.

Soweto is one of the largest black urban communities in South Africa. In many areas, poverty, poor street lighting, poor sanitation, lack of community and recreational facilities, and high-density population characterise this urban environment. Shortages of material resources and space, which determine overcrowding, have made bed-sharing and shift arrangements a familiar pattern to many subject to the effects of apartheid economics, both those in urban residential environments and those in residential labour compounds and hostels. To pursue a line of questioning which seemed to imply that proximity due to material necessity inevitably produces 'unnatural' practices can be seen as an extension of the homosexuality-as-colonial-defilement model. That the oppression of apartheid capitalism has produced inadequate and unacceptable housing conditions which are an offence to human rights is incontestable. However, to deduce from this that apartheid is the *cause* of homosexual practices that take place in these environments is to recapitulate the unhistorical version of 'homosex' as a white contamination of black culture, which thus justifies violent repression.

Given the above description of the way in which the theme of sexual abuse was embedded in the defence case, two questions clearly present themselves. Firstly, what was the basis for this claim? Secondly, what specifically was taken to constitute sexual abuse? The existing testimony is ambiguous and tenuous. Under cross-examination, Kgase confirmed that he had been tickled by Verryn in bed. He said that he did not particularly like this, and that he had told Verryn to desist, which he did. This is as close as one gets in the trial to a reported testimony by one of the abducted and assaulted witnesses detailing a specific form of physical encounter at the manse. The defence pursued the issue of the tickling with Kgase, from which line of questioning one can infer only that the court was being asked to accept that tickling in a bed-sharing situation, even though desisted from when not welcomed, constituted 'child abuse' and sexual assault.

In response to the homophobia generated by the trial, GLOW (the Gay and Lesbian Organisation of the Witwatersrand, which had several chapters operating within Soweto) took the lead with a prompt and formally organised campaign. On 13 March 1991, GLOW sent an open letter to the National Executive Committee of the ANC and bought advertising space to publish it in the national press. This letter specifically situated its opposition to the conduct of the trial defence with reference to Article 7(2) of the ANC's draft Bill of Rights, which stated that 'Discrimination on the grounds of gender, single parenthood, legitimacy of birth or sexual orientation shall be unlawful.' The letter referred to the anti-homosexual slogans displayed by ANC supporters outside the court, the damaging effects of failing to distinguish between rape and abuse, and the defence's use of allegations of homosexuality to detract from the real issues of the trial, stating that:

> we feel that the defence is attempting to capitalise on conventional and reactionary prejudices against homosexuals. This is particularly disturbing as this defence is being raised by the head of the ANC's Department of Social Welfare. The line of defence is irreconcilable with basic principles of human rights outlined in the ANC's proposed Bill of Rights....The ANC's failure to respond to the above, raises

doubts concerning its stated commitment to the recognition of lesbians and gay men.[29]

GLOW also announced the launch of a campaign to request progressive organisations, both local and international, 'to re-affirm their commitment to the protection of lesbian and gay rights in a future and democratic South Africa'.

The ANC National Executive Committee has yet to formally respond to this letter, or, indeed, make any public statement with specific reference to the homophobia generated by this trial, despite continuing developments in its general policy commitments to lesbian and gay rights. Around the time of the trial a large number of local ANC branches formally expressed concern about the homophobia attendant on the trial at the time, but despite this and the fact that the issue was raised at the 1991 National Policy Conference, it was apparently never officially recognised as a matter concerning 'sexual orientation' at leadership level. This failure might logically be ascribed to the threat the figure of Winnie Mandela herself was posing to the image of the ANC at the time. As the anxiety over the behaviour of the MUFC escalated and finally erupted irreversibly into the national public sphere through the revelations of the Jerry Richardson trial and Winnie's implication in the death of Stompie Moeketsi, the ANC leadership took internal action by forming the Winnie Mandela Crisis Committee. This committee, which included key figures in the ANC, was intended to perform the function of monitoring and regulating Winnie Mandela's activities, by both mediating in her frequent clashes with leading ANC activists and attempting to control the way in which her actions were represented in the press.

In reality, the committee ended up carrying the burden of responsibility for holding together the image of a disintegrating national icon who apparently refused to respond to its attempted interventions. It was the need to minimise the damage that Winnie Mandela could do to the ANC's national and international image that determined its failure to respond to the issue of the homophobia articulated by public figures aligned to its name during the trial. Whilst she was still perceived in the role of Nelson Mandela's wife, the ANC had at least to try to appear to be supporting her against charges brought by the state.

On 13 May 1991, Winnie Mandela was found guilty of four charges of kidnapping and four charges of being an accessory after the fact. She was served with a five-year jail sentence, subject to appeal. In April 1992, Nelson and Winnie Mandela officially announced their separation, and in August 1992, while her case was still on appeal, Winnie Mandela finally resigned from all leadership positions within the ANC. It is interesting to note that this resignation was precipitated by the leaking of a letter to *The Sunday Times*, allegedly from Mandela to her 28-year-old lover, Dali Mpofu, which led to further public demonisation of her as sexually voracious and politically irresponsible. This letter was apparently the final step in the demotion of Winnie Mandela from the Mother of the Nation to the liability of the nation. In addition, reasons for her resignation included allegations of her misuse of power in the ANC Women's League and her misappropriation of social welfare funding, both of which were still under investigation by the ANC at the time. While the homophobia of her defence certainly served to alienate her (and her counsel) further from some sectors of the white liberal establishment, and while it played a significant role within the ANC of drawing attention to the need for gay rights, it did not have anything explicitly to do with her resignation.

With the appeal court's final ruling in June 1993,[30] the Winnie Mandela trial was finally over. The political career of Winnie Mandela, however, was not. On 8 December 1993, she was re-elected president of the Women's League, defeating her opponent, Albertina Sisulu, by 224 votes. Commenting on Winnie Mandela's political comeback, Emma Gilbey has argued that:

> Her re-election took her back into the heart of the ANC's leadership, giving her an ex-officio place on the National Executive Committee. It would grant her an automatic right to speak at public meetings and on political platforms during the run-up to the April elections. It would bring her into far greater contact with her estranged husband than she would have enjoyed in recent months. Once again he was the ANC's premier man and she its woman. And she had done it without him and without the advantage of his support.[31]

In fact, as has been demonstrated thus far by the outcome of the 1994 elections, Winnie Mandela has not been enjoying the renewed support of the ANC at executive leadership level. Rather, that support has come significantly, although not exclusively, from precisely that sector whose members tended to end up in Winnie's house in Diepkloof Extension and at Paul Verryn's Orlando West manse — the disenfranchised, unemployed black youth of the PWV (Pretoria-Witwatersrand). Equally, Winnie Mandela's power base comes from the support of those experiencing the poor residential conditions of 'informal settlement', as demonstrated by the allegiance of the inhabitants of the Phola Park area. That such areas represent the chief constituencies of her power base is in part due to the fact that Winnie Mandela's militant style appeals to those sectors of grass-roots communities who feel their political needs have been compromised by the apparently more conciliatory tactics of leadership involved in the transitional politics of the national negotiating tables.

The demotion of Winnie Mandela in the early 1990s, from which she has so quickly recovered, was accompanied by a demonisation of her identity as both a black woman and an activist. This demonisation, just like the homophobic ethos peddled by her defence case, rested on the reification of the 'national family'. This was a discourse which Mandela herself exploited, but which equally was used to exploit her and to condition the terms of her transformation from the Mother of the Nation to (in the headlines of the mass media) the 'Mugger of the Nation'.

Early in 1991, breaking her press silence for the first time since the commencement of the trial, Winnie Mandela was reported by the *Argus* to have said that she had wanted to hold an 'indoor inquiry' into the allegations of sexual abuse she had heard about the Methodist minister Paul Verryn. In relation to this, she stated:

> He was doing the same kind of work that I was doing, providing food, shelter and educational facilities. For that I held him in high esteem. I intended to contain this problem among ourselves and I had hoped that Paul Verryn would allow himself to be assisted by a psychiatrist. I could not understand how a man who was doing such valuable work could at the same time abuse children who had no choice but to depend on him.[32]

The identification Winnie Mandela makes here between her own role and Verryn's is absolutely crucial to an understanding of the dynamics of the discourses which both demonised the figure of male homosexuality *and*, ultimately, made her perform the role of mother. The characterisation of those in receipt of food, shelter and educational facilities as 'dependent children' suggests that Mandela perceived both herself and Verryn as fulfilling roles symbolically mediated through the discourse of the family. Where the Methodist manse was presided over by a pastoral, male, 'white father' figure, the Diepkloof Extension home represented a household structure presided over by a black woman, styled as 'Mother' in relation to her 'dependants' (the MUFC) and the community. In terms of the trial, the sexual practices apparently implicit in the former site were situated in political and moral opposition to the latter, which was represented as a site of normative heterosexuality. The Winnie Mandela trial thus pitched its public address through the discourse of the family, straining and overdetermining Winnie Mandela's expected role as heterosexual and normative mother, and reproducing the oppressions of the heterosexist family. Violence and policing carried out 'in the name of the family' do not, therefore, represent aberrant behaviour deviating from an ideal familial norm. Rather, where they erupt into the public view, they perform the 'normative' state of the family, demonstrating the degree to which oppressive functions have been naturalised within it.

The above must be situated within the wider framework of the metaphorical 'slippage' of the discourse of the family into nationalist politics. As Homi Bhabha puts it: 'The nation fills the void left in the uprooting of communities and kin, and turns that loss into the language of metaphor.'[33] More specifically, Fanon suggests that the language of the family is a site of resistance to the dislocation and denial of social cohesion caused by colonisation:

> The very forms of organisation of the struggle will suggest to him [the colonised] a different vocabulary. Brother, sister, friend — these are words outlawed by the colonialist bourgeoisie.[34]

In the familial vocabulary of this trial, in which attention was centred on a national mother figure, the function that the category mother performed was, quite specifically, the protecting, disciplining and saving of 'children'. This saving of children narrative not only made homosexual practice inappropriate to 'youthful' sexuality, but explicitly defined homosexual practices as a product of abuse. This therefore excluded the possibility of a positive symbolic function for homosexuality in the national family. As husband and wife, estranged or otherwise, the symbolic role of the Mandelas was clearly predicated upon the performance of heterosexuality and its accompanying genres of romance and tragedy.

The symbolism of the national family was also used to negate Winnie Mandela's political activism and her right to the expression of her sexuality. In this respect, the Winnie Mandela trial must be contextualised alongside the emerging evidence of Winnie Mandela's affair with Dali Mpofu and the imputed embezzlement of ANC funds which finally precipitated her estrangement from Nelson Mandela — another family saga between husband and wife. National and international mass-media imagery fetishised Winnie Mandela's sexuality and demonised her as 'disreputable', 'wicked', 'wayward' and 'betraying'. She was, we were told, 'a shrieking shrew of a wife' who reduced her husband to a 'guilty', 'doting', 'lovesick fool' whose political credibility was potentially undermined by the 'fatal attraction'[35] of his wife. Emplotting the themes of symbolic excess through sexuality, violence and political over-reaching, the following words of a foreign correspondent characterise this response to the dissolution of Winnie Mandela into 'bad mother' and unreliable wife:

> *Private Eye*...was not entirely exaggerating when it drew a line of descent for Mrs Mandela through Lucrezia Borgia, Myra Hindley and Lady Macbeth.[36]

Through a nationalisation of familial discourse, Winnie Mandela's sexuality and her relationship to violence became popularly characterised as a threat to national security, the implication at times being that the future of South Africa was dependent upon the final resolution of the Mandelas' marital problems.[37] Through the medium of such gendered rhetorical displacements, Winnie Mandela became a figure whose projected roles as mother and wife carried an overload of symbols encompassing even the interests of finance capital:

> She was personally a metaphor for an environment not suitable for business....A metaphor for *wilful* political violence (by 'the oppressed', rather than 'the oppressor') the *whims* of Mrs Mandela threatened to spill out of bounds beyond the mean streets of Soweto into acts of state [my italics].[38]

Winnie Mandela's rapid political recovery demonstrates the extent to which these forms of public discourse did not reflect the continuing nature of her local popularity. Given her political revival, rising from the ashes of a highly publicised demise, it is inadequate and reductive to dismiss the durability of Winnie Mandela as being purely dependent upon coercion, as such formulations express themselves precisely through the dubious mystifications outlined above. Popular memory may be short but, as Zackie Achmat has cogently argued, it is also historically complex and fluid: 'popular memories like their official counterparts are constant reinventions and dissolutions of identities and affiliations of community, class, language, nationality and gender.'[39] It is precisely this fluidity which needs to be explored, in its local context, in future studies of Winnie Mandela's political role.

Postscript

Following the first non-racial democratic elections in April 1994, the new South African constitution was ratified and passed into law on 8 May 1996. Lesbian and gay rights are nominally enshrined in this constitution, which makes discrimination on the grounds of sexual orientation unlawful. The constitution also guarantees to protect the rights of women to control their own fertility. Winnie Mandela's political fortunes have continued to rise and fall, with controversy accompanying her personal and political life. Demoted from the ministerial office to which she was appointed in the first cabinet, she remains an ANC member of parliament, now divorced from her husband the president. At a time when Nelson Mandela is effectively becoming a part-time leader, his romance with Graça Machel, widow of a former president of Mozambique, has been made more public. In September 1996, Nelson Mandela revealed that he is proposing to marry this mother of another country. At the time of writing Winnie Mandela's fortunes are in decline. However, Winnie Mandela is a leader who has frequently shown an ability to align herself with populist challenge, and the possibilities for her making another return to the centre of the political arena should not be underestimated.

13. The Farewell Dance
Women in the Bulgarian Transition
Dimitrina Petrova

Should we be surprised? Most of the symbolic images of Communism, produced by the bizarre culture of the 'transition to democracy', are female images. Never mind that in the Bulgarian language, as in all other Slavic languages, in which nouns have gender, 'Communism' is masculine while 'democracy' is feminine. Take the political pop songs in Bulgaria, a country known for its musical genius. In one of the most popular hits, *Give Me Divorce*, democracy (male) demands divorce, after a long unhappy marriage, from Communism (female). Democracy is personified in the masculine body of a member of the Union of Democratic Forces (UDF), the non-Communist coalition in Bulgaria:

> We are sitting now for round-table talks
> In a cafe in our neighbourhood,
> You, member of our old [Communist] Party
> And I — of UDF.

And the refrain, its melody declamatory and solemn, echoing the thousands of voices of 1990 democratic rallies, continues:

> Give me divorce, give me divorce
> And don't harass me any more,
> Take the panel flat and the Trabant
> But leave the breathing space to me.

Exactly: divorce was the key word of the show, the inspirational climax in the singing *vox populi*, the cherished point omega at the core of the revolution.

In another emblematic song, chosen by one of the democratic parties for its campaign in the 1991 election, the proclaimed male philosophy is, 'Don't promise me anything for tomorrow/ Because tomorrow begins today'; the woman to whom this warning is addressed is Communism, or perhaps the Communist Party, or what we want to leave behind, or all that.

The greatest hit of the Bulgarian transition, the *Farewell Dance*, provided the ultimate vision: 'Bye-bye, my darling' — sings a male chorus, in hilarious sailor style, while Communist Party officials, portly military officers, state security agents, naive young activists and ordinary men, are dancing, one by one, their farewell waltz with their past. Their past is played by a beautiful woman, a red-mouthed vamp, in a long red dress, wearing a red domino mask, her head crowned with a red star.

This was the memorable October 1991 party political broadcast of the UDF, believed to have won them votes in the parliamentary election that took power away from the Communists — for a short while, until the gradual Communist comeback, which Adam Michnik dubbed 'the velvet restoration', began a year later. We loved the *Farewell Dance*. I myself — a woman, an intellectual, a liberal — was elated by the refrain:

> A farewell waltz,
> Bye-bye my darling,
> You will haunt me for ever
> Even though your name is new.

In 1990, the Communists renamed themselves 'socialists' in Bulgaria, as they did elsewhere in Eastern Europe. But if that manoeuvre could pass for a redirection of strategy in other places, we thought we knew better, our domestic Communists being recognised experts in the business of name changing. Six years earlier, they had renamed one million Turks in the course of just one winter, using such tools as tanks and truncheons, and the Turkish minority of Bulgaria disappeared.

Undoubtedly, the song had many sentimental meanings, especially for those of us who had accounts to settle with the former regime. I eventually settled no accounts, pledged not to seek revenge and to employ tolerance as my guide, and thus, unfit for macho Balkan politics, ended up in the human rights movement, advocating the rights of the Gypsies. But, to this day, when I hum the *Farewell Dance*, it feels so wonderful. It feels like liberty. And I didn't even notice, until much later, that the Big Lie, the Evil, the Past, the Woman, was being overcome by the Truth, the Good, the Future, the Man.

Should we be surprised? One thing is sure: if a future regime, for example a nationalist dictatorship, replaces the unconsolidated democracy about which hardly anyone cares in my country, I know to which sex that future regime will belong.

The post-1989, post-Communist culture developed a great number of purifying techniques, including lustration (removing former communists from top positions by a special law) and political manipulation of the secret police files. But the revolution is ironic by definition, by the very sense of its Latin name. The post-Communist exorcism of the spirits of the past blatantly masked the social essence of the year 1989: the liberation of the dominant class.

One of the fundamental aspects of the collapse of Communism was not just the demise, as it is often misunderstood, but the *liberation* of the Communist *nomenclatura* from all restricting obstacles — the economic irrationalities, the political legitimation crisis, and the ideological bans from participation in the global elite. To paraphrase that beautiful old English song, *Where have all the Communists gone*? They have not gone to graveyards every one, to be sure. (*When will they ever learn?*) Not only did the Communist elite return, in person and in progeny, to the economy, to politics, and even to such areas as the human rights movement, but the 'vampires' of Communism — the thought habits — are of course still with us.

It may be very arbitrary that we in Bulgaria visualised not only the Communist Party but Communism itself, or life under Communism, as a woman. In other places, people's imagination may have been more sublimated. Still, cognitive intuition of historic time is gendered: we have only to look deeper into the symbols and artifacts of our culture to see this. If someone undertook such a project — to look into the songs, caricatures, posters and happenings of the 'transition' — there would be exciting results. In the strange geometry of 'revolutionary' constructions, historic time was morally divided into Evil (past, feminine) and Good (future, masculine). There are many cases in ancient cultures (remember for example the Chinese *yin* and *yang*) of metaphysical dichotomies being gendered. But there is a more general question here: why are rationalisations of the historic process, such as the 'transition to democracy', gendered? Is gender constitutive of the categories by which we grasp political history?

The 'transition' is a rational construct covering, or wrapping, a metaphor. The metaphor, however, makes use of mythic elements, and myth is never gender-free. Myth is about origins, about a primary bond of maternal and paternal forces, and about procreation. In essence, myth as a form of rationality is a gendered interpretation and a familial perspective on the universe.

What makes the 'transition' mythic is that it engages the metaphor of birth: one society died, another society was born. When the social universe we inhabited was shattered, we subconsciously drew upon archaic identity values. No wonder, then, that successful labour ends in the cry, *It's a boy*!

I certainly made a long jump back to the well to fetch water for my garden. But then, didn't that mysterious 'man-democracy' make a long jump forward to land in our collective fantasy? Or did he just fall from the sky?

Social scientists will be divided, in many future debates, over the nature of the 'Communist' societies, or 'Soviet-type systems', in Eastern Europe, which came to an end in the late 1980s. But one could hardly expect them to question one fact: that these societies never abandoned domination, exploitation and patriarchy (hence the social-historical-cultural possibility of the *Farewell Dance*). Official Communist ideology, whose bible was Stalin's *Short Course*, contained in its *corpus immobile* the fossils of the 'emancipation' and 'equality' of women, and the Utopia of the all-round development of the human personality — Utopia because the general tendency of social development was towards the ever-deeper division of labour.

Soviet-Marxist ideology distorted or simply ignored whole layers within meaning of Marx's categories of 'emancipation' and 'equality'. Still less was it possible for meanings originating in the non-Marxist, libertarian socialist tradition to be incorporated into the official ideology. For women in Bulgaria, the superimposition of allegedly Marxist ideology on to a Soviet-type social system produced two schematic role models: I will call them the Woman on a Tractor of the 1950s and the Woman Secretary of the 1980s. These ladies were respectively the grandmother and the mother of the *Farewell Dance Vamp* of 1991, the one with the red domino mask in the merry carnival of the revolution.

The grandmother, Woman on a Tractor, looks at us from the early communist newspapers and magazines covering 'socialist competition'. She wore overalls, had weathered hands and used no make-up. She worked in heavy metallurgy plants, waved down from the scaffolding of construction sites, operated 20 looms in the textile factory, milked cows on the co-operative farm, and drove her roaring 'Belarus' tractor towards the bright future. She was in the business of the 'construction of socialism'. Being a wife and mother was also an important part of her role, but the state and the party took care to turn the children into reliable builders of socialism. She was left with the less serious task of raising them, together with the comrade women of the nursery and the kindergarten.

Granted, the early Communist governments of Bulgaria in the 1940s and 1950s made an idealistic attempt to emancipate women, albeit through the machinery of male-supremacist institutions. On paper, women were entitled to equal rights — political, civil and economic. Reproductive rights were protected through monthly payments and paid leave for birth and childcare, free medical assistance and, later on, free medicines for children. But all these achievements, which the official Communist women functionaries advertised at international conferences, were ambiguous.

Communist government support for motherhood was, in reality, underpinned by ethnic imperatives. In Bulgaria, there were considerable Turkish and Gypsy minorities, among whom the birth rate had been higher than among ethnic Bulgarians. The Communist government tried to encourage Bulgarian women to have more children by social policy measures, but also by certain restrictions on the right to abortion. Until 1990, abortion was not allowed to married women without children or with one child. Motherhood was eulogised as a precondition of womanhood.

In theory, nothing prevented Woman on a Tractor from being really equal with men. In reality, despite the fact that women in Bulgaria were, after two decades of Communism, as well educated and qualified as men, and accounted for close to 50 per cent of the labour force, they were unequal in the workplace, both in terms of employment opportunity, pay and promotion. The prestige of certain occupations was dependent on whether they were male-dominated or not. For example, the proportion of women in the teaching and medical professions grew to reach over 70 per cent by the 1980s; because of the relatively low salaries women received, these two occupations were among the least prestigious ones. They still are.

Official values such as 'equality of women' and 'all-round personal fulfilment of women' were not internalised and remained foreign to the Communist culture. Women themselves, even when they realised that there is more to equal rights and emancipation than law, remained passive. And law alone could not exclude the numerous forms of discrimination against women, as a result of which the general pattern of social stratification was again gender-specific.

In public life and politics, Woman on a Tractor featured as an object to be photographed for the newspaper, and also as a figure on the platform at meetings and party congresses. True, she had no real voice in decision making. But at least there were those informal women's quotas of about 15-20 per cent — never declared, but somehow always observed — in official party and state bodies. For some time, one woman in the Politburo, comrade Tsola Dragoicheva, a former activist from the antifascist resistance, had real power, but this can happen once men decide to play the game of tokenism. The whole atmosphere discouraged Woman on a Tractor from opting for a public career.

'Public' may actually be a misleading term in this context: can one speak of a 'public sphere' in a totalitarian society? The intention of the latter was to destroy the dualism of public and private spaces and to achieve homogeneity in everything: no social classes, no spheres, no divisions, no structures, no interest groups — only the individuals *vis à vis* the totality. Not that public and private spaces were absent: they remained, but underwent metamorphosis. Private space was invalidated by the total vulnerability of every person under the gaze of the 'System'. Ten-year-old Pavlik Morozovs reported on their parents. Public space in its turn became a matter of mere appearance: beyond the outward, visible, ritualistic layer was the hidden, opaque underlayer, accessible only to the key players. All the important decisions were made in the underlayer, and were 'legitimised' outside, in the quasi-public space, at the congresses, the plenums and the meetings. Elections were cosmetic too, as they disguised the real mechanisms of decision making. It therefore was not an achievement that 20 per cent of the members of public forums were women, as those forums themselves were only the symbolic dress of the body politic.

Formally equal with men, Woman on a Tractor was expected to 'function' simultaneously in three different social roles (to 'struggle on three fronts', in the early communist lexicon): mother and wife, diligent worker and good Communist. Society recognized women as fully developed personalities only when all three roles were performed 'harmoniously'. The role model of the 'socialist' woman featured by the women's magazines was a creature, hardly ever existent in real life, who had achieved this triple fulfilment. But perhaps she did exist! Woman on a Tractor was always so humble! Her modesty was part of her always quiet heroism, the most important element of her beauty — exactly the opposite of her outrageous granddaughter, right?

Role models always exit the stage one day. At some point in the ongoing tragicomedy of Communism, in the late 1960s and during the 1970s, the response of women to the call of the Woman on a Tractor began to change. There came the complaint that it is impossible to 'carry three watermelons under one arm'. This must have been one of the most quiet and most successful revolts in the history of women. Generally, women had no interpretative framework which would allow them to understand the impossibility of this triple performance as resulting from the low living standards, the backward cultural context, or the exploitative, male-dominated social structure. They tended, more and more, to think that the 'triple fulfilment' expectation which had dumped the triple burden on their shoulders had been a wrong target in principle, from the very beginning. The emancipation of women was now increasingly compromised. Woman on a Tractor was receding. Her daughter, Woman Secretary, stepped in.

Sometimes changes in Eastern Europe in relation to women are presented as if, up to 1989, women had been victims of forced emancipation, which was immediately replaced by a new 'democratic' doctrine. This is far from what has in fact been going on: the process of redefinition of women's roles was already under way in late Communist society, then officially calling itself the 'stage of the construction of Developed Socialist Society'. Today's mainstream stereotypes about women's roles, conservative and right-wing as they are, did not emerge overnight in 1989; they were articulated much earlier and simply reinforced by the 'transition'. Woman Secretary had been around for at least a decade.

During the late 1970s and early 1980s, the official communist indoctrination of women changed its message. Step by step, a more conservative, basically anti-feminist ideology, of essentialist inspiration, was elaborated. It implied the recognition that the early socialist promise to women had been inadequate and Utopian, and was therefore in need of serious reconsideration.

Woman Secretary looked down upon her mother with terror. According to the daughter, there was no point in getting up at dawn to hurry for the first shift in the factory, and the tractor was definitely a nightmare. Woman Secretary's definition of success was to crawl out of the mud. She was educated, worked in an office next door to the Director and carried nail polish in her purse. Through inertia, newspapers and magazines continued to see her in all walks of life — in industry, science, education, medicine, the Party. But in essence, what she was, no matter where, her home included, was Woman Secretary. Which man was her boss was all that mattered.

Sociologists are sure that there was a process of mass upward mobility for the larger part of the population of Bulgaria, as a result of the communist project of industrialisation and urbanisation of the once rural, underdeveloped and defeated nation. Woman Secretary was the outcome of this large-scale upward mobility. Most working-class women gave education to their daughters, and, with it, more opportunities and a better life.

Woman Secretary, unlike her mother, knew that she was unhappy to be born female: so many obligations to be fulfilled, and in return permanent exhaustion and nerves on the verge of breakdown. She was sitting in offices with phones never silent, running to meetings, jumping into trains and planes, and still clearly realising that, despite all her efforts, she would never be equal with men. So then Woman Secretary unconsciously employed the principle of the vixen and the grapes. She did not want the damned equality any more. And she silently drafted her new Utopia.

Emancipation now started to be seen as an official fabrication of yesterday, but now out of season, something that just made life more difficult. In the words of Silva Rakhneva, a key figure in the women's press over many years:

> if our shoulders are bent with exhaustion, if our eyes never smile, if our lips are tightly set — it is because we lack recognition. It is because behind our backs we are reproached — for the emancipation that we ourselves fabricated. And which we cherished. To the point of being today less feminine, less admired, less appreciated. Just contrary to what we once wanted.
>
> It will take some time until we suppress protest in ourselves. We shall scatter, each of us taking her own path. Different. Filled with children's laughter. Inspired by men's love. Enjoying many professional victories. To each according to what she wishes. The world cannot do without us. But the world certainly has had enough of seeing us in jeans and shirts, dragging kids along to the kindergarten, running to catch trams and trolleys, loaded down with shopping bags, rushing into the workplace at the last minute, choked with embarrassment: what to do first?
>
> We don't like ourselves. *At last*, we can admit this.[1]

Happiness, Woman Secretary thought, consisted of children's laughter and men's love. Alternatively, it could mean professional success. Or, above all, with some luck and by using her brains, Woman Secretary dreamed of building a life that took a piece of both cakes. Unlike her idealistic mother, she thought there is nothing wrong with personal enrichment. And, also unlike her mother, she tried to avoid at least the third 'watermelon', participation in the rituals of official Communism. At this stage, she was not really punished. At the expense of this withdrawal, Woman Secretary became an active networker, weaving the web of the unofficial, second economy, and, with it, of unofficial culture.

The official women's organisation, the Committee of the Movement of Bulgarian Women, an auxiliary to the ruling Communist Party, began to launch the new ideology as early as the late 1970s. Communist women functionaries, leaders of a non-existent women's 'movement', motivated, I believe, by a sincere concern for women, in essence abandoned women's long-term interests, together with the 'socialist promise'. Today, this seems justified as part of the larger process of the delegitimisation of Communism.

In the 1980s the very concepts of emancipation and equality were already being used ironically by official women's publications. The media had already created two caricatures of the 'emancipated woman'. One, reflecting the Eastern idea of the degenerate Western capitalist way of life, depicted the 'liberated' woman smoking a cigarette, extravagantly dressed, using a lot of make-up, sitting in cafés for hours, neglecting her children, promiscuous. The other, reflecting the nausea at the thought of tractors, looms and scaffolding, was the 'equal' woman, presented as ugly and unattractive, hardworking but personally unhappy, heroically struggling on all three fronts of women's fulfilment and left with nothing at the end of the road. The only time this self-sacrificing creature could have for herself was a remnant left over from other people's needs. The 'equal' woman was pictured as a self-mutilated creature, one who, to her sorrow, had deprived herself of her own femininity. The lesson was clear: combine family and career if you can, but to be a beautiful woman is your true profession.

This ideological swing from the socialist promise to a conservative anti-feminism in the late 1970s, as part of the developing legitimacy crisis of Soviet-type systems, prepared the general preconditions for the boom in right-wing value orientations that we have been witnessing since 1989.

I think that progress in the status of women in post-Communist society must involve retaining all the formal legislative achievements of the past and building on them. New developments would be focused on equal opportunity projects, and here post-Communist women can learn a great deal from the experience of Western women, insofar as the social and economic conditions under which they live are more or less of the same nature. The failure of the 'socialist promise', however, makes this option very problematical. The Western women's movement has traditionally had left-wing values. The idea of being left-wing, in Eastern Europe, is connected with the former Communists. Women in the East who are open-minded, non-cynical and committed to democracy are suspicious of all that is on the left, except, maybe, the Western women's movement.

Women are likely to suffer disproportionately more than men in the transition to a market economy. In the first two years of post-Communism, unemployment rates grew among women faster than among men; female unemployment was at least 20 per cent higher than male in 1991. Women's jobs were located mainly at the lower levels of firms' hierarchies. State protection of women's rights was loosened; gender segregation of the labour market tended to become deeper and increasingly hostile to women's career options. Single mothers were the most vulnerable category of women. Those who had somewhat better chances in the labour market, especially in small businesses, were educated, young, single, attractive, ambitious, competitive women — those who could perform the role of the ideal business secretary. But both the caring mother and the business secretary lived in a new environment — the universe of competition, whose most striking novelty was financial insecurity, the feeling that sudden bankruptcy is always around the corner.

According to an opinion poll carried out by The Centre for the Study of Democracy (Sofia) in October 1991 and representative of the whole Bulgarian population, only 8.1 per cent of the women in the sample expected a rise in their living standards over the following year (as against 13.1 per cent of the men). 43.1 per cent of the women expressed a fear that they might lose their jobs (as against 38.5 per cent of the men). 46.6 per cent of the women definitely preferred to work in a state-owned enterprise, while 22.3 per cent preferred a private employer (the respective figures for the men are 40.9 per cent and 33.8 per cent). 42.7 per cent of the women said they had neither intention nor desire to start a private business of any sort (as against 35.8 per cent of the men). Women's lower self-esteem was shown in the fact that 32 per cent of the women said they could not influence the course of their life (compared to 25.7 per cent of the men). Only 16.9 per cent of the women thought that their life is now full of new opportunities (compared to 26.7 per cent of the men).[2]

Women in Bulgaria want to work. Only one fifth of women (as against one third of men) think that women should stay at home and not work. Even if they were fully financially secure, 70 per cent of working women would still prefer to work full-time. But, as opinion polls demonstrate, they still do not want to govern. The clean sweep made by the free elections has reduced women's political participation and increased gender gaps in the public sphere. In June 1990, only 34 women were elected to the first post-Communist parliament (8.5 per cent of the seats). And the second post-Communist parliamentary election in October 1991 did not change this proportion.

It is unlikely that the newly emerging parliamentary democracy can in itself guarantee women's rights and freedoms. In the specific conditions that apply in the Balkans, the societal transformation that is taking place is not based on a reduction of arrogance, discrimination and neglect with respect to women: quite the contrary. The invisibility of women in the public sphere is growing, with the 'help' of the male-dominated media. The different forms of eroticisation of women's oppression (pornography in particular) are flooding everyday life.

Changes in the social system also mean substantial changes in the structures of everyday life. The traditional family pattern, the breadwinner-housewife arrangement, which, though never seriously challenged, was to a certain degree eroded under Communism, is now reinforced. This is due mostly to growing unemployment and to the drop in living standards. Accordingly, there is a tendency for the number of divorces to decrease, as the crisis mobilises the family for survival. The economic factors that stabilise the traditional family pattern are accompanied by the regressive reorientation of women's attitudes to gender roles.

The social security system has been shattered. Monthly benefits paid to mothers for childcare have now become totally inadequate. The most devastating effects of the economic crisis fall on the lives of minority women, Gypsies in particular, many of whom are driven to the edge — of hunger, death, suicide, or crime. Experienced foreign observers in some Gypsy housing areas claim that they have never seen such terrible poverty, even in Third World countries.

Violence against women is reportedly much higher than in the past decade, in line with the dramatic general growth of crime. There are no shelters yet for battered women, nor telephone hotlines. Women in the street are easy victims of robbery, even during the day. No wonder that the overwhelming majority of the people want the death penalty applied more often, and urge that law and order be the first priority of the government.

Because of the rapid and very visible stratification of Bulgarian society, a substantial proportion of women at present have physical survival as their number one priority. The prevailing mood among women is sadness, malice, bitterness and envy for those few who make it big. This, paradoxically, is combined with respect and admiration for the new rich. These are mixed feelings, leading to humiliation. And, day after day, the gap between poor and rich is opening wider and wider. The atmosphere is full of hostility and helplessness. In these times, Bulgaria has become the country of hatred.

This will not last for ever. Beyond this epoch of early post-communism, which is so reminiscent of the darkest days of early British capitalism, there will come a different, more mutually concerned way of living. It seems very far away, especially now, when the failure of communism is taken to mean the failure of each and every effort to transcend capitalism. So we can only try to keep the flame burning, the small flame of sympathy, of simple concern for others. Sisterhood may play a powerful part in this commitment. But the idea and the feeling of sisterhood have been absent from our society for a long time.

Under Communism, one precondition of a woman's well-being was the absence of other women. Objectively, the relations between women were determined by intra-gender competition. It was not only men's benevolence which was the 'goal' of such competition, but small achievements on the level of everyday life, owing to the misery and hardships of carrying on the household routine. Women thought that, without other women, queues would be shorter and there would be more space in the tram. There, in the queues and crowded trams, the Bulgarian woman's positive attitude to other women was systematically eroded. The other woman was the person who would steal 'my husband' or at least shake her carpets out on her terrace over the washing I had just hung out on a lower storey of the odious 'socialist' block of flats.

The structural expression of this lack of sisterhood is the lack of spontaneous grass-roots women's activities or voluntary associations which are the elements of civil society. The Democratic Union of Women is, regrettably, no more than a left-over of the Communist, official, state-controlled organisation, continuing to play a conservative part. Besides it, there are no significant organisations; even if there are some small, promising ones, their activity is not covered by the media. Building a civil society at the grass-roots is the priority for the women's movement in Eastern Europe.

This process might be fostered by institutionalising women's studies, a field that has been unknown until now. The issues that are most likely to mobilise women at present are women's unemployment and women's health. The women's movement, which is now at its formative stage in Bulgaria, should choose a combined strategy of the amplification of civil society and pragmatic, old-fashioned politics. A small official women's lobby will not make a difference unless a broader grass-roots movement of great moral vigour provides a constant voice from below. Some women will certainly try the institutional mode of empowerment; others will take the long road of local activism outside the official political sphere. The women's movement as a whole should opt for both.

What we make of our post-Communist lives now is up to us. We have all the tools and resources we need. The choice is ours. Our Farewell Dance Vamp is among our resources, because she has a message for us: if you don t like the role, take part in writing the script.

14. From Asexuality to Gender Differences in Modern China

Min Dongchao

At Beijing University's first 'International Conference on Women's Studies' in 1992, two papers on the subject of Chinese gender issues caused an argument. The opinion of one paper was that the victory of the revolution in 1949 had changed the status and concept of the femininity of Chinese women. There was an emphasis on 'asexuality'. Male and female did not transmit messages about sexual difference in public places; Chinese women thought of themselves as people alongside men and equal in the workplace. The second paper argued that gender differentiation in Chinese society should be divided into two periods: one from 1949 to 1979, when gender distinction was reduced, the other period from 1979 until the present day when gender distinction has become sharper.[1]

I agreed with the opinion of the second paper basically because gender differentiation has became more and more obvious from 1979. The condition of 'asexuality' of women was more obvious in the period 1949-79. As for the mainstream of thought on gender in traditional Chinese culture, I think that before 1949 the concept of *Nanzunnubei* — that women are inferior to men — was more dominant than the idea of the 'asexuality' of women. The question of why and how the concept of *Nanzunnubei* shifted to that of 'asexuality' and then reappeared again after 1979 will be discussed in this chapter, as will be the reactions of Chinese women to these changes.

The basic pattern of traditional Chinese culture in its classical form was *Lizhizhixu*, the rule of propriety, by which a hierarchy was established on the basis of kinship, juxtaposing superior and inferior, for instance, emperor and prince, father and son, husband and wife. Humans were not individuals, but parts of the social order. Women were placed at the lowest level. In ancient China, a male-centred society, the concept of

Nanzunnubei that women are inferior to men, became the established orthodoxy and the code of women's conduct. Women, who were in an inferior position, were bound by the highest code: 'The Three Obediences' and 'The Four Virtues'. The former referred to women's subjection to the authority of her father when young, of her husband when married and of her son when widowed, while the latter consisted of general virtue: she should be reticent in words, clean and pleasing in appearance and skilled in the performance of household duties. By and by, the concept of restraint and unselfishness was intensified and developed into the principle of women's submission. In short, the ideas 'women inferior to men', 'The Three Obediences' and 'The Four Virtues' were the core of the traditional Chinese concept of femininity.

After China went through the experience of becoming a modern society, and in particular because of the criticism of traditional Chinese culture launched by the May Fourth Movement in 1919, the conceptualisation of human rights moved closer to that of Western humanism. Chinese radicals began to realise that a person should exist as an independent and free being, and should be individually respected. Women discovered in a radically negative way that 'women were not instruments to carry on the family name', and 'women should not be regarded as playthings'.[2] For the first time in history, Chinese women as a collective body asserted that women were also human beings, and that men and women should be equal. Such a call undoubtedly revolutionised the traditional gender concept of *Nanzunnubei*.

The cultural revolution advocated during the May Fourth Movement and especially the ideologies that broke with the traditional gender concept were applauded by some intellectuals and young students, but they were not accepted by Chinese society. Given the lack of support, the break-up of the May Fourth Movement and the ebbing of the feminist movement were predictable.

After this cultural discontinuity, the women's movement in China took another direction: advancing the development of women's liberation through the socialist political struggle. When they joined the war of national revolution with men, most Chinese women acquired various rights equal to those of men, and the ideal of gender equality seemed to come closer to being achieved.

The year 1949 saw the foundation of the People's Republic of China, which further extended women's emancipation. In the course of transforming the old society, New China enforced a number of laws, orders, regulations and policies, stipulating and guaranteeing that women should enjoy political, economic, educational and social rights.

In 1950, the new marriage law was the first law passed after the founding of the People's Republic; its main purpose was to liberate women, eradicate the concept of *Nanzunnubei* and encourage women to free themselves from arranged and mercenary marriages. In 1953, the state launched the 'Enforcing the New Marriage Law' campaign.

In 1954, the first constitution was published. One of its terms stated that 'women are entitled to equal rights with men in every aspect of political, economic, cultural, educational, social and domestic life.' The concept of gender equality which is considered a symbol of women's liberation was publicly accepted by the state.

In 1958, a new campaign to build socialism began in China. The government called for women to take on work outside their homes and almost all able-bodied women began to participate in the public labour force. It became generally understood in China that the basic prerequisite for women's liberation was that women take part in production and achieve a measure of economic independence.

Beside these social reforms, eliminating concepts of gender differences such as *Nanzunnubei* was an important task. Research has shown that from 1950 to 1980, there were 30 leading articles in the *People's Daily* which celebrated International Women's Day.[3] Only two articles were about marriage and conceded women's special claims. All of them were about revolution, and called on women to take part in 'productive' activities. If you replaced the word 'women' with 'comrades', it would not affect the content of these articles.[4]

It cannot be denied that the founders of the Republic regarded 'women's emancipation' as one of the aims of the revolution and a mark of social progress, since 'women's problems' were part of the system that the revolution sought to overthrow. After the success of the revolution, one of their first aims was to liberate women, setting them free from the shackles of the feudal authorities of religion, clan and husband and turning them into a socialist labour force. Through the above-mentioned laws and policies, Chinese women achieved unprecedented social liberation and personal freedom for a short period. This achievement is generally acknowledged by those women who experienced the social reformation in the 1950s and 1960s.

On the other hand, we should realise that this women's liberation, though giving far more value to women's social rights and position, was achieved only at the cost of women's self-awareness. For this reason, some people called it *chaoqian*, or too-rapid liberation.[5] Since little attention was given to transforming and reconstructing women's intelligence, psychological state, personality and values, women lacked clear awareness of themselves. As a result, the traditional gender concept continued to exist, though in variant forms. Although *Nanzunnubei* was criticised as feudal ideology, gender equality effectively meant that women should take men as their models in every way. At the time, it brought about social progress, but this equality also had obvious disadvantages.

First of all, under the cover of gender equality, natural sex differences were ignored. Women were made to work in the fields, which required great physical strength. At one time, 'iron-girl teams' and 'March Eighth teams' worked all over the country to erect power transmission lines on pylons. The health of many women was damaged, and so was their enthusiasm for self-liberation. Women who had taken part in productive activities during the 1950s and 1960s were asked 'When did you become conscious of yourself as a woman?'. Some answered that it was after starting work. In doing physical labour, they found that differences in physical strength really existed between men and women. The two sexes were quite different from one another. However, under the slogan 'women can do whatever men do', they had to strain their effort and strength. Consequently, they felt exhausted in both mind and body.[6]

Secondly, the tendency towards masculinising women went to extremes. Women who worked outside their homes found that the world they were facing was one full of values adopted by men. If a woman wanted to be accepted and respected, she must behave like a man. There were no other choices. Fen Xiaotian has produced statistics on the types of women who have featured in the magazine *Chinese Women* since 1949 which show that the women characters in the 1950s and 1960s were mainly young, poorly educated workers and peasants. Most of them were Party or Youth League members who had worked hard and had thus been selected as model labourers.[7] The same characteristics could also be found in the women who appeared in the novels, dramas and films of the period. It can be said that the model Chinese woman of that era was an asexual being, without gender identity.

It was also quite popular for women to masculinise themselves. At one time, Chinese women made an effort to imitate men's behaviour, language and even clothing, and to repress their natural sexual features. This extreme imitation became quite a fashion during the so-called Cultural Revolution throughout China, when the Chinese people were described as a 'blue sea' or 'green sea' from the colour of the uniform that both sexes were wearing at that time. Thus we may see how history turned the idea of 'women being inferior to men' into the masculinisation of women.

The equality that accepted men's behaviour as the standard meant that Chinese women's self-awareness remained weak. Though 'The Three Obediences' and 'The Four Virtues' were not publicly advocated, the spirit of restraint and self-sacrifice in traditional femininity lingered on. In spite of devoting themselves to family, husband and children, women were also supposed to work hard for the nation and revolution, without even considering their own development. Since women themselves lacked self-awareness, they were unable to make full use of their acquired rights. Maria Mies has analysed this phenomenon in some developing countries, where

> remarkable steps in the direction of women's liberation were possible because they were necessary for the general struggle. These successes, however, cannot be interpreted as the result of a profound subjective and objective change in men-women relations....They do not necessarily bring about a profound change of consciousness.[8]

Because the Chinese Communist Party and state conducted the process of changing the gender concept during this period, gender difference was eliminated to a great extent from public institutions and ideology. However, in places that were farther from the public sphere, such as rural areas and the family, the gender difference was bigger. The traditional concept of *Nanzunnubei* which could not be eradicated by administrative order, was still embedded deep in the Chinese social psychology; given a chance, it would reappear again.

In 1979, the period of economic reform was launched. China shifted from a state-controlled socialist economy to a socialist market economy. The system of competition was introduced into people's lives and destroyed the old balanced social order. Chinese women began to feel that the guarantees provided by the socialist system were weakened. This was largely due to the fact that, because of longer periods of absence for pregnancy and childcare, women were unable to measure up to male competition. Women were the first to be withdrawn from employment. Female university graduates had difficulty finding work in either state or private enterprises. Other women's problems appeared, such as the low participation rate of women in politics and the high rate of female illiteracy. The traditional gender concept reappeared through the back door of 'equal competition' and 'economic development first'. Chinese women suddenly discovered that they were surrounded by the traditional prejudices against them. In the new atmosphere of competition, they felt oppressed as women for the first time. Gender consciousness thus finally and inevitably emerged, along with the unavoidable conflict between women's awareness of their gender oppression and *Nanzunnubei*. This conflict may help us to understand the crucial questions now facing Chinese women: I would like to take a discussion of women's political life in China as an example of the tension between the two concepts of gender.

What sparked the discussion was a report carried in *Chinese Women's Daily* on 23 October 1990. It told a story about a woman named Xiang Hua, who was deputy head of a remote county. The first advice the head of the county gave her was to move her family to the county, the reason being that it was quite difficult for a woman without a family at her side to work in the county government, since most of her inferiors were male. Xiang Hua accepted the advice and moved her family to the county town. She performed outstandingly at work, while also trying to maintain her status as a virtuous wife and good mother at home. No matter how busy she was, once she was at home she always cooked and washed. Nevertheless, her husband felt psychologically inferior to his high-ranking wife and picked a number of quarrels in the county government building. Xiang Hua meekly submitted and endured this humiliation in order to keep the family intact, fearing that rumours would affect her work. She thought about divorce, but again feared that this would end her career. Life to her was a difficult equation to solve. Many women in political life in China had similar problems.

More than 20 articles were published during the discussion, most of them written by women.[9] Many encouraged Xiang Hua 'to be courageous', 'to overcome oneself', to have a healthy personality, to struggle if necessary; only in this way could women's participation have significance. The opinions about women's political lives expressed in these articles were those of women whose gender consciousness had already been awakened. The other three or four articles might have been written by men; the writers thought that 'Xiang Hua's tragedy was produced by herself', and furthermore 'at the time she worked well therefore she should have kept in mind her husband's emotional needs'. Quite amusingly, one of the articles was written by the husband of the head of a rural township. This article, entitled 'It is also hard to solve the equation of the husband who has a head of a county as a wife', revealed men's predicament under the influence of the traditional attitude of 'husband high, wife glorious'. If a wife had a higher social position than her husband, people around her would talk disapprovingly, while the husband would feel embarrassed to face the world because he would lose the prestige of a man.

If we take this discussion a step further and put it against the background of Chinese society and its traditional culture, we find that *Nanzunnubei* still operates widely. Society, like Xiang Hua herself, still adopts a double standard in appraising men and women. Women like Xiang Hua need to work like a man in order to be regarded as successful; at home, on the other hand, they are required to be virtuous wives and good mothers, like traditional women. Even so, people feel reluctant to accept that a woman can occupy a higher position than her husband. In contrast, people judge a man's success only in terms of his social position, without consideration of his family life. Against such a social and cultural background, the pressure upon women like Xiang Hua is extremely heavy. Though they try their best to work like men, deep in their mind they are burdened by restraint, passivity and unselfishness. Thus, Xiang Hua's equation is hard to solve, not only because of the social culture but also because of her own internal contradictions.

Questions in relation to women's political life reflect only one aspect of the conflict between the two gender concepts. Such a conflict is also acute in other fields. The weakening of the original protective system for women and the reappearance of *Nanzunnubei* in reality has challenged the Communist Party theory of women's liberation and forced women to reconsider their own problems. Women's self-sacrifice has begun to be replaced by self-awareness. These changes are being revealed in the following ways:

1. *A series of actions taken by the All-China Women's Federation — the leading women's organisation in China.* The Women's Federation used to focus its attention on women's duties, encouraging them to take part in proletarian revolution and productive activities. But with the development of economic reform, it has shifted its focus.

At its fifth congress, held in 1983, the Women's Federation issued the slogan of women's 'Four Selfs'— self-respect, self-love, self-possession and self-improvement. This was an unprecedented action, although disciplining oneself for social duty still remained part of self-love and self-respect. The 'Four Selfs' showed that the Federation intended to set a new model of self-improvement and independence for women, emphasising women's self-protection backed by the law, instead of a reliance on the protection of society and the Women's Federation itself. Besides this, the Federation particularly pointed out that the rights of women reformers and outstanding achievers should be guaranteed. The Women's Federation has made considerable progress, from the mere protection of women's subsistence rights to defending their right to development. At its sixth congress in 1989, the 'Four Selfs' were revised to become self-respect, self-support, self-confidence and self-strengthening, and the original feature of disciplining oneself within social rules was abandoned. Women were encouraged to shake off the thought of dependence upon others and to strengthen their independent consciousness.[10]

Because of the special position of the Women's Federation, which has established its network at all levels of government, in all parts of the country, its actions have of course played an important role in transforming the concept of gender and advancing the women's movement at grass-roots level.[11]

2. *The awakening of self-awareness in Chinese women intellectuals who are pioneers in establishing a new gender concept.* Chinese women intellectuals have been beneficiaries of social liberation through legislation, and yet have also explored its limitations. Their problems, in the words of Li Xiaojiang

> may not be the typical ones among ordinary women, but record the pilgrimage of Chinese women and the awakening of their self-awareness, and reflect what they have encountered on their way forward and point out the direction they have pursued, thus reflecting the characteristics of contemporary China.[12]

In the course of their search, there has been no stage of radical criticism of male-centred culture, as in the Western feminist movement. Rather, they have focused on redefining their own orientation by analysing their relationship with men and with society.

Such a transition may be seen from a number of novels written by female writers during this new era. Here, however, I should like to describe some women intellectuals whom I have interviewed as examples to illustrate this transition. These women's ages range from 40 to 80. They are teachers, doctors, film directors and suchlike. For most of them, their gender consciousness was aroused during the 1980s. On the whole, they have gone through a process of development from being oriented by others (usually male), to an awakening of self-awareness, to locating themselves by understanding their relationship with men and with society.

When talking about the development of her self-awareness, a 60-year-old university professor said:

> The family education I received during my childhood was Confucian, in which father emphasised that man should respect himself, should struggle and should respect his elders. I have been deeply influenced by this. On the other hand, however, my father did not tell me what girls should not do. So I was able to go to a new-style school with my brothers when I was young.
>
> At that time, I was an obedient daughter at home and an outstanding student at school. The opinions of others were important to me. I was always obeying others' requirements, without ever considering if these requirements were reasonable. So, after 1949, when I was asked to give up a teaching position which I enjoyed and become a Party official, I obeyed. Now I realise that there is a close link between the education of Confucian obedience that I received when I was young and what the Party required me to be, 'an obedient instrument', which I did not feel any difficulty in accepting when I became a Party member. I was living without my 'self'.
>
> After China opened its door and started economic reform, my self-awareness began to awake under the influence of people's emancipation and I had an urge to realise my own value. So at the age of 50, I started from the very beginning, taking up teaching and researching. Especially after I began to do research on women's history, my urge to pursue self-development became even stronger.[13]

Some of the intellectual women experiencing a new awakening have been directly influenced by Western culture, and have seen themselves in a comparative light. They have discovered that for women in particular there exist great differences between Chinese and Western culture. One 40-year-old woman with a doctoral degree said:

> The Western feminist works that I have read point out that to be a complete female should include being a mother, having love and having a profession. But they do not mention being a wife, which in the West takes on a meaning quite different from in our culture. Chinese culture emphasises the role of the woman as a wife. Here, women's responsibilities and duties are focused, whilst the love in Western culture focuses more on women's personal feelings. During the era in which I got married [the 1970s], 'love' could not be voiced.

The things that you considered when looking for a spouse were his family background, honesty, etc. Emotional feelings were repressed.

My marriage is not a happy one, mainly because I have no spiritual exchange with my husband. My mother-in-law is not satisfied with me. She thinks that, as a daughter-in-law, I should listen to my husband's family and, as a wife, should not be better than my husband as far as social position is concerned. My mother has lived her life in such a way, listening to my father in every way without making decisions of her own. This has affected me a great deal. I have always vowed that I wouldn't repeat my mother's life!

Since my self-awareness awakened, I have changed in every aspect. In the past I thought housework was a kind of sacrifice. If I had no time to do it, I would feel guilty towards my husband and children. I often lost my temper with my children. Later, I managed to change the situation and took a step forward to meet the pressures around me. I enrolled as a graduate student working for the doctorate degree. I was a student like my children. Since that time, the family atmosphere has improved a lot. I make time to buy vegetables, cook meals and clean rooms. I want to set an example to my children, showing them that their mother can do well both in studies and housework. Sometimes, I will talk with my children instead of only looking after their material needs and forcing them to do their lessons.

I suffered during the Cultural Revolution, so I did not dare speak much at work. Now, I have begun to express my opinions about things such as the repression some professors have directed toward younger teachers or the unhealthy tendency in the science and technology field. I do not feel nervous or worried any longer.[14]

From the experience of such women, we have seen the new gender concept forming. It inherits and retains the valuable characteristics of Chinese traditional culture, such as the emphasis on unremitting struggle, hard work and sacrifice. At the same time, it absorbs the emphasis in foreign culture on individual development and the spirit of independence. It casts off the idea of 'women as inferior to men' and emphasises co-operation with men and with society. This new gender concept is progressive in comparison with the old 'equality between men and women', which actually took a male way of being as standard.

The aspirations of these women intellectuals may seem to other Chinese women to overstep the mark, and they may not be widely accepted for the time being. However, the current economic transformation in China must have a great effect upon the lives of most people. The changes in the mode of work and life, affecting millions of women farmers and women workers, are also leading to a gradual enhancement of their consciousness and their independent spirit. In the long run, women intellectuals and women workers will be able to come closer together in their growing self-awareness.

Humanity and Difference

15. Naked Human Nature and the Draperies of Custom
Wollstonecraft on Equality and Democracy
Kate Soper

It is always tempting to suppose that major thinkers of the past owe their continued influence and pertinence to the coherence of the body of argument they bequeathed, and to seek, in one's retrospection upon their work, to discover its essential unity and synthesis. But in yielding to this temptation it is easy to overlook the significance of the tensions in their writing, and I think this point may have especial relevance in the case of Mary Wollstonecraft. For it is, I suggest, a mercurial quality or instability in her writing that accounts for the continued fascination with it and allows *A Vindication of the Rights of Woman*, in particular, to figure as something more than a historical monument — as a source book still for feminist and democratic thinking.

Two of the more striking aspects of its argument, in fact, are its restlessness, rather than its seamless analytical coherence, and the many unresolved, if not contradictory, points in its dialectic. To offer but one or two instances here: the *Rights of Woman* both presumes and subverts a class-divided society. It claims to be addressed to the 'middle classes', regards domestic servants as a permanent institution, and recommends an educational segregation between richer and poorer strata. But it is also, of course, deeply opposed to the hierarchy of wealth and privilege, punctuated with tirades against the 'pestiferous purple' of monarchy, church and aristocracy, and sometimes close to being Marxist *avant la lettre* in its attacks on private property. (In her text on the *Vindication of the Rights of Men*, we might note, Wollstonecraft paradoxically cues Marx's fulminations in *On the Jewish Question* against the 'bourgeois egoism' of the American Declaration of Rights, with her assault on 'Security of Property! Behold in a few words, the definition of English liberty!')[1]

Yet, if Wollstonecraft is embryonically socialist in her polemic against property, she also accepts the standard assumptions of the day concerning the nature of the individual and the role of civic virtue in politics, and subscribes to cultural and aesthetic arguments based on elitist conceptions of taste and sensibility. In many ways, in fact, her attack on the abuses of aristo- or plutocracy can be viewed as a plea for the establishment of meritocracy, of a society in which it is personal worth and natural merit that win the esteem and honours which currently accrue to the specious and artificial distinctions of birth and wealth; and this tendency to recognise differential natural endowment creates a tension with those dimensions of her argument that point more directly towards the role of socio-economic factors in determining personal achievement.

Split then, as it is, between a liberal-humanist and a more socialist approach to equality, the *Rights of Woman* is likewise complex from any feminist point of view. For it seems to straddle or incorporate within it — in ways that can seem quite idiosyncratic when viewed from our current perspective — different strands of argument to be found in contemporary feminism. Obviously, it is an argument for equality based on a belief that there is no disparity between souls, and none between their embodiment save that of physical strength, an endowment which Wollstonecraft cannot allow gives men any claim to superiority in the qualities that matter — those of reason and capacity for virtue. It is an equal opportunities argument, then, insofar as its rhetorical move is to say, 'inferiority not proven until found guilty', until, that is, women have been given the opportunities that men have enjoyed and are still found wanting. Hence her suggestion that her epoch must wait

> Till kings and nobles, enlightened by state, throw off their gaudy trappings; and if then women do not resign the arbitrary power of beauty — they will prove they have *less* mind than man.[2]

Yet it is also an argument that acknowledges an essential difference of roles between the sexes, and which might even be said to offer us a version of 'maternal' feminism. There is much in the *Rights of Woman* which suggests that the enfeeblement and male-dependency of women is traceable to their own self-dereliction, to a failure to attend to that maternal dimension of being wherein the female can regain her autonomy and stand on a par with man in terms of dignity and self-respect. Deploring the frothy frivolity of women of fashion, she tells us she

> has often wished, with Dr Johnson, to place some of them in a little

shop with half a dozen children looking up to their languid countenances for support. I am much mistaken if some latent vigour would not give health and spirit to their eyes, and some lines drawn by the exercise of reason on blank cheeks, which before were only undulated by dimples, might restore lost dignity to the character, or rather enable it to attain the true dignity of its nature.[3]

However, underlying and subverting any such pious adherence to the binary gender framework of thinking is another strain altogether: one that brings her project closer to contemporary aspirations to transcend this grid, and which is most poignantly expressed in that 'wild wish' to 'see the distinction of sex confounded in society, unless where love animates the behaviour'.[4] Quite what she has in mind here, it is true, is a little unclear, as indeed are her views on love itself, which only go to add to the perplexities of the book. (Love, of its nature, must be transitory, 'a master and mistress of a family should not continue to love each other with passion'; unhappy marriages are often advantageous to the family, and the neglected wife is, in general, the better mother.[5] — all of which are highly debatable, if not downright mistaken, claims.)

Rethinking Liberalism

The relevance to our own times of the tensions within Wollstonecraft's views on love and sexuality has, on the whole, received more attention in commentary on her work than have the complexities of her political philosophy and their bearing on contemporary debates around questions of citizenship and democracy. I propose, therefore, to focus on the latter here, relating my argument in the first instance to the welcome attempt by Virginia Sapiro in a recent work to rectify the relative neglect of Wollstonecraft's arguments on democracy and to establish the claims of the *Rights of Woman* to be treated as a significant contribution to political theory.[6] Sapiro's general thesis is that Wollstonecraft invites a rethinking of liberal theory along more democratic lines, and she argues in this connection that a violence has been done to Wollstonecraft by those interpreters who view her only as a Lockean liberal and fail to attend to her republicanism. But her main claim for Wollstonecraft's contribution to the democratisation of liberalism concerns the impact of the argument of the *Rights of Woman*; this, she claims, extends beyond the demand that women as well as men be absorbed into liberal theory's conception of citizens and citizenship, going on to challenge the hallowed division between 'public' and 'private' spheres observed by even the most radical versions of liberalism. What Wollstonecraft offered, we are told, is a 'means of stretching the liberal temperament to incorporate into political thinking explicit concern for the quality of personal relations and day-to-day conditions of the lives of citizens'.[7] Sapiro thus sees Wollstonecraft as a kind of proto-theorist of the idea of the 'personal' being the 'political'.

Yet it is questionable, I think, how far we can defend such a view of her originality in terms which presume that her thought is unproblematically locatable within a tradition of liberalism. For, to the extent that Wollstonecraft can be credited with inaugurating the feminist challenge to the 'public'–'private' division of spheres (and I shall shortly argue, in fact, that there are some reasons to qualify this picture of her contribution), she would surely have to be viewed as challenging a fundamental tenet of liberal thinking rather than merely 'stretching' its temperament. Moreover, there may be some problem in viewing even what she most certainly does demand, namely that formal rights of citizenship be extended to women, as a democratisation of the liberalism of her day, rather than as a direct affront to its philosophy. In part, what is at issue here is the definition to be placed on the term 'liberal theory', and the extent to which we are essentially identifying this with the formulation given it in the nineteenth century, notably by Mill and Bentham. To the extent that we can speak of 'liberalism' in Wollstonecraft's day, it is in reference to a political philosophy which drew its character from its privileging of a male, property-owning elite to such a degree that Wollstonecraft's argument might be better viewed as a radical assault upon its presumptions than as a democratic extension of its principles. Equally, it is difficult to view Wollstonecraft's argument as fitting comfortably into any classic Millian mode (not to speak of the historical objections to the projection of the later theory back onto her own).

It is certainly true that her call for female citizenship is perfectly consistent with Millian liberalism. Indeed, it is a central plank of Mill's own argument against the subjection of women that this represents a barbaric anachronism in contradiction with the very logic of liberal theory. So, far from it threatening liberalism, Mill views the emancipation of women as bringing the practice of society into conformity with its principles.[8] Yet, given the extent to which Mill's theory is rooted in the division of private and public, its key concern being the protection of the individual from the incursions of the state, there may be a problem here, too, in regarding any erosion of this distinction, of the kind attributed to Wollstonecraft, as extending rather than subverting its principles. In other words, I think we have to ask how far you can stretch the 'liberal temperament' so as to incorporate the 'personal' within the 'political', without profoundly disturbing its equanimity. To the extent that Wollstonecraft may be said to initiate a line of feminist dissent from a 'separate spheres' conception within political philosophy, her thought, I suggest, is more resistant than Sapiro allows to being viewed as a contribution to liberal theory.

But, as suggested earlier, there are reasons to be cautious about crediting Wollstonecraft with any extensive transgression of the public-private divide, at least if we are interpreting this in the sense of her challenging its gendered value system and priorities. It is true that the *Rights of Woman* directs attention to the obstacles that the allocation of women to the 'private' zone places in the way of their becoming the independent citizens she would wish them to be; and in the process it sheds much light on the effects of disqualifying reproduction from the sphere of the political. But this, of course, is rather different from an explicit targeting of the public-private divide as a barrier to democracy. Moreover, it has to be recognised that much of the argument of the *Rights of Woman* does in fact presume, even depends upon, the idea of men and women having different respective tasks and duties — those of nurturing being accepted by her to be more naturally those of the female (and, indeed, as we have seen, all the better performed if she is neglected by her spouse). Third, I think it is relevant to the issue to consider the extent to which Wollstonecraft's conception of what constitutes 'duty' and civic virtue is imbued with patriarchalist assumptions, for one may certainly argue that neither in her political nor in her aesthetic conceptions is she disputing the privileging of the activities and attributes associated with the public domain, and thus with masculinity. Hence her plea that women might every day 'become more and more masculine'.[9] In other words, though she certainly draws attention to the effects of so defining the 'political' as to exclude all concern with sexuality, reproduction and personal relations, she does so on the basis of arguments that themselves embody the male bias of the public-private discrimination. Indeed, so deeply was the category of 'citizenship', and even that of 'humanity' itself, bound up with the idea of masculinity, that it is difficult to see how Wollstonecraft could have done otherwise than denigrate the feminine in her very demand for civic recognition of the female. As Barbara

Taylor has pointed out, 'so clearly gendered was the concept of the free citizen that Wollstonecraft's own attempts to employ it on women's behalf constantly drew her away from a discourse of humanity to one of masculine identification'. The dilemma of Wollstonecraft's feminism lay in the fact that 'it was impossible for women to speak as citizens without speaking *against* their womanhood'.[10]

This tension is also manifest in Wollstonecraft's support for the aims and aesthetic principles of the movement for 'civic humanism' in the arts, given the movement's exclusion of the female as a political subject or arbiter of taste. As John Barrell has convincingly argued, 'in the civic humanist theory of art, and the various mutations of it, women are denied citizenship and denied it absolutely, in the republic of taste as in the political republic.' The movement denied women membership of the 'republic of taste' on the grounds that since they had no public identity in the political republic they were incapable of public virtue; its theories of art all presumed that an ability to grasp the relations of general and particular was fundamental to correct taste, and exclusive to the male.[11]

Wollstonecraft, of course, contests this exclusion and allows Mary in the novel of that name to instantiate a 'male' preference for history painting (the inculcator of public virtue) over portraiture (concerned only with the 'personal' and particular likenesses). But this only goes to confirm Wollstonecraft's acceptance of the gendered values of 'civic humanism', and, one might add, at a more implicit level, of some of its class assumptions. Centred as it was originally on gentlemen of property and leisure, its aesthetic criteria reflected a presumption of their innately superior sensibility — specifically, in their privileging of a creative representation in art over the servile imitations of nature which the more 'mechanical' mind (the mentality, that is, associated with the mechanic or workman) contrived and favoured. Wollstonecraft's own liking for this aesthetic is evident not only in *Mary*, but also in her essay on 'Poetry' and in her approval for the non-mechanical quality of Greek statuary in the *Rights of Woman*:

> I observed that it was not mechanical, because a whole was produced — a model of that grand simplicity, of those concurring energies, which arrest our attention and command our reverence. For only insipid lifeless beauty is produced by a servile copy of even beautiful nature.[12]

In her discussion of Wollstonecraft's support for 'civic humanism', Sapiro notes the way in which, in the hands of Blake, Barry and others, including Wollstonecraft herself, this aesthetic was directed towards the creation of a more egalitarian culture, and she emphasises that it is a slavishness to authority and 'master copies' that Wollstonecraft is rejecting in her dismissal of mechanical servitude. The point is well taken. My point is that a full assessment of Wollstonecraft s positioning on the public-private divide must concern itself not only with her expressed sentiments, but with the extent of her implicit reliance on its masculine ideas and values. In this sense, I would contest Sapiro's claim that she offers a 'dynamic resolution' of the public-private division[13] — indeed, I am not sure that any of us to date have managed that. What is significant, I suggest, about Wollstonecraft's political contribution is not that it 'resolves' the tensions of this opposition, but that she is so clearly wrestling with issues that have remained an abiding source of frustration and difficulty in feminist thought.

Democracy and Difference

I shall turn now to some more wide-ranging thoughts about the pertinence of Wollstonecraft's argument on democracy to contemporary debates. Any demand for equality of participation or representation presupposes both a sameness and a difference between persons. On the basis of what is shared in common (for example, humanity) we are asked to overlook certain differences (for example, of sex, race, colour, wealth, etc.) as being pertinent to the question of entitlement. Wollstonecraft s refusal to recognise what she terms 'unnatural distinctions' (of rank and property) as grounds for differential treatment conforms to this model. However, there is a good deal of theory on offer today which claims to be the more democratic for its rejection of any appeal to sameness (on the grounds that there is no nature held in common by all members of humankind) and for its respect for the plurality of identities (or the indefinite differences that obtain between persons and cultures). Such approaches have been critical of the Enlightenment humanism that Wollstonecraft's argument exemplifies, claiming that it necessarily represents a form of Western-centric cultural imperialism, an attempt to project Western values and concepts of human identity and needs onto other peoples. Far from being democratic, it is argued, such humanism is disrespectful of other cultural preferences and practices and has served to legitimate colonial policies in the past and patronising interferences in the present, which have been destructive of the traditions and mores of non-Western communities.

On the basis of these kinds of argument, post-modernist critics of the Enlightenment have persistently denounced the pretensions of universalist discourse and invited us to suppose that there is something inherently counter-democratic in the very impulse to political representation: to attempt to speak on behalf of the 'other' is, so it is implied, always to be at risk of foisting our own culturally specific concept of human needs and values upon these 'others', and thus of denying their 'right' to self-identification. Representative, dare one say it, of this form of 'democratic' sensibility is Derrida's admonition in a recent interview:

> There would be no event, no history, unless a 'come hither' opened out and addressed itself to someone, to someone else whom I cannot and must not define in advance — not as subject, self-consciousness, nor even as animal, God, person, man or woman, living or dead....The one to whom 'come hither' is addressed cannot be defined in advance. This absolute hospitality is offered to the outsider, the stranger, the new arrival. Absolute arrivals must not be required to begin by stating their identity; I must not insist that they say who they are, and whether they are going to integrate themselves or not; nor should I lay down conditions for offering them hospitality, for whether or not I shall be able to 'assimilate' them into the family, the nation or the state.[14]

But while one can appreciate the force of this critical impulse as a counter to the framework of thinking that has tended, for example, to govern Western policies on immigration, the ultimate implications for political practice of the anti-universalist critique of Enlightenment humanism are, to say the least, problematic, and the nature of the controversies it has generated are well exemplified in the responses to the Salman Rushdie case or in feminist debates around such issues as female circumcision. A succinct illustration of the ways in which these implications have been registered in the discussion of 'democracy' among university teachers is provided by Martha Nussbaum in a recent article: in the course of an international conference on value and technology, a paper was given by a French anthropologist in which regret was expressed that the introduction of smallpox vaccine to India by the British has eradicated the cult of Sittala Devi, the goddess to whom the local community had been used to pray in order to avert smallpox. When it was objected that it was surely better to be healthy than ill, the answer was given that Western medicine could think only in terms of binary oppositions of health and illness, life and death, and was hence blind to the radical otherness of other cultures.[15]

Now, there is no doubt of the abuses that have been perpetrated under the cover of liberal humanist rhetoric, or of the extent to which the interests of specific power elites have been hypocritically protected by a projection of these as universal to human society at large. But we must surely ask what it is we are doing when we expose the iniquities of Western imperialism, or the forms of cultural dominion on our own doorstep, if it is not deploring the failure of such practices to observe the humanity, dignity and rights of those they tyrannise. In other words, it is difficult to see how we can offer any coherent criticism of oppression without, at least tacitly, acknowledging a communality of human needs. If we bend the stick so far in favour of difference and cultural relativity that we deny any universal moral values or common qualities of being human, then not only do we undermine the very grounds of any empathetic solidarity with the sufferings of others, but we are also invited to view any and every distinction of persons as intrinsic to them, as an indissoluble aspect of their individual identity.

Let us note, moreover — to return now to the disputes of the eighteenth century — the parallels between the post-modernist emphasis on the irreducible plurality of identities and the arguments with which Edmund Burke defended tradition against the likes of Wollstonecraft, with their upstart disdain for the 'draperies' of custom. From Burke's perspective, Wollstonecraft is indeed a destroyer of cultural difference, bent on denuding society of those distinctions that are of its very essence and endow it with its cultural richness. Thus, he professes, he cannot relate to 'human actions and human concerns, in a simple view of the object, as it stands stripped of every relation, in all the nakedness and solitude of metaphysical abstraction'.[16] For Burke, what distinguishes man from beast, culture from nature, is precisely that humanity is differentiated, its culture functioning as the sanctum of such difference:

> All the pleasing illusions, which made power gentle, and obedience liberal, which harmonised the different shades of life, and which, by a bland assimilation, incorporated into politics the sentiments which beautify and soften private society, are to be dissolved by this new conquering empire of light and reason. All the decent drapery of life

is to be rudely torn off. All the super-added ideas, furnished from the wardrobe of moral imagination, which the heart owns, and the understanding ratifies, as necessary to cover the defects of our naked shivering nature, and to raise it to dignity in our own estimation, are to be exploded as ridiculous, absurd, and antiquated fashion.[17]

Wollstonecraft, for her part, was happy to plead guilty to these charges, in a polemic against the 'gorgeous drapery' in which Burke had 'enwrapped his tyrannic principles', a polemic through which she seeks both to expose the principles themselves and to denude them of their rhetorical garb. For Wollstonecraft, Burke's eloquence masks a profound irrationalism, a defence of bigotry in the name of reverence for cultural tradition, whose logical implication would be that slavery ought never to have been abolished: because, as she puts it, 'our ignorant forefathers, not understanding the *native dignity* of man, sanctioned a traffic that outrages every suggestion of reason and religion, we are to submit to the inhuman custom.'[18]

It is, perhaps, a little mischievous to associate the conservative Burke with contemporary defenders of cultural relativism, given the difference in their political motivations: Burke's to preserve aristocratic privilege, the latter's to check the 'imperialising' power of Western discourse. But I would ask for the comparison to be indulged on the grounds that it does serve to dramatise the tensions, together with the potentially reactionary dimensions, of those positions that we have been invited to view as wholly positive ruptures with Enlightenment humanism. Moreover, the fact that certain parallels can be drawn here should give pause for thought to all those who would spontaneously acclaim Wollstonecraft's contribution to feminist and democratic theory, while subscribing to postmodernist theoretical positions very much at odds with hers.

In illustration of the tensions I have in mind here, one might cite the case of Foucault, whose influence on feminism is very extensive at the present time but from whose perspective Wollstonecraft's argument looks decidedly dubious. Wollstonecraft claims to be speaking for 'nature' and 'reason', concepts which for Foucault have no intrinsic meaning or purchase on truth, and which have to be analysed as themselves the historic, and in principle always mutable, construct of discourses such as Wollstonecraft's own. Where Wollstonecraft seeks to disperse ignorance and superstition, Foucault emphasises what he has termed the 'disciplinary' effects of the appeals to 'truth', 'reason' and 'knowledge': the ways in which discourses laying claim to scientific status serve as means of social control and policing of the individual. Where Wollstonecraft wants independence and the observance of human rights, Foucault presents the discourses of autonomy and human rights as the vehicle of processes of 'subjectivisation' through which individuals have been co-opted and manipulated in the name of emancipation and self-realisation.

To point to this clash between Wollstonecraft's realism and Foucauldian relativism is not to deny that a Foucaultian approach to the *Rights of Woman* can shed some insights on the ways in which the text is conditioned by its historical context, and reflects, for the most part unknowingly, the modes of thought and speech in circulation at the time of its writing. We might note, too, that he has illuminated the collusive role of individuals in their own oppression in ways that we can recognise as pertinent to the analysis of those forms of female compliance with cultural expectations (for instance of women's appearance, comportment and capacity) which Wollstonecraft exposes and condemns. In the light of Foucault's insistence that wherever there is power there is also resistance, it is always open to the Foucaultian to argue that Wollstonecraft's argument must be viewed as constituting precisely such a discourse of resistance to the presiding norms of patriarchal power. But we should note, too, that there is a profound tension between the Foucaultian emphasis on the discursivity of power relations (on the extent, that is, to which they exist only in virtue of being expressed and perceived as such) and Wollstonecraft's assumption that she is speaking to forms of power and oppression that pre-exist her own discourse upon them and which have determinate effects on the experience of women quite independent of her articulation of them. For Wollstonecraft, the denial of the rights of women — like the traffic in slavery — is not immoral in virtue of the discourse that condemns it as such, but in virtue of the kinds of experience to which these oppressive conditions condemn the subject, since these involve, in her essentialist conception of human nature, a denial of the fundamental dignity of the person. From her perspective, feminist resistance is not to be construed as the arrival and imposition of a contingent and relative norm — as a new development in the discourse of democracy — but as a protest against structures of social power which are political in the sense of exercising power over the lives of women whether or not they are expressly articulated in a political discourse such as her own.

This is also the source of the related tension we might note between the ontological framework of her argument for the extension of the 'rights of man', and the anti-essentialism of the late twentieth-century project (most fully elaborated in the writings of Ernesto Laclau and Chantal Mouffe) to 'radicalise' liberal democracy.[19] For, while Wollstonecraft's fundamental appeal is to affronted 'human nature', the theorists of 'radical democracy' have rejected any such invocation of a common human nature or 'general principle or substratum' of an anthropological character.[20] In the argument of Laclau and Mouffe, oppressive relations are such not in virtue of their assault upon a pre-given 'natural' self, but in virtue of their being discursively constituted as oppressive.[21] 'The struggle against subordination,' they have claimed, 'cannot be the result of subordination itself', and relations of subordination — for instance between men and women, master and slaves — in effect become sites of victimisation and oppression only at the point of emergence of a 'democratic' discourse which pronounces them to be not simply relations of difference, but relations of inequality:

> It is only to the extent that the positive differential character of the subordinated subject position is subverted that an antagonism can emerge. 'Serf', 'slave', and so on, do not designate in themselves antagonistic positions, it is only in the terms of a different discursive formation, such as the 'rights inherent to every human being', that the differential positivity of these categories can be subverted and the subordination constructed as oppression. This means that there is no relation of oppression without the presence of a discursive 'exterior' from which the discourse of subordination can be interrupted. The logic of equivalence in this sense displaces the effects of some discourses towards others. If, as was the case with women until the seventeenth century, the ensemble of discourses which constructed them as subjects fixed them purely and simply in a subordinated position, feminism as a movement of struggle against women's subordination could not emerge. Our thesis is that it is only from the moment when democratic discourse becomes available to articulate the different forms of resistance to subordination that the conditions will exist to make possible the struggle against types of inequality. In the case of women we may cite as an example the role played in England by Mary Wollstonecraft, whose book *Vindication of the Rights of Women* [sic], published in 1792, determined the birth of feminism through the use made in it of the democratic discourse, which was thus displaced from the field of political equality between citizens to the field of equality between the sexes.[22]

Now I would suggest, in fact, that there is a certain equivocation in this formulation of their argument. On the one hand, we are invited to accept that relations of what they term 'subordination' are essentially relations of difference, whose distinctively 'oppressive' character comes into being only through a discourse which claims that the subordinated grouping is victimised or 'oppressed' within them, and cannot be accounted for in terms of the suffering of those who — prior to the emergence of this discourse — experience their condition as oppressive. On the other hand, in the latter part of the quotation, we are referred to the 'different forms of resistance to subordination', which, it is implied, pre-exist the 'discourse of equality' and find their expression or representation within it. Here what is being recognised, it would seem, is precisely that subjective experience of a relationship of 'subordination' *as* 'oppressive' — the individual feeling her condition to be a denial of her essential self — which Laclau and Mouffe are elsewhere insisting is 'constructed' only in the discourse that transforms the relationship of subordination into one of oppression. Laclau and Mouffe want both to deny the priority of any pre-discursive, naturally given sense of victimisation, and at the same time implicitly to recognise that, without some reference to it, no compelling and coherent explanation can be given of the emergence and political attractions of any particular 'discourse of equality' (in this specific example, of Wollstonecraft's feminist appeal). On the one hand, we are invited to accept that it is only in and through the discourses of democracy that the 'desire' for more egalitarian treatment is constructed; on the other hand, it is only by way of a smuggled reference to the 'resistance' by such a pre-constructed desiring individual that they can ultimately hope to explain the appeal of the 'logic of equivalence' itself. This vacillation, I suggest, is indicative of their tacit recognition of the inherent difficulties of attempting to dispense altogether with any reference to an 'anthropological substratum' in the theorisation of political power.

However, if we acknowledge what Laclau and Mouffe themselves appear to want to emphasise, namely the transformative role of the discourse of inequality, then they would be crediting the *Rights of Woman* with not so much bringing to light but constituting the oppression of women. But this is, of course, an analysis very much at odds with the argument of the book itself, which is indeed based in an 'anthropological substratum' and leaves us in little doubt that it views slavery (or the subordination of women) not as becoming an affront to humanity at the point where they are denounced as such, but as intrinsically wrong in virtue of their assault on the 'native dignity' of men and women. Equally, I suspect that Wollstonecraft would have been rather resistant to the notion that until she took up her pen, relations between the sexes were merely 'differential'; if confronted with a 'discourse theory' account of the role of the *Rights of Woman*, she might well have wanted to point out that it is one thing to recognise its inaugural role in constituting 'feminism' as a distinctive discourse of resistance, another to suppose that it was itself constitutive of the 'oppressive' character of the female condition it sought to articulate and represent.

Lastly, let us note in this connection that it is on the basis of their analysis of the contingency and discourse-dependency of all political struggles that Laclau and Mouffe proceed to pit their idea of radical democracy against the classic Jacobin model based around a unified conception of human nature and citizenship.[23] Linked as it was to a positive and unified concept of human nature, earlier democratic thought, they argue, tended to constitute a single, 'public' space of citizenship, within which that 'nature' had to manifest the effects of its radical freedom and equality. But the 'logic of equivalence' unleashed by the democratic revolution has overspilled so far into the space of the 'private', politicising as it has done so social relations previously excluded from the 'public' political domain, that it has exploded, so they claim, 'the idea and the reality itself of a unique space of constitution of the political':

> What we are witnessing is a politicisation far more radical than any we have known in the past, because it tends to dissolve the distinction between the public and the private, not in terms of the encroachment on the private by a unified public space, but in terms of a proliferation of radically new and different political spaces. We are confronted with the emergence of a *plurality of subjects*, whose forms of constitution and diversity it is only possible to think if we relinquish the category of the 'subject' as a unified and unifying essence.[24]

But if 'radical' democracy is conceived as an *indefinite* proliferation of 'subject-places' constituted through a continuous 'politicisation' of relations previously held to be purely 'differential', what prevents it from collapsing into anarchy or becoming the site of endless interpersonal abrasions and antagonism? What stops any and every difference of persons becoming a ground of contestation and staking its claim to 'democratic' recognition? What can provide the bases for the forms of solidarity and equality essential to the coherence of the concept of democracy and to the reality of its practice?

Laclau and Mouffe are not so naive as to fail to see this problem, and indeed it exercises them very considerably: hence their concern to distinguish the pluralist logic of 'radical democracy' from that of post-modernism. Mouffe herself has written, for example, that:

> a radical-democratic project has also to be distinguished from other forms of 'postmodern' politics which emphasise heterogeneity, dissemination and incommensurability and for which pluralism understood as a valorisation of all difference should be total. Such an extreme form of pluralism...could never provide the framework for a political regime. For the recognition of plurality not to lead to a complete *indifferentiation* and *indifference*, criteria must exist to decide between what is admissible and what is not.[25]

The legitimisation of every difference is indeed incompatible with democracy, and, unless one is prepared to accept this, one is deprived of any arguments against a Burkeian defence of hierarchy. Why should the king not be respected for his regal difference, the queen for her queenliness, the man for his mastery, and so forth? On the other hand, I do not see how one can justify any limits one would place on pluralism without invoking something more in the way of a unified subject or common humanity than Laclau and Mouffe are prepared to allow. It is not enough to imply, as they do, that citizenship and participation in democracy are a matter of being 'constructed' through the discourse of equality and freedom and subscribing to its rules. For how could there be any plausible defence of that discourse and its 'rules' that did not argue that some properties are more intrinsic to being human than others? How is it possible to conceptualise 'equality' and 'freedom' without accepting something of the abstraction back to human nature that Burke found so deplorable in Wollstonecraft's argument? Democracy, in short, cannot be grounded or legitimised purely at the level of its own discourse, and Wollstonecraft's own discourse on equality remains a pertinent reminder of this.

16. Mary Wollstonecraft, Feminism and Humanism
A Spectrum of Reading

Himani Bannerji

Some years have passed since feminism has gained currency and a degree of respectability in the West. No longer inhabiting social, political and intellectual margins, in various adapted forms and effects it has gained a niche for itself even in governments, businesses and public institutions. The generalisation of feminism among women is wide enough to have reached the point of divergent claims and contests regarding the meaning of the concept, its agents and practices. The current atmosphere among Western feminists is ridden with strife not only along class lines but also over orientations of difference based on 'race', sexuality, religion and so on, in any number of combinations. These struggles over difference and representation have made it apparent that we may not have a common feminist vision and that shifting the emphasis from the singularity of the common noun 'woman' into the plurality of 'women' has not really done the trick.[1] In fact, we may even have come to a time when we may routinely need to put a quotation mark around the word 'woman' since some critics have claimed this to be an entity created by discourse rather than a referent for an existing social subject.[2] Why, then, in this situation should we, non-white women living in the West, marked by our own forms of difference and representation, begin to read Mary Wollstonecraft, an eighteenth-century woman, a writer of the Enlightenment, whom present-day white middle-class feminists have as their 'foremother'? By doing so, are we not increasing our subservience to a white middle-class women's movement and its version of feminism?

This chapter attempts to show why, in spite of many reservations, I consider *A Vindication of the Rights of Woman*[3] a classic text for the possibilities it offers of understanding Western feminist theory and politics. I will chart different readings of this text at different biographical and political moments of my life, highlighting both its problems and its contributions to developing a more effective feminism in our time. Here, my reading itself becomes a critical methodology, as an act of conscious retrieval, connection and formulation which historicises and socialises the text. This is not a gesture of self-indulgent personal disclosure, but rather an epistemological venture which implies that the social ontology of both the writer and the reader (their social being in historical and personal times) not only shapes their intellectual/political views but also provides the necessary ground for a social and critically active form of reading. This method, which sees writing and reading as contingent social acts and forms, does not, however, advocate arbitrariness and randomness. It simply attempts to situate both the text and the reader in lived time and history, so that the full value of the text, its relevance not only to the past but also to the present, may become apparent. In establishing this reader-writer relationship I offer three possible ways of reading *The Rights of Woman*. They are: (a) reading as identification; (b) reading as difference; and (c) reading as negotiation.

Reading as Identification

There are certain books to which we return for this or that reason over a long period of time, each return both measures the distance we have covered in our own lives and reveals a hitherto unnoticed dimension of the text. One such book is Mary Wollstonecraft's *A Vindication of the Rights of Woman*.

The very first time that I set my eyes on the *Rights of Woman* was in my mid teens. It was one of a number of books left for me by our departing headmistress, Miss Kathleen N. Bradley, when she returned to England, completing her assignment for the education of girls in the colonies and ex-colonies of the British Empire. Thus my memory of this book, with its yellowing pages and a pleasant musty smell, is tied up with that of our redoubtable spinster headmistress, who pursued the cause of reason among girls and young women with a formidable zeal. Often she, together with our other similarly inspired local teachers, spoke to us, or exhorted us, to cultivate our faculty for reason. Though careful in their enunciations, they managed to convey to us the view that marriage and a serious life of reason were not mutually compatible, but that a good married life was itself impossible without some cultivation of that noblest of faculties. They suggested to us — the children of the upper classes — that their less affluent and often spinster's lives in pursuit of education were more worthy than the lives of wealthy matrons who did not have an inclination or vocation for reason. It was within the framework of education that they spelled out our rights and duties, citing the development of reason as the difference between an animal and a human being. And they spoke in the language of light, of rationality contrasted with stupefying sensuality. They advocated reading 'good books', texts by social reformers, both national and international. As a result, Mary Wollstonecraft's *Rights of Woman* and John Stuart Mill's *The Subjection of Women* rubbed shoulders with the essays of Rabindranath Tagore[4] and Sir Sayyid Ahmad.[5] On the Foundation Day of our school, we heard about the connection of nationalism and independence with women's education. 'No nation', it was announced to the students from the podium of the assembly hall, 'progresses without the advancement of education among its women.' It was in such an environment that I made the acquaintance of Mary Wollstonecraft. Miss Bradley 'hoped', in her note, that I would both learn from and enjoy reading this book: instruction and delight — an old pedagogic maxim!

So the way in which I came across Mary Wollstonecraft, the historic situation in which I first read the *Rights of Woman*, did not make her an 'other' for me. Not only did the world in which I grew up support and produce thinkers like her, but its social organisation abundantly supported her reasons and impulses for writing it. Pleas for social reform, rationality and women's education had become established discourses in Bengal since the nineteenth century, and their justification continued to exist in my personal environment. There were women at the foundation of my life — my mother, grandmother, aunts and other female relatives of the older generations — who were deprived of education (not through a lack of wealth), of remunerative labour and of public life of any kind. These women generally viewed the lives of their school-going daughters with protective support, and occasionally with envy and suspicion. Just at the time when I was growing up, women's novels and short stories resonated with themes of women's education and independence; stories of mothers and daughters abounded. Thus there was a world of uneven development which contained our mothers, our women teachers, those secular 'nuns of reason', and us, the educated daughters and potential wives of professionals, to be brought up in the lores of intellectual conjugality. Nothing could have been a more ideal environment for a young woman reading the *Rights of Woman*.

The world of my childhood and youth in an upper-class/caste Hindu family resembled Wollstonecraft's severely gendered world, with its sharp demarcation between the public and the private spheres. These similarities came through in spite of the details specific to the social and economic worlds of upper- and middle-class Europeans — especially of the English. Though patriarchy in my world was less sexual and translated more into male-centred kinship hierarchies, the organisation of everyday life as described in the *Rights of Woman* was familiar to me. Gender division of labour and morality lay at the bottom of the daily practices and ideologies of both her world and mine. To be a woman or a girl in these worlds were scripted matters. A 'girl' in my class environment, which meant a 'good girl', rarely did anything alone which involved the public sphere and men. Like the well-brought-up girls and women in the *Rights of Woman*, we did not go unescorted for visits, except to relatives or in the most immediate neighbourhood. We did not go to markets and shops, nor for solitary long walks, did not take part in energetic play in general, did not stay out, unless specially permitted, after sundown, and often did not work for a living. After a certain age, unlike European women, Bengali women were not encouraged to go to social gatherings attended by non-kin men, except on official or ritual occasions. The university, with its co-educational schooling, was an exception.

There were double messages in my world. There were simultaneous pleas for women's education and emancipation while actualities of preventive moral regulations textured our lives. But this contradiction settled somewhat if one attended closely to what was being conveyed both with and without words: the message was that education and reason were important matters for women to become better wives and mothers. In other words, they were adjuncts to decent domesticity. That argument underlay some aspects of Mary Wollstonecraft's text, as well. She, like the social reformers of Bengal, spoke in favour of women's cultivation of reason mainly as a source of improvement for the overall quality of domestic life. Thus, women's education was seen both by us and her as a 'motherhood' issue, even while women's economic dependence was a matter of some importance.[6] Though I resented this belief that 'real work' for women lay in an apprenticeship to some kind of enlightened domesticity, rather than in learning for a profession, Wollstonecraft's thoughts were not alien or opaque to me.

My affinity for the *Rights of Woman* lay in issues of gender, evoking responses in me which were both experiential and historical. In our daily lives and cultural unconscious lay embedded the longing to know. The intensity of this longing is reflected in letters, memoirs, the rarely published women's autobiographies and hearsay dating all the way back to the nineteenth century. The following passage from *Amar Jiban* (*My Life*), the autobiography of Rasasundari Dasi (1806-1900), is similar to the writings of Wollstonecraft in its intense desire for knowledge. It also speaks of the immense obstacles that she faced in this, like most older women who surrounded me. This translated text is intended to serve as a parallel to the *Rights of Woman*, as a mirror for my reading of it. Rasasundari Dasi's passionate desire to read scriptural texts propelled her into an heroic project of self-instruction. Unable to seek help, since 'no woman learns to read and write', she tried to remember the alphabet which she had overheard from boy pupils in the schoolroom in childhood. She then tried to puzzle out the meaning of the words and lines. She tore a leaf from a book and hid it under the firewood in the kitchen:

> I had no time to study that page. At night it got too late by the time the cooking was finished. And no sooner were the chores all done then the children woke up. Is it possible to do anything else then? One would say, Ma, I want to pee; the other, Ma, I am hungry; the other, Ma, hold me; and another would wake and start crying. One had to console and look after them. And as night progressed sleep overcame [me] and there was no time left to study. I saw no way for me to learn....So when I cooked I kept the page in my left hand, and once in a while sneaked it within my veil to look at it. But what could mere glancing accomplish? I could not even recognise the full alphabet....In those days my eldest son used to write on palm leaves. I hid a palm leaf as well. I would look at this palm leaf first and then the page from the book, and refer to my mental image of the alphabet. And then again I would try to compare this with how people talk. Some days passed in this way. I would occasionally take out the book's page, and then hide it under the logs lest anyone should see it![7]

This text perhaps shows what lay in my background and positively predisposed me to Mary Wollstonecraft. I felt myself to be a part of the history of debates on women and learning since the mid nineteenth century, debates which by the end of the century had precipitated thousands of girls into schools.[8] This was not simply a colonial formation, but blended into indigenous rationalist traditions which stretched into the pre-colonial past.[9]

It was not a problem for me in those days that this preoccupation with reason, rationality and reform were essentially the middle-classes' concern, their way of forming a class consciousness by elaborating moral regulations.[10] But I never thought of these issues in terms of class discourse, nor in terms of colonial discourse. In my world, which was organised around the location of women and men in private and public spheres, I echoed longings of other women and girls to be out in the world. And the getting of knowledge seemed to be the way to that public space; in fact it was accomplished in that public space. At this stage of my life, the only contradictions that I felt deeply were ones of gender and patriarchy. The overwhelming proscription of sexuality, the chastity belt of moral regulations pertaining to 'good' Hindu girls from a 'respectable' family, was my immediate and biggest barrier. The only difference and otherness I knew well was from 'man'. I could not see 'class' in Bengal, with its particular colonial inflexion, because I was in it and of it. This form of class was my everyday life, my condition of being, in which I was just beginning to enunciate my own particular personality.

The cry for a gender-neutral, transcendent and yet critical reason that rose from the pages of the *Rights of Woman* went straight to my heart. I could not think of either knowledge or justice as a sexed matter, since difference led only to inequality. I agreed with Wollstonecraft that morality was a matter not of manners but rather of criticism and conscience. The critical, ethical imperatives of the *Rights of Woman* gave a different twist to my own individualistic urge for liberty, since freedom as understood by Wollstonecraft was not a simple manifestation of an individualist will. It was a product of ethical self-improvement, and thus not to be confused with hedonistic selfishness. Thinking in terms of a vindication of rights of both women (and men) seemed like a great opening in the social enclosure produced by the iron laws of gender.

Reading as Difference

By the time I took another serious look at *A Vindication of the Rights of Woman*, I was much older, and more significantly I had been living in the West for many years. The Marxism I brought with me from India had now acquired feminist, anti-racist dimensions. I was earning my living by teaching part-time in women's studies and the social sciences. In this changed context of my life, my reading of the *Rights of Woman* also changed, as colours and patterns reconfigurate in a kaleidoscope.

I then read it from the perspective of difference with which I identified.

What I mean by 'difference' here is not the cultural traits and values that I brought with me from India. Rather it is a difference created outside of me, by a relational and interpretative framework which ascribes 'race' and stereotyped ethnicity, produced in the context of colonial histories and imperialist relations peculiar to the West. This 'difference' has more to do with relations of ruling[11] and with a hegemonic racist common sense,[12] than with my own sense of difference as a cultural entity.[13] This 'raced' or ethnicised otherness is not gender-neutral: it types us, both non-white and white women and men, differently from each other. It provides the modalities, the organising principles, of social and cultural forms through which class comes into being.[14]

As I explored this difference it became evident that definitions of 'self' and 'other', even in the context of Enlightenment 'universals', such as the notion of the 'human', are deeply socio-cultural and historical. The concrete content of the notion 'human' turns out to be a bourgeois, white, Christian, European male, who provided the ideal type against which European women and inhabitants of the non-European world were measured and found wanting. Thus the actual historical affiliation of humanism to domination, in spite of the former's metaphysics of equality in reason and political rights, prompts us to make a distinction between the universalism of the idea of the human and its actual articulation and deployment. This pathology of the Enlightenment and of rationalism became distinctly visible from my present perspective of difference and distanced both the *Rights of Woman* and Wollstonecraft from me. She had become an eighteenth-century white European woman, who shared the colonial ideologies of her time. I was now situated in an historical and political relationship of criticism and even antagonism towards her.

This reading through the lens of difference made me aware of the *Rights of Woman* as a text not only of reform but of Utopianism, with polarities of the ideal and the debased paralleling the exalted possible and the fallen actual. Her contemporary society, Wollstonecraft felt, lay in a state of degeneration, in sore need of improvement. In this grand narrative movement of morality, the language, images and values she associated with various types of difference became crucial.

I was impressed by the impassioned and figurative richness of Wollstonecraft's prose. Not a page of the *Rights of Woman* goes by without charged and constellated metaphors, descriptions and anecdotes, which make her sentiments, criticism and advice glow with vividness and conviction. I thought this to be curious for a rationalist text, and it seemed important to explore the role of these figures of speech in Wollstonecraft's social theory and vision, particularly with respect to themes of racialised forms of difference.

From this point of view, the *Rights of Woman* is marked by the iconic centrality of 'slavery' used in various metaphoric and analogical ways. It is not an exaggeration to say that it serves as an interpretive and organisational device of the text. This theme of slavery, in all its vivid details, variations and political consequences, reveals a binary aspect of liberty or freedom; Wollstonecraft shifts from a metaphoric level to the actual, alluding to economic slavery while accommodating sexual slavery as an analogy of heterosexual familial relations. Thus metaphors, similes and analogies of bondage, ranging from sadism to sadomasochism, deriving from the thematic complex of slavery, provide the point of departure for her reform and Utopian proposals. Without this figurative layer underwriting its philosophical and moral arguments, the *Rights of Woman*, which is otherwise a rather repetitive and formless text, would not have its internal coherence or sense of urgency. Like many other political and moral texts, it subsists on a connotative level, signalling its wider political concerns through a figurative discourse. It is this rather than a deductive and expositional mode which helps Wollstonecraft to present her social criticism and political theory.

This importance of a figurative, signifying device for a text of Enlightenment political theory might seem exaggerated. But this same claim has been made by Nancy L. Stepan in the context of scientific writing, with its dependence on metaphor, analogies and models in putting across its message.[15] If this is the case with science from at least the eighteenth century onwards, then it seems possible to argue that without this metaphor of slavery in its various interactive and illuminative forms Wollstonecraft would not have been able to accomplish her task in the *Rights of Woman*.

Wollstonecraft, after all, was neither alone nor the first in using the metaphor of slavery in political theory. Indeed, the political theory of radical democracy rested on this discourse of slavery and other forms of bondage. This metaphor emanated from actual long-standing practices of European feudalism and colonial capitalism. But, ironically, it also thematised and projected the democratic aspirations of the slave-owning classes themselves, relying on unfree labour to provide the emotive, conceptual and figurative signs for their own conditions of domination. In the case of Mary Wollstonecraft, the obvious comparison lies with Jean-Jacques Rousseau, though the metaphor of slavery continues to be effective for later revolutionary writing.[16] This double-edged use of slavery as metaphor or an allegory of bondage and freedom is able to encapsulate a multilayered oppression, while opening a space for imagining resistance. In the political theory of the eighteenth and nineteenth centuries, this constellation of metaphors of 'slavery' thus borders on the notion of class and class struggle.

This importance of slavery as the central discursive figure in the *Rights of Woman* has not been explored by many. Even as insightful a text as Virginia Sapiro's *A Vindication of Virtue* does not dwell on it in any significant way.[17] Infrequently, writers such as Moira Ferguson, motivated by an interest in the abolition of slavery, mark out its importance for Wollstonecraft.[18] Yet most interpreters have not seen her as much more than a critic of patriarchy and gender, or at best a 'rights' theorist. But the warp and weft of universality and difference which texture the *Rights of Woman* extend beyond gender to other relations of domination, and its Utopian vision, composed of the ideal and the fallen, needs the metaphor of slavery to convey these ideas. Figures of African slaves, oriental sultans, women of harems or seraglios and the allegedly tyrannical precepts of 'mahometanism' are all deployed to chart the trajectory of her narrative. These allusions and images blend with Wollstonecraft's descriptions of European upper/middle-class women's lives. This theme of slavery is further augmented with allusions to domestic creatures such as fawning spaniels, canaries in gilded cages, and beasts of burden such as donkeys. These are 'interactive metaphors' of bondage which rebound on other components of the text and create a meaning which is both concrete and subliminal.[19]

This pervasive and yet unproblematised use of the concept and metaphors of slavery by both male and female thinkers of the European Enlightenment is somewhat disturbing. Is it possible that, in spite of her support for the abolitionists and of the Haitian revolution, Wollstonecraft may have shared some of the racist and orientalist political unconscious of her time? The answer is a basic 'yes', even though there are qualifications to be made. Wollstonecraft's use of the Haitian revolution to warn the European bourgeoisie of an impending apocalypse of 'mobs' or her condescending review of the African writer Olaudah Equiano[20] may be seen as versions of racism. This applies also to stereotypes of ignorance and savagery that she attributes to black slaves. This is not negated by

Wollstonecraft's equation of white women with black slaves or by the use of slavery as a source of subversion and resistance. The word 'slave' is ambivalently developed through this text to imply both an innocent victim and a corrupt and morally degraded human being. Words such as 'slave', 'enslave', 'slavish' perform a judgemental function in the text's moral narrative and are indiscriminately used, Wollstonecraft's abolitionist views notwithstanding.[21]

This use of the image of black slavery to depict the condition of white middle-class women is also questionable in terms of Wollstonecraft's presumptions regarding the morality of black slaves, since here analogy becomes statement. She pronounces judgements upon psychological deformations brought about by patriarchy, and in the same breath imputes the same traits of weakness, cunning, seduction, manipulation and hunger for power to the actually enslaved black population. She can ignore actual slavery and its non-voluntary nature, together with the violence and irreducible antagonism it generates, because she is distant from black slaves and less interested in them than in white women, and yet she also feels entitled both to construct and to speak 'for' them. Thus it becomes apparent that she is using slavery primarily as an illuminating, persuasive device to project and combat the oppression of middle- or upper-class women of her time. It is this illustrative and heuristic appropriation however, which lends moral and emotional strength to the case of European women's fight for their 'rights'. This idiom of slavery consistently marks Western discourse on 'the subjection of women'.[22] Once more the slave serves the cause of the master class.

This association between 'race', gender and sexuality became increasingly normalised from Wollstonecraft's time onwards within a discourse on sexuality in European women, and became associated with blackness, with particular reference to African women and the institution of slavery.[23] In both its versions, of meek submissiveness and aggressive or seductive female lust, female sexuality could be fitted, as by Wollstonecraft, within the scope of a European racist understanding of African men and women through the institution of slavery. A self-contradictory perception of Africans and black slaves, of both obsequiousness and aggression, is pervasive in the *Rights of Woman*, and takes on a sexual quality as she compares white women with black male slaves. This equation of black men with white women continues to this day, and is criticised consistently by black feminists.[24]

This elision of gender subordination and economic slavery obscures the actuality that, even when both involve inequality of power, the two are composed of different modes or mores. A man and a woman, as lovers or husband and wife or father and daughter, have radically different modalities or practices of power than the ones obtaining between slaves and their masters or mistresses. Familial relations are nominally voluntary in many cases, and contain possibilities of economic and emotional investment and joint privileges. The personal moralities that are enjoined in the patriarchal family are not integral to the master-slave relationship. Thus patronage, in the sense of concubinage or children's protection extended by the master to a female slave, for example, is not comparable to that extended by a husband to a wife. In slavery, neither conjugality nor common parentage nor property can be held together; relations are not contractual or voluntary. Under such circumstances, the conflation of slavery and gender relations leads to the erasure of the actuality of slavery as a practice, as well as of African experiences and histories in bondage.

The use of slavery in the *Rights of Woman* has another dimension, drawing on what Edward Said calls 'orientalism'.[25] An imagined Orient, reputed in Christian Europe as a domain of sexual slavery and sensual excess, provides Wollstonecraft with her richest images of a degenerate world. Whereas there is ambivalence about black slavery, the Orient is portrayed as wholly static, intrinsically immoral, enervated and inert. This construction of the sensual and despotic Orient, which is extended from the theme of slavery, is played off against the violence of economic slavery, and both forms together supply metaphors and analogies for Wollstonecraft's moral vision.

Throughout the *Rights of Woman*, moral degeneration in European families is imagined through the discourse of the Orient as a brothel. The eighteenth-century European imagination projected the Orient as the quintessential space for sexual vices and male domination.[26] Images of the seraglio, the odalisque, the lustful sultan and a whole paraphernalia of orientalist construction are present in art, literature and the moral tracts or sermons of the time. The paintings of Ingres, for example, or French preconceptions about Egypt during the Napoleonic invasion and after, are indicative of a perception of the Orient as a hypersexual space; moreover, they come with the proviso of oriental women's complicity in their own degradation. Their subjection is thus seen as an intrinsic aspect of their own immorality and sensuality. In the *Rights of Woman*, Wollstonecraft repeatedly speaks of European husbands as sexually insatiable despotic sultans, and of their complying wives as their slaves. In these harem-like familial spaces of gender slavery, although there is no sound of lashes, there are bribes and flatteries, which dull the souls of European women into becoming dolls or spaniels of men. Female power is thus solely that of an 'oriental' seductress and manipulator, who gains her petty privileges through self-degradation.

This orientalist discourse, which provides Wollstonecraft with a theatre of sensuality, deliberately invites the reader's moral contempt. This imagined social enclosure contains no possibility of rupture or liberation. Here, the wills of the female slave and the sultan/master fuse into a relationship of degraded pleasure. In contrast to this, economic slavery, with its brutalities and unconsenting nature, has openings built into the very structure of its violence and the resulting resistance. Thus it functions as the negative pole of the voluntary degradation projected onto the Orient. This schema holds throughout the text, in spite of Wollstonecraft's sporadic negative comments on Africans as 'savages' with their superficial intellect and childish love of ornaments.[27] As against the static 'Oriental' world of tradition, the moral dynamism of black slavery could be seen as blending with the Enlightenment's project of 'improvement'. This politico-philosophical rhetoric offered Wollstonecraft a ready set of metaphors of inertia and resistance. Metaphors of 'savagery', including that of the 'noble savage', with their associations of both the pristine and the primitive, allowed Wollstonecraft a redemptive view of nature and helped her and others to connect 'rights' arguments based on nature with their enthusiasm for reason, as reason was seen to be a natural attribute. Moreover, for a pedagogue like Wollstonecraft, 'the savage' could be inserted into the Enlightenment project of 'improvement', whereas the oriental remained a traditionalist 'other'.[28] This process was further facilitated by the fact that slavery imposed a burden of guilt, which Orientalism did not.

In this version of reading with difference, my primary emotion towards Wollstonecraft was obviously one of rejection. Her claims of universality and her metaphysical gestures had largely become a legitimation device for condemning societies and peoples whom Europe sought to dominate. What, after all, could be more particularistic than a text constructed through orientalist and racist metaphors and analogies, which in actuality privileged European men and women in the name of all humanity? This critique of the *Rights of Woman* obviously shares many premises with those of other feminists of colour who have made similar readings of European and North American feminist texts from the perspective of difference, inclusive of anti-colonial critiques.

Many of these feminists have put forward critiques of the European Enlightenment and of 'white' feminism as it now exists. Of course, motivated as they were by their sense of difference, they did not call for the building of a broader feminist movement. But, given how I felt after I was ascribed my 'difference', or constructed into an 'other', I was not perturbed by this. At this point, my choices seemed to lie between an erasing and dishonest essentialism and the relative and localised honesty of difference. Understandably, I chose the latter, and closed my copy of the *Rights of Woman*.

Reading as Negotiation

It may be thought that by now I had come to the end of my reading of the *Rights of Woman*. But there is still a reading left untried, which negotiates with a text without categorical acceptance or rejection. The purpose of this reading is to uncover aspects of a text which may be useful to a reader's project, mindful of both difference and affinity. From this point of view the value of a text lies in its methodological approach — in its epistemology, for example, or in the ways in which the problematic is framed — rather than in its specific or exact content. This is what I now propose in relation to the *Rights of Woman*, and my reading, as before, is determined by its time and by my social subjectivity and politics.

Having lived through a time when the politics of difference has produced results which are as disappointing as those of essentialism, I have decided to re-examine classic feminist texts such as the *Rights of Woman*. My purpose is to explore the possibilities of developing a feminist analysis and politics which are cognisant of difference as well as of the general concern for social justice. This means getting beyond single-issue formulations of 'race', gender and class, and segmented politics based on a reduced understanding of these issues. Such an expanded analysis translates into understanding capital (national and international) and class through a lens of difference, where difference is understood as being inherent not to individuals, but rather to identities created by social relations of domination. Not that the *Rights of Woman* exactly performs this task; but, in the way in which it is textured, through an interplay between the wrongs of women and those of society in general, it allows for an insight into the construction of difference in a general social context. Simultaneously critical of forms of power as disclosed through the inverse relationship between 'woman' and 'human', the *Rights of Woman* creates a complex problematic whose horizon can extend to revolutionary humanism. Wollstonecraft's critical formulations, peculiar to her Enlightenment roots, raise the possibility that universalist categories such as 'human', 'justice' and 'rights', with their strong ethical tone, may not, when in full articulation with a concrete or materialist social analysis, be as politically exhausted as we have recently thought.

The importance of social theorists such as Wollstonecraft, who can think both abstractly and concretely and signal to a collective politics, is particularly evident now. Neither the politics of representation and identity nor that of the formal equality of liberal humanism, both subsisting on the ground of the market and of international capitalist expansion, have provided acceptable options for a politics of social wellbeing. We are constantly confronted with political and economic crises in which capital and capitalist states show increasing violence, implicating the local and the global. Nation states and international finance come to comfortable agreements with each other, and huge capital accumulation rests on the dispossession, vagrancy and degradation of an overwhelming number of people all across the globe. All around the world, socialist and anti-imperialist forces are in retreat, and yet it is precisely now, when we need to think more comprehensively and act collectively, that our inclination and ability to do so have declined. Even feminists have not risen to this task. On the contrary, the militancy of women's movements, as of labour movements, has declined. In spite of their interest in women's agency, post-modernist feminist theorists have not effectively articulated women's wrongs with those of others. On the level of politics, the options have been either sectarian or open to co-option by the corporate sector or the state. Many feminists, as bureaucrats of international finance or aid consortiums, have become managers of structural adjustment and capitalist expansion. Others, concentrating on their difference, in the name of 'race' and representation, have ended up in the multicultural margins of the capitalist state or have entered into sealed political enclosures of identity politics.

This crisis of feminism is obviously a part of the overall retreat of the left, which has intensified since the dismantling of the Soviet Union and the unification of Germany. The rumour about the death of socialism and Marxism that these events generated has acted in the manner of a self-fulfilling prophecy. Intellectuals of the right, such as Francis Fukuyama, hastened to put forward the 'end of history' thesis,[29] while 'radical' cultural critics influenced by theories of deconstruction kept pace by advancing the 'end of the subject' thesis. Fear of collectivities, carefully nurtured throughout the Cold War and after in the name of the individual, freedom and democracy, achieved its end by producing radical theorists who, even when they spoke of agents and selves, emptied these selves of *social* subjectivities.[30] All this created not only ineffectual or sectarian politics but also an ethos of, if not a commitment to, the anti-political.

For these reasons, I feel the need to re-examine texts that spoke of larger social projects, such as those of humanism or class, and to reconsider feminism in that light. Otherwise feminism, practised as a politics of gender alone, has a built-in tendency to move to a position which serves vested group interests. It requires a conscious effort, therefore, to explore gender in ways which unravel the social relations and ideological fields within which the gendering occurs. This is a must for feminism if it is to become a genuinely *social* politics.

Mary Wollstonecraft's *Rights of Woman* is an important text from this epistemological and political position, in spite of her essentialism and Eurocentrism. This is because of the unusual use she makes of the Enlightenment's rationalist/humanist discourse in the cause of women and the kind of problematic she frames to situate the wrongs of women within the wider social relations of her time. The *Rights of Woman* poses the question of women in terms not only of English society and history, but also of Europe. It poses the particular issue of women's rights in the context of human or universal rights, in a continuum with the rights of unfree labour, including those of slaves. But this interest in humanism or universal rights is not derived from any commitment to an *a priori* principle, but rather from her empirical knowledge and personal experience of the injustice peculiar to the lives of women. Thus she approaches the universal from the standpoint of difference, of a critique of patriarchy, while grounding it in the social and the historical. From these epistemological elements she propounds an early thesis of women's standpoint, which she considers a valid stance for promulgating social morality and politics. On this premise, unorthodox for a universalist thinker, Wollstonecraft attempts to base a social and political theorisation — a fact that is perhaps not emphasised enough, except, rarely, in books such as Sapiro's *A Vindication of Virtue*.

The conventional reading of Wollstonecraft underestimates this methodological innovation and reduces her to either a romantic libertarian or a 'typical' Enlightenment thinker - a practitioner of abstraction or an advocate of disembodied reason. But her deployment of tenets of

Enlightenment which accommodate the subjective, the experiential and the empirical opens up the possibility that the Enlightenment may not be a monolithic body of ideas and politics, thereby allowing for a connection between, for example, certain aspects of Enlightenment thought and the Haitian revolution. Though the debacles and defeats of principles of reason in the colonial and patriarchal context are only too obvious, it is perhaps also important to note the revolutionary potential of humanism or universal rights when articulated in historicised projects of political justice. The works of Rousseau, Diderot, Condorcet and Wollstonecraft, for example, all show some of these emancipatory possibilities, while the French Revolution, through its composite and convoluted history, holds the Enlightenment's contradictory articulations and possibilities in suspension.[31]

Mary Wollstonecraft's distinctive and emancipatory use of the concept of reason, therefore, lies in her non-Cartesian approach, in a non-dualist relationship between reason and experience or subjectivity. Embodiment and location in society and history, and not any commitment to abstraction, are the necessary conditions for her interest in reason. This becomes clear when we consider her use of the concept of 'the human' as a measure of the oppression of women. The word 'human' here acquires a concreteness, since it implies a negation of the actual degrading conditions of being a woman in a given society. Socialisation to 'femininity' or womanhood becomes a process of dehumanisation, primarily through depriving 'woman' of the exercise of 'reason', which is simultaneously a moral, creative and critical faculty. Thus social transformation, from domination to equality, necessarily involves 'reason'. The demanding of 'human rights' or the 'rights of individuals', therefore becomes a mode of exercise of this 'reason' as a condition of being fully 'human'. This way of approaching or arriving at the universal, from the standpoint of women and experience, renders it difficult to place Wollstonecraft unproblematically among male 'rights' theorists.[32] The concrete awareness of difference and power which underpins her project of reason makes Wollstonecraft a rationalist/humanist with a difference.

This concreteness or grounded epistemology is conducted through the stylistics of Wollstonecraft's writing. The *Rights of Woman* is a surprisingly social and communicative text, full of images, metaphors, similes, analogies and anecdotes. It has the subjective quality of personal communication. Addressed by her to Talleyrand (by implication, to the revolutionary male elite of France) as her contribution to the educational philosophy of a revolutionary country, this text is charged with a sense of immediacy. Through this device she not only addresses the members of the French government, but also projects her ideal reader as politically engaged, as a social critic. This strategy substantiates the anti- or non-Cartesian character of the *Rights of Woman*, and thus redeems the book from being an 'in principle' argument.

This critical-political strategy makes Wollstonecraft an important author for those of us who wish to integrate identity and experience within an overall socio-historical analysis. Thus the positionality, the particularity of 'who' a knower or a political agent is becomes integral to what the knower seeks to know, or what can be known by her. By making social subjectivity material to knowledge, by connecting the personal and the rational, Wollstonecraft emerges as an Enlightenment thinker who can be called anti-dualist, in violation of the mind-body or experience-reason split conventional among male thinkers of the time.[33] The *Rights of Woman* is then the voice of a woman who has herself suffered the tyranny of gender and class. If she is a child of the Enlightenment, she is not of the right sex for a political thinker. By being a woman and writing political theory and social criticism from a woman's standpoint, she violates the conventional gender attribution of knowledge and political discourse of her time. The gendered private-public divide is challenged both by her own presence in a public, intellectual space, and by her claims in the domains of pedagogy and political theory. This transgression and her attempts at integration are equally present in her rearrangement of the relationship between the political and the personal, and in her anchoring of the public into the realm of the private.

That Wollstonecraft takes recourse to adapting a humanist discourse of reason rather than inventing a full-fledged discourse of her own is not surprising. This was, after all, the main language of social criticism and political theory of her time. Anti-clerical, dissenting and radical political traditions questioned time-honoured practices of hierarchy and servitude in this language of 'reason'. As such, 'reason' becomes a code word for a critical apparatus which is used to criticise, explain and interpret prevailing social and political conditions, and thus it ceases to be only a name for a faculty which transcends the social. Such an adaptation of reason makes it an entry point to intellectual democracy, since it is said to represent an ability equally present in every human being. The social character of reason, in this version, is evident, in that it needs cultivation to be equal to its own definition. It is this social character of reason, including its susceptibility to deformation, which is explored in the *Rights of Woman*, in terms both of general education and familial socialisation of the processes which construct, both practically and ideologically, the feminine and the masculine. Classroom education, child-rearing and children's play, parental and marital violence, seduction, and the inertia of aristocratic, bourgeois and petty-bourgeois lives, are all scrutinised through and in relation to this interpretation of 'reason'. Thus for Wollstonecraft 'reason' is not only a sign of abstract transcendence; it is also the critical instrument of theorisation and the point of entry into the social.

In rejecting dualism, Wollstonecraft also brings other antithetical concepts into formative relations. Thus passion and reason, the public and the private, and difference and similarity become constitutively related. This prevents us from characterising her as either a romantic or a rationalist, or from positing any direct correlation between romanticism or classicism and any particular brand of politics. Possibilities proliferate: we see that Edmund Burke's romanticism leads him finally to counter-revolution, whereas that of Rousseau leads to certain revolutionary stances, (which, however, encode the subordination of women). Wollstonecraft shares with Rousseau his determination to reconcile passion and reason, the use of metaphors and analogies from slavery, and his interest in a humanised form of 'reason'. In fact, it is by expanding this humanist core of Rousseau's philosophy that she questions his own discriminatory treatment of women and their absence from his proposal for democracy. Wollstonecraft takes up the Enlightenment's romantic passion for reason and adapts it to an argument against sexual, social and economic forms of slavery. This is consistent with her interest in the validation of emotive and experiential subjectivity and her argument for morality in the constitution of freedom.

In keeping with this approach, and confounding any attempts to label her as a rationalist, Wollstonecraft allows a place for feelings in her theorisation. In this she is helped by her use of the metaphors and analogies of slavery and resistance. This metaphoric textualisation exceeds the limits of her adapted rationalist discourse and expands the ideological space into the domains of personal and social life, experience and history. Unlike classicists, who demonise feelings, particularly those of women, common people or black slaves, Wollstonecraft does not see revolutions in terms of irrational excesses of mob violence. Through her legitimisation of emotions and experience she revolutionises the conventional cast of political drama. As such the elite of her society — kings and the aristocracy, masters of slaves and serfs, domineering husbands and fathers — are not her protagonists or heirs of 'reason', that is, upholders of justice and morality. Rather, it is the demonised and the dominated, women and slaves, admittedly under the leadership of the exceptionally few 'reasonable' men, who play key roles in her drama of social change. That this is so is particular to her project of reason and not due to any blindness on her part as to the corruptive powers of domination, or to any idealisation of the dominated. She is perfectly aware of moral and psychological deformities, such as practices of manipulation and blackmail, which, she claims, are resorted to by both European and oriental women and black slaves.[34]

The social basis of personal identity for Wollstonecraft is expressed by the connection she makes between property and propriety or personal morality. Had she not so often been viewed as solely concerned with gender, this would have been apparent. Her disagreement with Edmund Burke is partially on grounds of property.[35] Her support of radical democracy — of the Haitian revolution, for example — reflects more than romanticism; it makes a serious criticism of hierarchy and ownership in moral and political terms, even though she has some presumptions of a class organised society. In fact, her analogy between slaves and European women rests on this particular understanding of property. She questions the illegitimacy of such an appropriation of people, wealth and social privilege, of the laws and social institutions which allow this, and of the morality which governs such a social order. This approach may be construed as a modified form of subscription to the ideas of 'liberty', 'equality', and 'fraternity' that inspired the French revolution. Thus, since her criticism of patriarchy is connected to that of propriety and property, she may be more than a forerunner of bourgeois feminism. And, though her criticism of property is mainly ideological, she is not negligent in paying attention to poverty and its dehumanising effects. This bitingly critical dimension of her humanism has a revolutionary cast to it, although, like contemporary revolutionary humanist thinkers, she did not think in terms of class and class struggle. There is in her work a determined criticism of wealth and patriarchal power, and of the profoundly unethical imperatives they exert over society as a whole. It is here that she brings the category 'human' to a critical purpose. Through an infusion of a Utopian desire, it becomes the very ground and the ultimate validation of all political 'rights'. It is this meaning of the word 'human' to which she turns sometimes in the name of nature and sometimes in the name of God. In both cases, it implies creativity and perfectibility.[36] The role of reason in this enterprise is that of a critical and creative faculty which provides the ground for envisioning a practical, ethical knowledge. What one may know and how this knowledge might help to build a reasonable, that is a 'humanised' and 'enlightened' life, were her basic preoccupations. Thus her critical and political project went far beyond the confines of gender and partial good, toward the creation of a 'humanity' even for womankind.

Conclusion

If I were asked which of these three readings of the *Rights of Woman* is most accurate, I would be hard put to answer. Shifting the ground somewhat, I would suggest that they have all captured certain aspects of this text, which coexist simultaneously. Any active reading, we must remind ourselves, is an ability to see that a text is a middle space, a sort of social relationship between on the one hand a writer and her writing and on the other a reader and her context and form of reading. As such, neither writing nor reading is a private individual activity, independent of the time and space within which it occurs. Intentional, formal and contextual constraints continue to press both the writer and the reader. As such, my readings are very specific to different stages of my life, and yet in some form all respond to Wollstonecraft's preoccupations — for example with sameness and difference, with patriarchal and other modalities of power, with humanisation and degradation. Elements of my first reading and those of the second are subsumed in my third, which has come to terms with the previous ones. It is this complexity, rather than one 'true' reading, which must be kept in mind. The point is that Wollstonecraft's text is full of loops and fissures, her orientation to hegemonic forms of racism and orientalism coexists with her understanding of difference and inequality, and these propel her to a radical humanism — whose contours are contradictory. But there is also an overall integrity to her text, where a stance based on the universal presence of reason motivates her commitment to justice, not only for women but for other oppressed groups.

A Vindication of the Rights of Woman is not a monolithic text. It contains both the shortcomings and the emancipatory moments of Enlightenment thought. But its universalist/humanist stance, when qualified by the recognition of the construction of difference, is a useful one in current feminist theory and politics. In order to go beyond segmented politics, we may rely on notions such as 'justice', 'human' or 'woman', as long as we inform these generic notions with an awareness of social relations of power and lived history. Mary Wollstonecraft presents us with an example of this type of social and political theorisation, whereby the concept of universal justice is no longer a philosopher's category but can have arisen only from the experience of lived 'differences' created by inequalities of power. Situated thus, notions of democracy or human rights can address centuries of struggles by women and men against tyranny, brutality and various forms of exclusion. This is a conclusion I can reach without imposing a linearity on her thought, or papering over her contradictions, while, in the same process, saving the paradoxical integrity of my own reading.

Reference Notes

Introduction
Eileen Janes Yeo

1. Barbara Taylor, 'The Fantasy of Mary Wollstonecraft', opening plenary paper read to the Wollstonecraft 200 Conference, p.7, in the author's possession; the account of changing feminist views of Wollstonecraft is published in Barbara Taylor, 'An Impossible Heroine? Mary Wollstonecraft and Female Heroism', *Soundings*, issue 3, summer 1996.
2. See Eric Hobsbawm and Don Ranger, *The Invention of Tradition*, Cambridge, Cambridge University Press, 1983; for a useful discussion of selective tradition, Raymond Williams, *The Long Revolution* (1962), London, Hogarth Press, 1992, pp.50–9.
3. For the history of the term 'feminism', see Nancy Cott, *The Grounding of Modern Feminism*, New Haven, Yale University Press, 1987; Barbara Caine, *English Feminism, 1780-1990*, Oxford, Oxford University Press, 1997, which also explores the difficulties of constructing traditions.
4. Catherine Hall, 'Feminism and the Imperialist Other', Wollstonecraft 200 Conference paper, pp.1, 14, in the author's possession.
5. Ibid., pp.3–4, 11, for quotes and points in this paragraph.
6. At the Wollstonecraft 200 Conference, papers from Maya Korac about the former Yugoslavia and from Sarah Benton about Britain stressed the even more flagrant shrinking of gender options where masculinity is being constructed as the role of warrior-protector and women and children are made to constitute the protectorate. Especially in countries where ethnic nationalist projects predominate, women are being pushed more narrowly into the role of ethnic reproducer-mothers (and rape, as in Bosnia, has been used as a systematic way to pollute the enemy's stock): see Maya Korac, 'Women in the Balkan Wars', in Ken Coates (ed.), *Peace Register. Drawing the Peace Dividend*, Nottingham, Bertrand Russell Foundation, 1993; also her 'Understanding Ethnic-National Identity and its Meaning: Questions from Women's Experience', *Women's Studies International Forum*, vol. 18, nos 4–5, Summer 1995.
7. The Wollstonecraft 200 Conference catalysed several new initiatives including the formation of a Southern Region of the Women's History Network, which

has attracted women from all walks of life, and an expansion of networks with women in China, which resulted in the production of a book of East-West dialogue, Barbara Einhorn and Eileen Janes Yeo (eds), *Women and Market Societies: Crisis and Opportunity*, Aldershot, Edward Elgar, 1995, which was presented at the United Nations Fourth World Conference on Women.

1. For the Love of God
Religion and the Erotic Imagination in Wollstonecraft's Feminism
Barbara Taylor

This essay is part of a longer study of Wollstonecraft's feminism, to be published as *A Wild Wish: Mary Wollstonecraft and the Feminist Imagination*. My thanks to Sally Alexander, Norma Clarke, Lyndal Roper, Jacqueline Rose and Nick Stargardt for comments and critical encouragement.

1. Mary Wollstonecraft, *A Vindication of the Rights of Woman* (1792), Harmondsworth, Penguin, 1982, p.160.
2. Ann Snitow, 'A Gender Diary' in M. Hirsch and E. Fox Keller (eds), *Conflicts in Feminism*, London, Routledge, 1990, p.29.
3. William Godwin, *A Memoir of the Author of a Vindication of the Rights of Woman* (1798) Harmondsworth, Penguin, 1987, p.215.
4. Mary Wollstonecraft, *Thoughts on the Education of Daughters* (1787), London, William Pickering, 1989, p.33.
5. Mary Wollstonecraft, *Letters Written During a Short Residence in Sweden, Norway and Denmark* (1796), Harmondsworth, Penguin, 1987, p.106. Wollstonecraft is here describing the free-thinking mentality of the Norwegians, 'the least oppressed people of Europe'.
6. Godwin, *Memoir*, op. cit., p.215. This strong emphasis on Wollstonecraft's piety in the *Memoir* did not register with many readers, including one who claimed that Godwin's book gave 'a striking view of a Woman of fine talents...sinking a victim to the strength of her Passions & feelings because destitute of the support of Religious principles': James Woodrow, quoted in Gary Kelly, *Women, Writing and Revolution, 1790-1827*, Oxford, Clarendon Press, 1993, p.27.
7. Godwin, *Memoir*, op. cit., p.236.
8. Letter to William Godwin, 4 July 1797, in Ralph Wardle (ed.), *The Collected Letters of Mary Wollstonecraft*, Ithaca, Cornell University Press, 1979, p.404. According to Godwin, Wollstonecraft's religion 'was not calculated to be the torment of a sick bed' and thus 'not one word of a religious cast' fell from her lips as she lay dying (*Memoir*, op. cit., p.270). It is possible of course that none did so while her atheist husband was present but I also think it is possible that Wollstonecraft's faith in a personal God — her epistolary *cri de coeur* notwithstanding — may have become weaker in her final years. In a longer version of this essay, I intend to discuss the evidence for this in relation to her last novel, *Maria*.
9. Godwin, *Memoir*, op. cit., p.215.
10. Ibid., pp.272-3.
11. Wollstonecraft, *Rights of Woman*, op. cit., p.218.
12. Godwin, *Memoir*, op. cit., pp.276-7.

13   Letter to Rev Gabell, 13 September 1787, in Wardle (ed.), *Letters*, op. cit., p.162.
14   Mary Wollstonecraft, *Mary, a Fiction* (1788), Oxford, Oxford University Press, 1980, Advertisement.
15   Ibid.
16   Ibid., p.5.
17   Ibid., p.11.
18   Ibid., pp.11–12.
19   Ibid., p.68.
20   Letter to Everina Wollstonecraft, 22 March 1797, in Wardle (ed.), *Letters*, op. cit., p.385.
21   Wollstonecraft, *Mary*, op. cit., p.67.
22   Ibid., p.36.
23   Ibid., p.40.
24   Ibid., p.41.
25   Ibid.
26   Mary Astell, 'Some Reflections Upon Marriage' (1700), 1706 edn reprinted in Bridget Hill, *The First English Feminist*, Aldershot, Gower, 1986, p.84.
27   A Methodist woman preacher quoted in Leslie Church, *More About the Early Methodist People*, London, Epworth, 1949, p.168.
28   Wollstonecraft, *Rights of Woman*, op. cit., p.102.
29   Richard Price, *A Review of the Principal Questions in Morals* (1758), London, 1816, p.305.
30   Wollstonecraft, *Rights of Woman*, op. cit., p.122.
31   Ibid., p.119, and see also pp.210–11.
32   Ibid., p.101.
33   Ibid., p.305.
34   Ibid., p.201.
35   Ibid., p.133.
36   Ibid., p.134.
37   Ibid., p.146.
38   Ibid., p.119.
39   Ibid., pp.185–6.
40   Ibid., p.110.
41   Ibid., p.114; p.248.
42   Cora Kaplan, 'Wild Nights: Pleasure/Sexuality/Feminism', in her *Sea Changes*, London, Verso, 1986, p.41.
43   Mary Poovey, *The Proper Lady and the Woman Writer*, Chicago, University of Chicago Press, 1984.
44   Wollstonecraft, *Rights of Woman*, op. cit., pp.213–14.
45   Mary Wollstonecraft, *A Vindication of the Rights of Men* (1790), London, William Pickering, London, 1989, p.46.
46   James G. Turner, *One Flesh: Paradisiacal Marriage and Sexual Relations in the Age of Milton*, Oxford, Oxford University Press, 1987, p.32.
47   Quoted in ibid., p.32. For an influential discussion of the relationship between divine and earthly love in Christian theology, see Anders Nygren, *Agape and Eros* (1938), London, SPCK, 1953, and for the significance of Christian Platonism

in the formation of eighteenth-century British moral philosophy see John K. Sheriff, *The Good-Natured Man: the Evolution of a Moral Ideal, 1660-1880*, Alabama University Press, 1982.
48   Wollstonecraft, *Rights of Woman*, op. cit., p.169.
49   Jean-Jacques Rousseau, *Emile, or On Education* (1762), Harmondsworth, Penguin, 1991, p.333.
50   Ibid., p.405.
51   Mary Wollstonecraft, *The Wrongs of Woman: or, Maria* (1798), Oxford, Oxford University Press, 1980, p.99.
52   Ibid., p.189.
53   Wollstonecraft, *Rights of Woman*, op. cit., p.316
54   Letter to Gilbert Imlay, 12 June 1795; in Wardle (ed.), *Letters*, op. cit., p.291; and see also Wollstonecraft, *Rights of Woman*, op. cit., pp.247, 231.
55   Wollstonecraft, *Rights of Men*, op. cit., pp.46, 39, 34.
56   Letter to Gilbert Imlay, 30 December 1794, in Wardle (ed.) *Letters*, op. cit., p.273.
57   Letter to Gilbert Imlay, 13 June 1795, in ibid., p.292.
58   Letter to Gilbert Imlay, 27 November 1795, in ibid., p.321.
59   Wollstonecraft, *Rights of Men*, op. cit., pp.39–40.
60   Ibid., p.53.
61   Ibid., p.39.
62   Wollstonecraft, *Mary*, op. cit., p.5.
63   Letter to Gilbert Imlay, 26 August 1795, in Wardle (ed.), *Letters*, op. cit., p.310.
64   Letter to Gilbert Imlay, 3 July 1795, in ibid., p.302.
65   Jean-Jacques Rousseau, *La Nouvelle Héloïse* (1758), 1767 trans., London, p.128.
66   Wollstonecraft, *Rights of Woman*, op. cit., p.147.
67   Ibid., p.245, and see also p.240. The argument here is with Adam Smith's concept of conscience as an 'impartial spectator'.
68   Ibid., p.121.
69   Ibid., p.120.

2. The Imagination of Olympe de Gouges
Joan W. Scott

This chapter is the text of my 1992 conference paper. For further development of my ideas see, *Only Paradoxes to Offer: French Feminists and the Rights of Man*, Cambridge, MA, Harvard University Press, 1996.
1   Olympe de Gouges, *Réponse à la Justification de Maximilien Robespierre*, Paris, 1792, p.8; and de Gouges, *Compte Moral Rendu et Dernier Mot à mes Chers Amis*, Paris, n.d., p.5.
2   Darlene Gay Levy, Harriet Applewhite and Mary Johnson (eds), *Women in Revolutionary Paris, 1789-1795*, Urbana, University of Illinois Press, 1979, p.259.
3   *Almanach des Femmes*, 1853, p.15.
4   *L'Opinion des Femmes*, supplement to no.4, May 1849.
5   Richard Tuck, *Natural Rights Theories: Their Origin and Development*, Cambridge, Cambridge University Press, 1979, pp.5–6; see also the discussion in William Sewell, Jr., '*Le Citoyen/La Citoyenne*: Activity, Passivity, and the Revolutionary

Concept of Citizenship', in Colin Lucas (ed.), *The French Revolution and the Creation of Modern Political Culture*, vol.2, *The Political Culture of the French Revolution*, Oxford, Pergamon Press, 1988, p.110; and Pierre Rosanvallon, *Le Sacre du Citoyen: Histoire du Suffrage Universel en France*, Paris, Gallimard, 1992, pp.41–101.

6 Condorcet, 'On the Admission of Women to the Rights of Citizenship' (1790), in K.Michael. Baker (ed.), *Condorcet: Selected Writings*, Indianapolis, Bobbs-Merrill, 1976, p.98.

7 Keith Michael Baker, 'Defining the Public Sphere in Eighteenth-Century France: Variations on a Theme by Habermas', in Craig Calhoun (ed.), *Habermas and the Public Sphere*, Cambridge, MIT Press, 1992, pp.181–211; and Baker, 'Politics and Public Opinion Under the Old Regime: Some Reflections,' in Jack R. Censer and Jeremey D. Popkin (eds), *Press and Politics in Prerevolutionary France*, Berkeley, University of California Press, 1987, pp.204–46; Mona Ozouf, '*L'Opinion Publique*', in Keith Michael Baker (ed.), *The French Revolution and the Creation of Modern Political Culture*, vol.1, *The Political Culture of the Old Regime*, Oxford, Pergamon Press, 1987, pp.419–34; Daniel Gordon, '"Public Opinion" and the Civilizing Process in France: The Example of Morellet', in *Eighteenth-Century Studies*, vol.22, no.3, Spring 1989; Joan Landes, *Women and the Public Sphere in the Age of the French Revolution*, Ithaca, Cornell University Press, 1988; Roger Chartier, *Cultural Origins of the French Revolution*, Durham, Duke University Press, 1991; Dena Goodman, 'Public Sphere and Private Life: Toward a Synthesis of Current Historiographical Approaches to the Old Regime', in *History and Theory*, vol.31, no.1, 1992, pp.1–20. See also Goodman, 'Enlightenment Salons: The Convergence of Female and Philosophic Ambitions', in *Eighteenth-Century Studies*, vol.22, no.3, Spring 1989. Much of the discussion of public opinion alludes to Jurgen Habermas, *The Structural Transformation of the Public Sphere: An Inquiry into a Category of Bourgeois Society*, translated by Thomas Burger and Frederick Lawrence, Cambridge, Harvard University Press, 1989.

8 Nina Rattner Gelbart, *Feminine and Opposition Journalism in Old Regime France: Le Journal des Dames*, Berkeley, University of California Press, 1987, pp.212–13.

9 De Gouges, *Réponse à Robespierre*, op. cit., p.8.

10 Cited in Benoîte Groult, *Olympe de Gouges: Oeuvres*, Paris, Mercure de France, 1986, p.47.

11 Ibid., pp.88–92.

12 Voltaire, 'Imagination', in *Encyclopédie ou dictionnaire raisonné des sciences, arts et des métiers*, 17 vols, Neufchâtel, 1751–65, vol.8, p.561.

13 Jean-Jacques Rousseau, *Emile*, cited in Linda Zerilli, *Signifying Woman: Culture and Chaos in Rousseau, Burke and Mill*, Ithaca, Cornell University Press, 1994; Denis Diderot, 'Sur les femmes' (1772), in *Oeuvres*, vol.3, Paris, 1821, p.440.

14 See for example Olympe de Gouges, *Le Bonheur Primitif de l'Homme, ou les Rêveries Patriotiques*, Amsterdam, 1789, p.1.

15 Olympe de Gouges, *Réponse à Robespierre*, op.cit., p.8; and de Gouges, *Compte Moral*, op.cit., p.5. See also 'Procès d'Olympe de Gouges, Femme de Lettres, 12 brumaire an II', in A. Tuetey, *Répertoire Général des Sources Manuscrites de L'Histoire de Paris pendant La Révolution Française*, vol.10, Paris, Imprimerie Nouvelle, 1912, pp.156–64.

16 Olympe de Gouges, *Séance Royale: Motion de Monseigneur Le Duc d'Orléans, ou Les Songes Patriotiques*, Paris, 1789.
17 Groult, 'Introduction,' in *de Gouges: Oeuvres*, op. cit., p.46.
18 Levy, Applewhite and Johnson, *Women in Revolutionary Paris*, op. cit., p.219.
19 Cited in E. Lairtullier, *Les Femmes Célèbres de 1789 à 1795, et leur Influence dans la Révolution*, Paris, 1840, p.140.
20 Olympe de Gouges, 'Oeuvres de la Citoyenne de Gouges', n.d., p.15.
21 Denise Riley, 'Am I that Name?' *Feminism and the Category of 'Women' in History*, London, Macmillan, 1988.

3. Mary Does, Alice Doesn't
The Paradox of Female Reason in and for Feminist Theory
Joan B. Landes

I am grateful to the organisers of the conference 'Mary Wollstonecraft and 200 Years of Feminisms' for the opportunity to develop and present the ideas incorporated in this paper. I owe special thanks to Eileen Janes Yeo for her comments, and to Meredith Michaels and Theodore Norton for their insightful readings of this article.

1 Mary Wollstonecraft, *A Vindication of the Rights of Woman*, New York, W.W. Norton, 1975, p.3.
2 Rosi Braidotti, *Patterns of Dissonance: A Study of Women in Contemporary Philosophy*, New York, Routledge, 1991.
3 Lewis Carroll, *The Annotated Alice: Alice's Adventures in Wonderland and Through the Looking-Glass*, intro. and notes Martin Gardner, New York, New American Library, 1960.
4 Wollstonecraft, *Rights of Woman*, op. cit., p.5.
5 Ibid., p.3.
6 Ibid., p.7.
7 Ibid., p.6.
8 Carol Kay, 'Canon, Ideology, and Gender: Mary Wollstonecraft's Critique of Adam Smith', *New Political Science*, vol.15, Summer 1986, p.71.
9 According to Kay, Hobbes's 'sceptical denial of knowable universal moral truth and the natural meaning of moral words aided his denial of any natural political leadership. He even refused to admit that the family subsisted as a natural political entity; that is, he argued that the rule of wives by husbands, or of children by parents, is not established by the rational recognition of natural superiority, but by passionately motivated consent. In effect, he made all men like the women pictured in classical antiquity: creatures of passion not reason, of opinion, not knowledge, who must be ruled by arbitrary authority through consistent rules in a culture of timid conformity. For modern philosophy thereafter, woman is the paradigm of ideological man.' Ibid., p.70.
10 Ibid., p.71.
11 Wollstonecraft, *Rights of Woman*, op. cit., pp.3–4.
12 Ibid., p.5.
13 Ibid., p.11.

14 In a contrasting view of the 'central rhetorical thrust of the *Vindication*', Keith Michael Baker proposes that whereas she 'admits the hypothesis that women might be inferior to men (though similar in nature), Wollstonecraft works to undermine its plausibility.' Baker claims that Wollstonecraft derived her fundamental arguments for women's emancipation from the rationalist discourse of the social, rather than the republican discourse of virtue, the former of which is only 'contingently', the latter 'essentially' masculinist. However, Baker is not concerned with the problematic nature of reason within the rationalist discourse of the social, nor does he consider how reason is implicated in the differential assignment of rational abilities and social responsibilities between men and women which Wollstonecraft herself allows. Even if it were the case that social rationalism and republicanism were in actuality (not just hypothetically) distinct from one another, it is still important to set the 'feminine' or 'feminist' implications of social rationalism against the powerful countervailing efforts by social rationalists themselves to 'remasculinize' moral theory. Keith Michael Baker, 'Defining the Public Sphere in Eighteenth-Century France: Variations on a Theme by Habermas', in Craig Calhoun (ed.), *Habermas and the Public Sphere*, Cambridge, Mass., MIT Press, 1992, pp.205, 207.

15 Wollstonecraft, *Rights of Woman*, op. cit., p.26. In general, Wollstonecraft refuses the idea that men's superior physical constitution ought to be the basis for their greater virtue. As Carol Poston observes in her editorial note to this passage of the *Rights of Woman*, 'Men have more passions to contend with than women: "From the constitution of their bodies" could mean men's difficulty with sexual continence, as well as their superior physical size.' Ibid.

16 Mike Gane, *Harmless Lovers? Gender, Theory and Personal Relationships*, London, Routledge, 1993, p.80. Wollstonecraft, as cited by Gane.

17 Wollstonecraft, *Rights of Woman*, op. cit., p.6.

18 Timothy J. Reiss, 'Revolution in Bounds: Wollstonecraft, Women, and Reason', in Linda Kauffman (ed.), *Gender and Theory: Dialogues on Feminist Criticism*, Oxford and New York, Basil Blackwell, 1989, p.32. Wollstonecraft, as cited by Reiss.

19 Elizabeth Fox-Genovese, 'Introduction' to Samia I. Spencer (ed.), *French Women and the Enlightenment*, Bloomington, Indiana University Press, 1984, p.4.

20 See my *Women and the Public Sphere in the Age of the French Revolution*, Ithaca, N.Y., Cornell University Press, 1988, p.135; Mary Poovey, *The Proper Lady and the Woman Writer: Ideology as Style in the Works of Mary Wollstonecraft, Mary Shelley, and Jane Austen*, Chicago, University of Chicago Press, 1984; Cora Kaplan, *Sea Changes: Culture and Feminism*, London, Verso, 1986.

21 Wollstonecraft, *Rights of Woman*, op. cit., p.10.

22 Ibid., p.4.

23 Kay, 'Canon', op. cit., pp.69, 72.

24 Wollstonecraft, cited by Gane, *Harmless Lovers*, op. cit., p.68.

25 Moira Gatens, '"The Oppressed State of My Sex": Wollstonecraft on Reason, Feeling and Equality', in Mary Lyndon Shanley and Carole Pateman (eds), *Feminist Interpretations and Political Theory*, University Park, Pennsylvania State University, 1991, p.127.

26 Braidotti, *Patterns*, op. cit., p.282.

27 In the title of her 1984 work *Alice Doesn't*, borrowed from a movement leaflet,

Teresa de Lauretis invokes the name of Lewis Carroll's dream child (along with other Alices real and fictional) to symbolise feminism's refusal of the existing social relations, given definitions and cultural values, and to affirm the collective project of feminism — the political and personal ties of shared experience that join women to a movement. However, she concludes her first chapter 'Through the Looking-Glass', with a warning against reading her title as a citation to Carroll's book or its heroine. Rather, the first chapter is meant to be a citation to the first section of Sheila Rowbotham's *Woman's Consciousness, Man's World*, an account of 'the male non-experience' of the specific material situation of women. Luce Irigaray, too, fashions her own Alice (not Lewis Carroll's) in 'Through the Looking-Glass, from the Other Side', the opening essay of *This Sex Which is Not One*. All qualifications aside, however, Alice resonates throughout each of these works, and, I would argue, each of these writers intends her presence to be felt by her readers. See Teresa de Lauretis, *Alice Doesn't: Feminism, Semiotics, Cinema*, Bloomington, Indiana University Press, 1984, p.36; Sheila Rowbotham, *Woman's Consciousness, Man's World*, Harmondsworth, Penguin, 1973; Luce Irigaray, This Sex Which is Not One, trans. Catherine Porter, Ithaca, N.Y., Cornell University Press, 1985.

28 Alison Lurie, *Don't Tell the Grownups: Subversive Children's Literature*, Boston, Little, Brown, 1990, p.7.
29 Braidotti, *Patterns*, op. cit., p.219.
30 Gilles Deleuze, *The Logic of Sense*, trans. Mark Lester with Charles Stivale, ed. Constantin V. Boundas, New York, Columbia University Press, 1990, p.117.
31 Carroll, *Through the Looking-Glass*, op. cit., chapter 6; *Alice's Adventures in Wonderland*, op. cit., chapter 5.
32 William Empson, 'Alice in Wonderland: The Child as Swain' in Robert Phillips (ed.), *Aspects of Alice: Lewis Carroll's Dreamchild as Seen Through the Critics' Looking-Glasses, 1865-1971*, Harmondsworth, Penguin, 1971, pp.400–33.
33 Jan Gordon makes this point, without drawing the connection to Hobbes. See her 'The Alice Books and the Metaphors of Victorian Childhood', in *Aspects of Alice*, op. cit., pp.127–52.
34 Ibid., p.146. I would not discount Alice's experiences even if what she learns experientially is, as Gordon says, 'to distrust her sense altogether', ibid.
35 See: *Lewis Carroll's Symbolic Logic*, ed. and intro. William Warren Bartley III, New York, Clarkson N. Potter, 1977.
36 Carroll, *Through the Looking-Glass*, op. cit., chapter 4.
37 See Genevieve Lloyd, *The Man of Reason: 'Male' and 'Female' in Western Philosophy*, Minneapolis, University of Minnesota Press, 1984; Braidotti, *Patterns*, op. cit., p.219.
38 Hegel's rational ontology captures best the ethical, political, and intellectual privileges claimed by modern Western man at woman's expense: distinguishing between the two sexes, he writes, 'in relation to externality, the former is powerful and active, the latter passive and subjective. It follows that man has his actual substantive life in the state, in learning, and so forth, as well as in labour and struggle with the external world and with himself so that it is only out of his diremption that he fights his way to self-subsistent unity with himself. In the family he has a tranquil intuition of this unity, and there he lives a subjective

ethical life on the plane of feeling. Woman, on the other hand, has her substantive destiny in the family, and to be imbued with family piety is her ethical frame of mind.' G.W.F. Hegel, *Philosophy of Right*, trans. and ed. T.M. Knox, Oxford, Oxford University Press, 1973, para. 166.

39 Letter from Wollstonecraft to Godwin, cited in Moira Gatens, 'The Oppressed State', op. cit., p.125.

40 Teresa de Lauretis, 'Upping the Anti (*sic*) in Feminist Theory', in Marianne Hirsch and Evelyn Fox Keller (eds), *Conflicts in Feminism*, New York, Routledge, 1990, p.226. See also Rosi Braidotti, 'Embodiment, Sexual Difference, and the Nomadic Subject', *Hypatia*, vol.8, no.1, Winter 1993, p.10.

41 Rosi Braidotti, 'Toward a New Nomadism: Feminist Deleuzian Tracks; or, Metaphysics and Metabolism', in Constantin V. Boundas and Dorothea Olkowski (eds), *Gilles Deleuze and the Theatre of Philosophy*, New York, Routledge, 1994, p.182.

42 Braidotti, 'New Nomadism', op. cit., p.168.

43 Braidotti attributes this perspective on philosophy, and also thought, to Gilles Deleuze. She states, 'For Deleuze, thought is made of sense and value: it is the force, or level of intensity, that fixes the value of an idea, not its adequation to a preestablished normative model. Philosophy as critique of negative, reactive values is also the critique of the dogmatic image of thought; it expresses the force, the activity of the thinking process in terms of a typology of forces (Nietzsche) or an ethology of passions (Spinoza)....Thinking, in other words, is to a very large extent unconscious, in that it expresses the desire to know, and this desire is that which cannot be adequately expressed in language, simply because it is that which sustains language. Through this intensive theory of the thinking process, Deleuze points to the prephilosophical foundations of philosophy.' Braidotti, 'New Nomadism', op. cit., p.165.

4. Wanting Protection
Fair Ladies, Sensibility and Romance
Mary Nyquist

1 Mary Wollstonecraft, *A Vindication of the Rights of Men*, 2nd edn, ed. Eleanor Nicholes, New York, Delmar, Scholars' Facsimiles & Reprints, 1975, pp.136, 111, 112. For a discussion of how tensions between romanticism, rationalism and radicalism are played out in *Wrongs of Woman*, see Mitzi Myers, 'Unfinished Business: Wollstonecraft's Maria', *The Wordsworth Circle*, vol.11, no.2, 1980, pp.107–14; and Mary Poovey, who explores the contradictory claims of bourgeois sentimentalism in 'Mary Wollstonecraft: The Gender of Genres in Late Eighteenth-Century England', *Novel*, no.15, 1982, pp.111–26.

2 In chapter 5 below, which outlines the often self-contradictory character of Wollstonecraft's views on female and colonial slavery, Moira Ferguson argues that Wollstonecraft occasionally suggests an identification between British and African women in the *Rights of Woman* (see pp.96ff.). My own reading of the passages in question leads me to think Wollstonecraft does not entertain this identification. For a detailed treatment of the interrelationship among British

colonialist, feminist and anti-slavery discourses, see Ferguson's *Subject to Others: British Women Writers and Colonial Slavery, 1670-1834*, London, Routledge, 1992. For a sense of how the issues Wollstonecraft raises are relevant to current debates and struggles, see, for example, Maria Lugones's characterisation of White/Anglo 'infantilisation of judgement' when confronted with white racism, in 'Hablando Cara a Cara/Speaking Face to Face: An Exploration of Ethnocentric Racism', in Gloria Anzaldua (ed.), *Making Face, Making Soul/Haciendo Caras: Creative and Critical Perspectives by Women of Colour*, San Francisco, Aunt Lute Foundation Books, 1990, pp.52–4. Elizabeth Spelman takes up the issue of 'women's inhumanity to other women' in 'The Virtue of Feeling and the Feeling of Virtue', in Claudia Card (ed.), *Feminist Ethics*, Lawrence, University of Kansas Press, 1991, pp.213–32.
3 Samuel Richardson, *Sir Charles Grandison*, ed. Jocelyn Harris, Oxford, Oxford University Press, 1986, vol.6, pp.248–9.
4 Thomas Holcroft, *Anna St. Ives*, ed. Peter Faulkner, London, Oxford University Press, 1970, pp.423, 465. Wollstonecraft, 'On Poetry: Contributions to the *Analytical Review*', in Janet Todd and Marilyn Butler (eds), *The Works of Mary Wollstonecraft*, London, William Pickering, 1989, vol.7, pp.439–40.
5 William Godwin, *Things as They Are, or The Adventures of Caleb Williams*, ed. David McCracken, Oxford, Oxford University Press, 1982, pp.57, 73.
6 Mitzi Myers explores the pedagogical uses to which Wollstonecraft puts autobiographical materials in 'Pedagogy as Self-Expression in Mary Wollstonecraft: Exorcising the Past, Finding a Voice', in Shari Benstock (ed.), *The Private Self: Theory and Practice of Women's Autobiographical Writings*, Chapel Hill, University of North Carolina Press, 1988, pp.192–210. One of the few critical studies to consider *Things as They Are* and *Wrongs of Woman* together, Tillottama Rajan's 'Wollstonecraft and Godwin: Reading the Secrets of the Political Novel', in *Studies in Romanticism*, vol.27, no.2, 1988, pp.221–52 examines polemical, narrative and autobiographical motives as they affect the interpretative process. In another highly innovative essay, 'Autonarration and Genotext in Mary Hays's *Memoirs of Emma Courtney*', *Studies in Romanticism*, vol.12, 1993, pp.162, 157, Rajan analyses the discourses of subjectivity at work in the *Memoirs*, arguing that Emma's desire is 'at once metaphysical, political and sexual', and that 'if her desire is not initially political, it becomes the site of her emergence as a political subject'.
7 Cited in Claire Tomalin, *The Life and Death of Mary Wollstonecraft*, rev. edn, London, Penguin, 1992, p.212. Tomalin has an interesting discussion of Holcroft and Hays, pp.246, 47.
8 Mary Wollstonecraft, *A Vindication of the Rights of Woman*, 2nd edn, Harmondsworth, Penguin, 1983, p.153.
9 Ibid., pp.117, 118. When referring to a second volume on laws respecting women (p.257), Wollstonecraft specifies coverture, a central concern of *Wrongs of Woman*.
10 *Rights of Woman*, op. cit., p.259.
11 Mary Wollstonecraft, *The Wrongs of Woman; or, Maria*, in *Mary, Maria and Matilda*, ed. Janet Todd, London, Penguin, 1992, pp.85, 131.
12 Ibid., p.124.

13 Mary Hays, *Memoirs of Emma Courtney*, ed. Gina Luria, New York and London, Garland, 1974, vol.2, p.53.
14 Ibid., vol.1, pp.35, 36.
15 Ibid., pp.64, 70, 78.
16 Ibid., pp.112, 113.
17 Wollstonecraft, *Wrongs of Woman*, op. cit., p.78. Holcroft, *Anna St Ives*, op. cit., p.148, reminds its readers of St Preux's association with *preux chevaliers* or chivalric ideology. A chaste, restrained, thoroughly principled St Preux, Frank Henley at one point counsels a discriminating reading of Rousseau's narrative of transgressive desire (p.242).
18 Hays, *Memoirs*, op. cit., vol.1, p.8; Wollstonecraft, *Wrongs of Woman*, op. cit., p.59.
19 Ibid., p.72.
20 Ibid., p.74.
21 Wollstonecraft, *Rights of Woman*, op. cit., pp.224, 225.
22 Wollstonecraft, *Wrongs of Woman*, op. cit., p.138.
23 Hays, *Memoirs*, op. cit., vol.1, p.8.
24 Wollstonecraft, *Wrongs of Woman*, op. cit., p.144.
25 Ibid., pp.59, 114.
26 Ibid., pp.114.
27 Ibid., p.142.
28 Ibid., pp.144, 117, 120, 145.
29 These questions become even more urgent when considered against the English legislative debates that occurred when women's marital status was addressed in the mid 1850s. In 'Covered but Not Bound: Caroline Norton and the 1857 Matrimonial Causes Act', Mary Poovey argues that Norton gives her own experience the form of melodrama, and exploits a class-bound idealisation of domesticity, together with the ideology of separate spheres. Positioning herself as an opponent of 'equal rights' feminism, Norton appeals in a direct, reactionary fashion to what I am calling the ideology of patriarchal protection in requesting *civil* protection: 'Masculine superiority is incontestable; and with the superiority should come protection....Women have one *right* (perhaps only that one). They have a right—founded on nature, equity, and religion—to the protection of man. Power is on the side of men—power of body, power of mind, power of position. With that power should come, not only the fact, but the *instinct* of protection.' Cited in Poovey, *Uneven Developments: The Ideological Work of Gender in Mid-Victorian England*, Chicago, University of Chicago Press, 1988, p.69.
30 Wollstonecraft, *Wrongs of Woman*, op. cit., p.85.
31 Ibid., pp.85, 109, 116.
32 Ibid., p.124.
33 Mary Ann Radcliffe, *The Female Advocate, or An Attempt to Recover the Rights of Women from Male Usurpation*, ed. Gina Luria, New York, Garland, 1974, p.469.
34 Wollstonecraft, *Wrongs of Woman*, op. cit., p.129.
35 Ibid, pp.79, 59, 60.
36 Ibid., p.139.

5. Mary Wollstonecraft and the Problematic of Slavery
Moira Ferguson

1 Mary Wollstonecraft, *Thoughts on the Education of Daughters with Reflections on Female Conduct, in the more Important Duties of Life*, London, J. Johnson, 1787, p.63.
2 Mary Wollstonecraft, *Mary, a Fiction*, 1788, reprinted as *Mary and The Wrongs of Woman*, Oxford, Oxford University Press, 1976, p.49. Writers as diverse as Katherine Philips, the Duchess of Newcastle, Aphra Behn, Mrs Taylor, Lady Chudleigh, Sarah Fyge Field Egerton, Anne Finch, the Countess of Winchelsea, Elizabeth Rowe, Elizabeth Tollett and many more frequently employed the metaphor of slavery to express the subjugation of women; marriage was far and away the foremost situation in which women described themselves or other women as 'enslaved.' Note also that Wollstonecraft refers to the Spartans' perpetual subjugation in Lacedaemonian society of the Helots, state serfs bound to the soil, with no political rights. See Benjamin Shimron, *Late Sparta: The Spartan Revolution 243-146 BC*, Arethusa Monographs III, Buffalo, State University of New York, Department of Classics, 1972, p.96; H. Mitchell, *Sparta*, London, Cambridge University Press, 1952, pp.75–84; Douglas MacDowell, *Spartan Law*, Edinburgh, Scottish Academic Press, 1986, pp.23–5, 31–42.
3 Reginald Coupland, *The British Anti-Slavery Movement*, 1933, London, Frank Cass, 1964, p.68.
4 Thomas Clarkson, *The History of the Rise, Progress, and Accomplishment of the Abolition of the African Slave-Trade by the British Parliament*, vol.1, London, Longman, Hurst, Rees and Orme, 1808, pp.276–85 and *passim*.
5 Michael Craton, *Sinews of Empire. A Short History of British Slavery*, New York, Anchor Books, 1974, especially chapter 5.
6 Emily Sunstein, *A Different Face: The Life of Mary Wollstonecraft*, New York, Harper and Row, 1975, p.171.
7 Olaudah Equiano, *The Interesting Narrative of the Life of Olaudah Equiano, or Gustavus Vassa the African, Written by Himself*, vol.1, printed and sold by the author, 1789, reprinted in Paul Edwards (ed.), *Equiano's Travels: His Autobiography: The Interesting Narrative of ... Olaudah Equiano etc.*, London, Heinemann, 1967.
8 Mary Wollstonecraft (Mr Cresswick), *The Female Reader, or Miscellaneous Pieces in Prose and Verse*, London, printed for Joseph Johnson, 1789. 'The History of Inkle and Yarico', pp.29–31; 'Negro Woman', p.171; 'On Slavery' (from 'The Task'), pp.321–2.
9 *The Analytical Review, or History of Literature, Domestic and Foreign*, London, Joseph Johnson, vol.5, September 1789, pp.98–103; October, 1789, pp.227–32; appendix, pp.574–7.
10 Edmund Burke, *Reflections on the Revolution in France*, 1790, reprinted New York, Doubleday, 1961; Richard Price, *A Discourse on the Love of Our Country, Delivered on Nov. 4, 1789*, Dublin, T. Cadell, 1790.
11 Mary Wollstonecraft, *A Vindication of the Rights of Men, in a Letter to the Right Honourable Edmund Burke; Occasioned by His Reflections on the Revolution in France*, 2nd edn, London, Printed for Joseph Johnson, 1790.
12 Claire Tomalin, *The Life and Death of Mary Wollstonecraft*, New York and London,

Harcourt Brace Jovanovich, 1974.
13 Wollstonecraft, *Rights of Men*, op. cit., pp.23–4.
14 Ibid., p.76.
15 Ibid., pp.45, 59.
16 Moira Ferguson, *First Feminists. British Women Writers 1578-1799*, Bloomington, Indiana University Press, 1985, p.399; Catherine Macaulay Graham, *Letters on Education. With Observation on Religions and Metaphysical Subjects* (1790), New York, Garland, 1974.
17 Ferguson, *First Feminists*, op. cit., pp.403–4.
18 Christian Gotthilf Salzmann, *Elements of Morality for the Use of Children*, London, Joseph Johnson,1790.
19 Craton, *Sinews*, op. cit., p.261.
20 C.L.R. James, *The Black Jacobins, Toussaint L'Ouverture and the San Domingo Revolution*, New York, Vintage, 1963, p.ix.
21 Frank Klingberg, *The Anti-Slavery Movement in England: A Study in English Humanitarianism*, New Haven, Yale University Press, 1926, pp.88–95.
22 Mary Wollstonecraft, *A Vindication of the Rights of Woman*, London, Joseph Johnson, 1792, pp.37, 138.
23 Ibid., pp.44, 83.
24 Ibid., p.167.
25 Ibid.
26 Ibid., pp.82–3.
27 Cora Kaplan, *Sea Changes: Essays on Culture and Feminism*, London, Verso, 1986, p.48.
28 *Analytical Review*, vol.2, 1788, pp.431–9; see also Samuel Stanhope Smith, *An Essay on the Causes of the Variety of Complexion and Figure in the Human Species* (1787), 2nd edn, New York, Williams and Whiting, 1810.
29 Hannah More's renowned opinions on women constitute one of Mary Wollstonecraft's significant textual silences, but most notably in the second *Vindication*. When Wollstonecraft vociferously applauds women's assumption of more prominent socio-cultural roles, she implicitly intertextualises More's opposition to this advice. See also Sylvia Harcstark Myers, *The Bluestocking Circle: Women, Friendship, and the Life of the Mind in Eighteenth-Century England*, Oxford, Clarendon Press, 1990, pp.260–2.
30 However, despite Wollstonecraft's argument that ethnic differences are due to climate and social conditions, *à la* Stanhope Smith, and her unilateral commitment to abolition, she remains ambivalent about black equality. Her acceptance of a system that operates on the differential between owners and workers and on the basis of certain assumptions about European superiority can never square with an absolute human liberation. Everything is measured against the model of a European society that regards African society as the other. Wollstonecraft may eurocentrically contend that people in other cultures would be clever and civilised if they were brought up as she was, but her review of Olaudah Equiano's narratives gives the lie even to that belief: 'We shall only observe, that if these volumes do not exhibit extraordinary intellectual powers, sufficient to wipe off the stigma, yet the activity and ingenuity, which conspicuously appear in the character of Gustavus, [i.e. Equiano] place him on a par

with the general mass of men, who fill the subordinate factions in a more civilized society than that which he was thrown into at his birth.' *Analytical Review*, vol.4, May 1789, p.28.
31 Ibid.
32 Equiano, *Equiano's Travels*, op. cit., p.69.
33 Ibid., p.121.
34 Wollstonecraft, *Female Reader*, op. cit., p.31. Aside from her commentary on Equiano's and Yarico's experiences, among others, Wollstonecraft also recognized other ways in which sexuality oppresses white women. She had dealt on a personal level with her sister Eliza's post-natal depression by effecting Eliza's separation from her husband, Hugh Skeys. She felt, it seems, as if Skeys were responsible for her sister's condition; she treated him, more or less, as a male predator, a villain of sorts. Similarly, the *Rights of Woman* appeared at a time in her own life when she was immersed in a difficult personal situation; the choices open to a woman who wants to work and to love — she was discovering — were very limited.
35 Wollstonecraft, *Rights of Woman*, op. cit., p.144.
36 Winthrop Jordan, *White Over Black: American Attitudes Toward the Negro, 1552-1812*, Chapel Hill, University of North Carolina Press, 1968, pp.150–4.
37 Wollstonecraft, *Rights of Woman*, op. cit., pp.144–5.
38 Ibid., p.17.
39 Remember, too, that, psychologically, Wollstonecraft's attack on male sexuality could mark a displaced attack on Fuseli, whose male sexuality had engendered her own inner turmoil. Mary Poovey's argument that 'men's [and not women's] insatiable appetites' are Wollstonecraft's target is worth considering in the light of her passion for the Swiss painter: Mary Poovey, *The Proper Lady and the Woman Writer. Ideology as Style in Works of Mary Wollstonecraft, Mary Shelley, and Jane Austen*, Chicago, University of Chicago Press, 1984, pp.71–6 and *passim*. See also discussions of displacement in Anna Freud, *The Ego and the Mechanisms of Defence*, New York, International Universities Press, 1966, pp.155–6 and *passim*.
40 Wollstonecraft, *Rights of Woman*, op. cit., p.47.

6. It Ain't all Black and White
Delia Jarrett-Macauley

1 Lauretta Ngcobo, *Let it be Told*, London, Virago, 1988.
2 The phrase is Zora Neale Hurston's and comes from her novel *Their Eyes were Watching God*, in which the main character's grandmother aptly describes the black woman's position as such. However, within Neale Hurston's fiction black women show how they rebel against and challenge this position: they are not 'victims'.
3 Toni Morrison, 'Rootedness: The Ancestor as Foundation', in Mari Evans (ed.), *Black Women Writers*, London, Pluto, 1985, p.342.
4 'A Stir for Seacole', quoted in Ziggi Alexander and Audrey Dewjee (eds), *The Wonderful Adventures of Mary Seacole in Many Lands*, London, Falling Wall Press, 1984, p.235.

5   In 1992, *Mary Seacole Teacher's Pack and Learning Resources* was co-produced by the Black Cultural Archives of Brixton, South London, and the Florence Nightingale Museum so that materials related to her life could be included within the National Curriculum at Key Stages 1–4. The project owed much to the efforts of Connie Mark, President of the Friends of Mary Seacole, who had campaigned for her inclusion in the National Curriculum.
6   See Dorothy Sterling, *Black Foremothers*, New York, Feminist Press, 1988, pp.37ff.
7   See for both presence and absences, Peter Fryer, *Staying Power: The History of Black People in Britain*, London, Pluto, 1984.
8   Ben Bousquet and Colin Douglas, *West Indian Women at War*, London, Lawrence and Wishart, 1991, p.ix.
9   Ibid., p.113.
10 'Disloyal to Civilisation: Feminism, Racism, Gynphobia' (1978), in Adrienne Rich, *On Lies, Secrets and Silence: Selected Prose 1966-1978*, London, Virago, 1980, pp.281ff.
11 Ibid.
12 Claude McKay, *A Long Way from Home*, London, Pluto Press, 1985, pp.74ff.
13 Ibid., p.76.
14 Rasheed Araeen, *Making Myself Visible*, London, Kala, 1984, pp.100ff. June Henfrey and Ian Law (eds), *A History of Race and Racism in Liverpool, 1660–1950*, Liverpool, Merseyside Community Relations Council, 1981.
15 Pratibha Parmar, *Feminist Review*, no.31, 1989, p.56.
16 See also Amryl Johnson's poetry *Long Road to Nowhere*, London, Virago, 1985.
17 Ngcobo, *Let it be Told*, op. cit., p.36.
18 Patricia Hill Collins, *Black Feminist Thought: Knowledge, Consciousness and the Politics of Empowerment*, London, Harper Collins, 1990, p.14.
19 See, for example, Patricia Mohammed and Catherine Shepherd (eds), *Gender in Caribbean Development*, University of West Indies, Mona, Jamaica, St Augustine, Trinidad and Tobago, Cave Hill, Barbados, 1988; Pat Ellis (ed.), *Women of the Caribbean*, London and New Jersey, Zed, 1986.
20 Delia Jarrett-Macauley, *The Life of Una Marson, 1905-1965*, Manchester, Manchester University Press, forthcoming.
21 Kamau Brathwaite, *Contradictory Omens: Cultural Diversity and Integration in the Caribbean*, Kingston, Savacou, 1985, p.6.
22 Fryer, *Staying Power*, op. cit., pp.146–65.
23 Audre Lorde, *A Burst of Light*, London, Sheba, 1988, p.64.

7. *Some Contradictions of Social Motherhood*
Eileen Janes Yeo

1   Mary Wollstonecraft, *A Vindication of the Rights of Woman* (1792), London, Penguin, 1992, pp. 263, 264. Blake's *London* for 'mind forg'd manacles'.
2   For a helpful discussion, see Joan Scott, 'Deconstructing Equality-Versus-Difference: or the Uses of Post-Structuralist Theory for Feminism', *Feminist Studies*, vol.14, no.1, 1988.
3   For example, Seth Koven and Sonya Michel (eds), *Mothers of a New World:*

Maternalist Politics and the Origins of Welfare States, New York, Routledge, 1993; Gisela Bock and Pat Thane (eds), *Maternity and Gender Policies: Women and the Rise of the European Welfare States, 1880s-1950s*, Routledge, London, 1991.

4   My conference paper dealt with 'Three Faces of Maternal Feminism' and some of its arguments appear in my *Contest for Social Science: Relations and Representations of Gender and Class*, London, Rivers Oram, 1996, ch.9. My present work on *Meanings of Motherhood in Europe and America* will further develop this chapter.

5   Carolyn Steedman, *Landscape for a Good Woman: A Story of Two Lives*, London, Virago, 1986, was an important milestone.

6   See Martha Vicinus, *Independent Women: Work and Community for Single Women, 1850-1920*, London, Virago, 1985, pp.293–4.

7   Quoted in D. Kelly Weisberg, 'Barred from the Bar: Women and Legal Education in the United States 1870-1890', in Nancy Cott (ed.), *History of Women in the United States*, Munich, Saur, 1993, vol.8, p.169.

8   W.R. Greg, 'Why are Women Redundant?', *National Review*, vol.15, 1862.

9   Mary Carpenter, 'Women's Work in the Reformatory Movement', *English Woman's Journal*, vol.1, 1858, pp.291–2.

10 Quoted in Irene Stoehr, 'Housework and Motherhood: Debates and Policies in the Women's Movement in Imperial Germany and the Weimar Republic', in Bock and Thane, *Maternity*, op. cit., p.222.

11 Quoted in Ann Taylor Allen, *Feminism and Motherhood in Germany, 1800-1914*, New Brunswick, Rutgers University Press, 1991, p.95.

12 Octavia Hill, 'District Visiting', in *Our Common Land*, London, Macmillan, 1877, pp.24–5. For Alice Salomon on motherliness and social peace, see Christoph Sachsse, 'Social Mothers: The Bourgeois Women's Movement and German Welfare-State Formation, 1890-1929', in Koven and Michel, *Mothers*, op. cit., p.146.

13 Linda Gordon, 'Black and White Visions of Welfare: Women's Welfare Activism, 1890-1945', *Journal of American History*, vol.78, 1991, pp.571ff, shows that of 76 white activists, 86 per cent were college-educated, the great majority were social workers in the widest sense, 'only 34 per cent had ever been married and only 18 per cent remained married during their peak political activity'; this pattern of singlehood continued and in 1920, only 12 per cent of all professional women were married.

14 Cohn quoted in Eileen Boris, 'The Power of Motherhood: Black and White Activist Women Redefine the "Political"', in Koven and Rose, *Mothers*, op. cit., p.230. For Britain, see A. Davin, 'Imperialism and the Cult of Motherhood', *History Workshop*, no.5, Spring, 1978; for Germany, see Sachsse, 'Social Mothers', op. cit., pp.139ff.

15 Barbara Bodichon, *Women and Work*, London, Bosworth and Harrison, 1857, p.51; Ellen Key, *The Woman Movement*, trans. Mamah Borthwick, New York and London, G.P. Putnam's Sons, 1912, pp.75–6.

16 For Britain, see Celia Davies, 'The Health Visitor as Mother's Friend: A Woman's Place in Public Health, 1900-14', *Journal of the Society for the Social History of Medicine*, vol.1, 1988; for Germany, Sachsse, 'Social Mothers', op. cit. pp.140, 147. For growth of women's professions on the social motherhood pattern, see my *Contest*, op. cit., pp.281, 221–3, 247–9. For women doctors, see note 18 below.

17 Rosalind Rosenberg, *Beyond Separate Spheres: Intellectual Roots of Modern Feminism*, New Haven, Yale University Press, 1982, pp.43–4 for the US; for kindergarten teachers in Germany, see Allen, *Feminism*, op. cit., pp.62ff and for the US, W. Leach, *True Love and Perfect Union: The Feminist Reform of Sex and Society*, New York, Basic Books, 1980, pp.331ff.
18 For Britain, see Meta Zimmeck, 'Strategies and Strategems for the Employment of Women in the British Civil Service, 1919-1939', *Historical Journal*, vol.27, 1984, pp.904–5, 909; E. Morley (ed.), *Women Workers in Seven Professions*, Routledge, London, 1914, pp. 256ff, 237–49 for civil service and pp. 155, 167 for British medical women. For America, see Kathryn Kish Sklar, in Koven and Rose, *Mothers*, op. cit.; Regina Morantz-Sanchez, *Sympathy and Science: Women Physicians in American Medicine*, New York, Oxford University Press, 1985, pp. 71, 280ff. For Germany, see Jean Quataert, 'Woman's Work and the Early Welfare State in Germany: Legislators, Bureaucrats, and Clients before the First World War', in Koven and Rose, *Mothers*, op. cit., pp.167–9; James Albisetti, 'Women and the Professions in Imperial Germany', in Ruth-Ellen Joeres and Mary Maynes (eds), *German Women in the Eighteenth and Nineteenth Centuries*, Indiana University Press, Bloomington, 1986, pp.94–6.
19 Quoted in Weisberg, 'Barred', op. cit., p.173; see also pp. 171ff.
20 Yeo, *Contest*, op. cit., pp.293–4 for Britain; Sachsse, 'Social Mothers', op. cit., pp. 147ff; Allen, *Feminism*, op. cit., pp. 212ff for Germany.
21 Sachsse, 'Social Mothers', op. cit., p.153.
22 Rosenberg, *Beyond*, op. cit., pp.48–9.
23 For my earlier uses of this 'typology', see 'Social Motherhood and the Sexual Communion of Labour in British Social Science, 1850-1950', *Women's History Review*, vol.1, no.1, 1992, pp.77ff; *Contest*, op. cit., chs 5, 9.
24 The best exposition of Klein's theories, delivered as training lectures at the British Psychoanalytic Association, is Hanna Segal, *Introduction to the Work of Melanie Klein*, London, Heinemann, 1964; also her *Klein*, Glasgow, Fontana, 1979.
25 C.G. Jung, 'Psychological Aspects of the Mother Archetype' (1938, revised 1954), in *The Archetypes and the Collective Unconscious*, London, Routledge, 1991, p.82; also his autobiography, *Memories, Dreams, Reflections*, London, W.M. Collins and Routledge & Kegan Paul, 1963.
26 Stephen Reynolds and Bob and Tom Woolley, *Seems So! A Working-class View of Politics*, Macmillan, London, 1911, p.278.
27 Eileen Boris, 'Power', op. cit., p.231.
28 Ibid., p.233.
29 M.E. Loane, *From Their Point of View*, London, Edward Arnold, 1908, p.92. For further reflections on the disciplining pose in early twentieth-century social work, see my *Contest*, op. cit., pp.250ff.
30 Ellen Ross, *Love and Toil: Motherhood in Outcast London, 1870-1918*, New York and Oxford, Oxford University Press, 1993, chs 5 and 7; Anna Davin, *Growing Up Poor*, London, Rivers Oram, 1995.
31 Eileen Boris, *Home to Work: Motherhood and the Politics of Industrial Home Work in the United States*, Cambridge, Cambridge University Press, 1994, pp. 104—8, 110—1, 122.
32 M.E. Loane, *The Next Street But One*, London, Edward Arnold, 1907, p.79; for

Loane on inspectors, see my *Contest*, op. cit., pp.272–3.
33 Margaret Sewell, 'Charity Organisation: a Retrospect', *Charity Organisation Review*, n.s., vol.11, 1902, p.146.
34 Gordon, 'Black and White', op. cit., p.577.
35 Hannah Mitchell, *The Hard Way Up*, London, Virago, 1977, chs 11ff for a socialist turning to suffrage campaigning.
36 Jean Quataert, *Reluctant Feminists in German Social Democracy, 1885-1917*, Princeton, Princeton University Press, 1979, pp. 99, 120, 239.
37 Molly Ladd-Taylor (ed.), *Raising a Baby the Government Way: Mothers' Letters to the Children's Bureau, 1915-1932*, New Brunswick, Rutgers University Press, 1986, pp.57, 148–53.
38 Women's Co-operative Guild, *Life as We Have Known It*, ed. Margaret Llewelyn Davies (1931), London, Virago, 1977, p.40.
39 Eleanor Hood to Margaret Llewelyn Davies, 5 October 1921, material illustrating the work of the Guild, British Library of Political and Economic Science, London School of Economics, vol.8, pp.46–7.

8. Working-Class Feminism?
The Women's Co-operative Guild, 1880s-1914
Gillian Scott

1 Alison Jaggar, *Feminist Politics and Human Nature*, Totowa, New Jersey, Rowan and Littlefield, 1983, p.4.
2 R. Nash, *The Position of Married Women*, Manchester, CWS Printing Works, 1907, p.9.
3 *New Statesman*, 21 June 1913.
4 Margaret Llewelyn Davies to Leonard Woolf, n.d. [Nov.1913?], Monks House Papers (MHP), University of Sussex.
5 Jean Gaffin and David Thoms, *Caring and Sharing The Centenary History of the Co-operative Women's Guild*, Co-operative Union Ltd, Manchester, 1983, p.13; G.D.H. Cole, A Century of Co-operation, London, George Allen and Unwin for the Co-operative Union, 1944, p.216.
6 Presidential Address, 8th Annual Guild Meeting, *Co-operative Congress Report (CCR)*, Manchester, CWS Printing Works, 1890, p.112.
7 Report of Women's Co-operative Guild Open Meeting, *CCR*, 1888, p.107; speech of newly-elected General Secretary, 7th annual Guild Meeting, *CCR*, 1889, p.106.
8 WCG, *How to Start and Work a Branch*, Kirkby Lonsdale, WCG, 1896, p.3.
9 *Co-operative News*, 10 June 1922, p.8.
10 Enid Stacey, 'A Century of Women's Rights', in A.R. Wallace, *Forecasts of the Coming Century by a Decade of Writers*, Manchester, The Labour Press Ltd, 1897, p.91.
11 M. Llewelyn Davies, article for *Norges Kvinder*, February 1931, typed MS, 'Material illustrating the work of the guild and kindred interests, manuscript, typed and printed papers, photographs, erstwhile property of Margaret Llewelyn Davies (1890-1944)', 11 vols., British Library of Political and Economic Science, vol.1, item 39, 1931.

12 The net worth of Margaret Llewelyn Davies's will at her death in 1944 was £20,725; her earliest acquisition of capital seems to have been a legacy of £3,000 from Charles Crompton in 1892, Joyce Bellamy and John Saville, *Dictionary of Labour Biography*, London, Macmillan, 1972, vol.1; 'The Morgue' MS chronicle of the Llewelyn Davies family 1750-1915, compiled by Peter Llewelyn Davies between 1945 and 1951, private collection, 7 vols., vol.4, pp.115 and 122 (thanks to Chrys Salt for access to this material).
13 Stacey, 'A Century', op. cit., p.93.
14 M.L. Davies to Barbara Stephens, n.d., 'The Morgue', vol.1, p.145.
15 *Co-operative News*, 3 June 1944, p.1.
16 Cole, *Co-operation*, op. cit., p.217.
17 M.L. Davies, 'MS article for *Norges Kvinder*', op. cit.
18 Ibid.
19 *Co-operative News*, 4 February 1899, p.114.
20 'The Women's Co-operative Guild, 1895-1916: A Review of Twenty-One Years' Work', *WCG Annual Congress Handbook*, London, WCG, 1916, pp.10–11.
21 *Co-operative News*, 4 February 1899, p.114.
22 'WCG: Twenty-One Years' Work', op. cit., pp.10–11.
23 See J. Brenner and M. Ramas, 'Rethinking Women's Oppression', *New Left Review*, no.144, 1984, pp.33–71 for a fuller discussion of this question.
24 Harriet Taylor Mill and John Stuart Mill, *Enfranchisement of Women and The Subjection of Women*, introduction by Kate Soper, London, Virago, 1983, pp.18, 88–9.
25 M. Llewelyn Davies, *The Women's Co-operative Guild 1883-1904*, Kirkby Lonsdale, WCG, 1904, p.151.
26 The obvious exception to this pattern was the widespread employment of women in the textile industry in Lancashire and Cheshire, see Jill Liddington and Jill Norris, *One Hand Tied Behind Us*, London, Virago, 1978, for details of the various domestic arrangements that made this possible.
27 M. Llewelyn Davies (ed.), *Maternity: Letters from Working Women* (1915), London, Virago, 1978, pp.8–9.
28 'Evidence of Miss M. Llewelyn Davies', *Minutes of Evidence Taken Before the Royal Commission on Divorce and Matrimonial Causes*, 1912, vol.3 (Cd. 6481) PP 1912-13, XX.
29 Davies, *Maternity*, op. cit.
30 'WCG: Twenty-One Years' Work', op. cit., p.11.
31 'Evidence of M.L. Davies', op. cit., pp.150–1.
32 M.L. Davies, *Maternity*, op. cit., pp.7–8.
33 M.L. Davies, 'Special Education, Divorce and Independence', MS article for German publication, n.d. [1933?], in 'Material illustrating the work of the Guild', vol.1, item 42.
34 *WCG Annual Congress, 1915, The Self-Government of the Guild*, London, Co-operative Printing Society, 1915, p.3.
35 M.L. Davies wrote in a letter to Leonard Woolf that as well as objecting to the Guild's support for divorce law reform, Co-operative officials had disliked the Guild's involvement with the suffrage movement; MLD to LW, n.d. [June 1914?], MHP. In 1913 the only party to oppose the amendment to the National Insurance

Act to make maternity benefit the property of women was Labour, on the grounds that it would weaken the union position in collective bargaining: *Co-operative News*, 16 August 1913, p.1038.
36. WCG, *Divorce Law Reform: the Majority Report of the Divorce Commission*, Central Committee paper for Spring Sectional Conferences, Manchester, WCG, 1913, p.24. Mutual incompatiblity did not become grounds for divorce until 1969.
37. General Secretary, Catholic Federation Diocese of Salford, to General Secretary, WCG, 22 October 1913, MHP.
38. *Annual Report of WCG 1913-14*, London, WCG, 1914, p.27.
39. C. Goodenough, *The Central Board and the Grant to the Women's Co-operative Guild*, Manchester, 1914, p.4.
40. *Co-operative Union Annual Report (CUAR)*, Manchester, CWS Printing Works, 1915, p.25.
41. 'Meeting of Central Board', *CUAR*, 1914, p.15.
42. M.L. Davies to Leonard Woolf, n.d., MHP.
43. *Co-operative News*, 20 June 1914, p.808.
44. *CUAR*, 1915, p.523.
45. M. Llewelyn Davies, *The Vote at Last! More Power to Co-operation*, London, Co-op Union Ltd., Political Pamphlet No.2, 1918, p.1.
46. *Annual Report of WCG, 1918-19*, p.2.
47. Priscilla Moulder, 'What the Women's Co-operative Guild is Doing for Working Women', *The Englishwoman*, April 1914, p.37.
48. M.L. Davies, *Maternity*, op. cit., pp.4–5.
49. M.L. Davies, MS article for *Norges Kvinder*, op. cit.
50. Ibid.

9. *Ernestine Rose (1810-92) and her Multiple Identities*
Françoise Basch

1. Elizabeth Cady Stanton, Susan B. Anthony, Matilda Joslyn Gage (eds), *The History of Woman Suffrage*, Rochester, Little and Ives, 1889, 6 vols, vol.1.
2. *The New York Herald*, 3 February 1850.
3. *London Daily News*, 9 August 1892.
4. The only full scale biography is Yuri Suhl, *Ernestine Rose and the Battle for Human Rights* (1959), republished as *Ernestine Rose, Woman's Rights Pioneer*, New York, Biblio Press, 1990, with an introduction by Rosalyn Baxandall and a foreword by me but otherwise not revised.
5. 'A Bit of Reminiscence', *The Woman Citizen*, 12 August 1922, Schlesinger Library, Cambridge, Mass.; 'The Fanny Goldstein Letter', American Jewish Archives, Cincinnati and The Library of Congress.
6. Barbara Taylor, *Eve and the New Jerusalem: Socialism and Feminism in the Nineteenth Century*, New York, Pantheon, 1983, p.39.
7. L.E. Barnard, 'Ernestine L. Rose', *History of Woman Suffrage*, op. cit., vol.1, p.88; Jenny D'Héricourt, 'Mrs. Ernestine L. Rose', *Boston Investigator*, 8 December 1869; Suhl, *Rose*, op. cit., p.275.
8. 'American Reformers — Infidels', *The Liberator*, vol.24, no.47, 24 November

1854, p.188.
9   Ernestine Rose, *A Lecture on Woman's Rights*, Boston, 19 October 1851, p.17.
10. *Proceedings of the National Woman's Rights Convention*, New York, 1853, p.33, and Syracuse, 1862, p.56.
11 L.G. Wells, *The Communal Skaneateles Experiment, 1843-1846*, pamphlet no.20, Worcester, Mass., American Antiquarian Society, 1953, pp.6, 8, 9.
12 *The Banner of Light*, 10 July 1858.
13 *History of Woman Suffrage*, op. cit., vol.1, p.237.
14 *Boston Investigator*, 12 October 1859.
15 Hypathia Bradlaugh Bonner in *National Reformer*, 14 August 1892.
16 *The Liberator*, 17 June 1853.
17 *Boston Investigator*, 12 December 1855.
18 'Naturalisation laws' were aimed at barring the foreign-born from American citizenship until they had resided in the United States for 21 years: M.U. Schappes, *Documentary History of the Jews in the United States*, New York, Schocken, 1950, pp.252, 286, 293, 342.
19 *History of Woman Suffrage*, op. cit., vol.1, pp.608–10.
20 'Diary of a Lecture Tour with Ernestine Rose to Washington, Baltimore and Philadelphia', 19 April 1854, Anthony Papers, Schlesinger Library; E. DuBois (ed.), *The Elizabeth Cady Stanton – Susan B. Anthony Reader: Correspondence, Writings, Speeches*, Boston, Northeastern University Press, revised edn, 1992, pp.74–7.
21 Third National Woman's Rights Convention at Syracuse, 8-10 September 1852; Schappes, *Documentary History*, op.cit., p.326.
22 *Boston Investigator*, 28 October 1863 for Seaver; 6 January, 10, 17 February, 2 March, 6 April. 1864 for Rose.
23 Ibid., 24 August 1892.

10. Ignota, the Unknown Woman
Elizabeth Clarke Wolstenholme Elmy, 1833-1918
Muriel Fielding

1   Elizabeth Wolstenholme Elmy, *The Emancipation of Women*, London, Women's Printing Society, 1888, p.3.
2   Ibid.
3   Sylvia Pankhurst, *The Suffragette Movement* (1931), London, Virago, 1972, p.32. For their union, see Sandra Holton, 'Victorian Feminism and Free Love: The Divers Matrimonials of Elizabeth Wolstenholme and Ben Elmy', *Victorian Studies*, vol.37, 1994.
4   Letter from Millicent Garrett Fawcett to Elizabeth Wolstenholme Elmy, 10 December 1875, Fawcett Library Autography Collection, London Guildhall University.
5   Lee Holcombe, *Wives and Property*, Oxford, University of Toronto Press, 1983, p.272.
6   Elizabeth Wolstenholme Elmy, *The Decision in the Clitheroe Case and its Consequences*, Manchester, Guardian Printing Works, 1891. The Clitheroe case related to R.

v. Jackson, 16 March 1891, when the judges found against Mrs Jackson, who was living apart from her husband, and decreed that it was his right to seize possession of his wife by force and detain her in his house until she rendered him conjugal rights. A Court of Appeal overturned this decision and declared that the personal slavery of the wife was no part of the law of England. Elizabeth Wolstenholme Elmy, *Woman and the Law*, Women's Emancipation Union, Congleton, 1896.

7 Ignota, 'Judicial Sex Bias' and 'Privilege v. Justice to Women', *Westminster Review*, vol.149, nos 2 and 3, February and March 1898, pp. 147–60, 279–88; vol.152, August 1899, pp. 128–41.

8 Letter from Elizabeth Wolstenholme Elmy to Harriet McIlquham, 21 May 1897, Elizabeth Wolstenholme Elmy Papers, British Library, Add. Mss. 47451.

11. Ada Nield Chew
An Uncomfortable Feminist
Gerry Holloway

1 Anne Phillips, *Divided Loyalties: Dilemmas of Sex and Class*, London, Virago, 1987, p.1.

2 The details of Ada's life come from her daughter, Doris Nield Chew's book *The Life and Writings of Ada Nield Chew Remembered and Collected by Doris Nield Chew*, London, Virago, 1982.

3 Ibid., p.77.

4 Ibid., p.81.

5 Ibid., p.37.

6 Ida Nield Chew, 'The Problem of the Married Working Woman', *Common Cause*, 6 March 1914.

7 I discuss this issue in more depth in my article '"Let the Women be Alive!": The Construction of the Married Working Woman in the Industrial Women's Movement 1890-1914' in the forthcoming collection Eileen Janes Yeo (ed.), 'Radical Femininity: Women's Self-Representation in Nineteenth- and Twentieth-Century Social Movements', Manchester University Press.

8 Philippa Levine, *Feminist Lives in Victorian England: Private Roles and Public Commitment*, Oxford, Basil Blackwell, 1990, p.158.

9 For an in-depth discussion of sisterhood see Rosemary Fuerer, 'The Meaning of "Sisterhood": The British Women's Movement and Protective Labour Legislation, 1870-1900', *Victorian Studies*, vol.31, no.2, 1988.

10 Ada Nield Chew, 'An Effective Plan of Campaign', *Common Cause*, 18 April 1912.

11 See Liz Stanley with Ann Morley, *The Life and Death of Emily Wilding Davison*, London, The Women's Press, 1988, for a fascinating example of how feminist networks worked in the Edwardian women's movement.

12 I argue this more fully in my 'A Common Cause? Class Dynamics in the Industrial Women's Movement, 1888-1918', PhD thesis, University of Sussex, 1995.

13 Chew, *Life*, op. cit. pp.34–5.

12. Leading a Normal Family?
Sexuality and Nation in the 1991 Winnie Mandela Trial
Rachel Holmes

Thank you Zackie Achmat, Jerry Brotton, Edwin Cameron, Mark Gevisser and Anne McClintock for your comments and contributions to my work on this material over the past four years.

1. Nelson Mandela announcing his separation from Winnie Mandela, April 1992, in Mark Galloway (Producer/Director), *Mandela: From Prisoner to President*, Yorkshire Televison, 1994.
2. Winnie Mandela described him as 'national property' in an interview in the Galloway documentary, op. cit.
3. For examples, see Emma Gilbey, *The Lady: The Life and Times of Winnie Mandela*, London, Vintage, 1994; and Nelson Mandela, *Long Walk to Freedom: The Autobiography of Nelson Mandela*, London, Little, Brown, 1994.
4. See Paul Trewhela's work on the Winnie Mandela Trial, particularly his essay 'The Mistrial of Winnie Mandela: A Problem of Justice', *Searchlight South Africa*, Johannesburg and London, vol.3, no.1 (no.9), 1992.
5. *Sowetan*, 12 February 1991.
6. This is a line Winnie Mandela has consistently maintained. Breaking her public silence on the murder of Stompei Seipei in the South African Parliament in August 1994, Winnie Mandela described how she had given refuge to fugitive youths who had been subjected to sexual abuse: 'I unhesitatingly fell in with a plan to rescue them and gave them refuge in my house and for that I was convicted for kidnapping,' she said. *Guardian*, 10 August 1994.
7. Testimony of Xoliswa Falati, Case No. 167/90, Rand Supreme Court, March 1991.
8. Gilbey, *The Lady*, op. cit., p.183.
9. The significance of this term should not be overlooked. For more detailed accounts of the history and significance of the practice of thigh sex in black male urban culture, see T. Dunbar Moodie with Vivienne Ndatshe and British Sibuyi, 'Migrancy and Male Sexuality on the South African Goldmines', in Duberman *et.al.* (eds), *Hidden From History: Reclaiming the Gay and Lesbian Past*, New York, New American Library, 1989; and, for an account of contemporary practices, Hugh McLean and Linda Ngcobo, 'Abangibhamayo Bathi Ngimnandi (Those Who Fuck Me Say I'm Tasty): Gay Sexuality in Reef Townships', in Mark Gevisser and Edwin Cameron (eds), *Defiant Desire: Gay and Lesbian Lives in South Africa*, Johannesburg, Ravan Press, 1994, London and New York, Routledge, 1995.
10. *Daily Dispatch*, 13 April 1991.
11. Cited in Gilbey, *The Lady*, op. cit., p.270.
12. Winnie Mandela, *Address to Toekumsrus Branch of the ANC Women's League*, ANC Women's League, 22 April 1991.
13. I have already discussed this issue in detail in my article, '"White Rapists Made Coloureds" (and Homosexuals): The Winnie Mandela Trial and the Politics of Race and Sexuality', in Gevisser, *Defiant Desire*, op. cit., pp.284–94.
14. My interpretation of the trial as a site of incitement of these discourses of sexu-

ality evidently draws upon Michel Foucault's theorisations in *The History of Sexuality*, vol.1, London, Peregrine, 1984.
15 I use the past tense here in order to register the challenge posed by the recent democratic elections to a seamless reproduction of the image of South Africa as *inherently* violent.
16 Trewhela, 'Mistrial', op. cit., p.33.
17 A charge that had frequently been made at community level against Richardson himself.
18 *Sowetan*, 8 March 1992.
19 Walter Benjamin, 'Critique of Violence', in P. Demetz (ed.), *Reflections*, New York, Schocken Books, 1986, p.132.
20 The Rivonia Trial, which began in October 1963, was the most infamous of South African state trails in the apartheid era. It subsequently led to the banning of the ANC and the long-term imprisonment of its key leaders, including Nelson Mandela.
21 Benjamin, 'Critique of Violence', op. cit., p.133.
22 Franz Fanon, *The Wretched of the Earth*, London, Penguin, 1963, p.40
23 Ibid., p.30
24 A practice known in MUFC community circles as 'Break Down'.
25 *City Press*, 17 March 1991.
26 *Argus*, 11 April 1991.
27 *The Sunday Times*, 10 March 1991.
28 *Sowetan*, 15 March 1991.
29 GLOW letter in the *Weekly Mail*, 25 March 1991.
30 In the appeal court, ruling Winnie Mandela's conviction for kidnapping was upheld, but the court did not find her to have been an accessory to the assaults. Her five-year jail sentence was commuted to two years' suspended sentence and a fine of R15,000, and she was ordered to pay compensation of R5,000 to each of the three surviving complainants. Although Falati's sentence was reduced to four years' imprisonment, only two were suspended, meaning that, unlike Winnie Mandela, Falati would have to serve time.
31 Gilbey, *The Lady*, op. cit., p.298.
32 *Argus*, 17 April 1991.
33 Homi Bhabha, 'DissemiNation', in Homi Bhabha (ed.), *Nation and Narration*, London, Routledge, 1990, p.291.
34 Fanon, *Wretched*, op. cit., p.36.
35 See *Daily Dispatch*, 16 May 1992; *Independent on Sunday*, 19 April 1992; *Weekend Guardian*, 25 April 1992.
36 John Carlin, *Independent on Sunday*, 19 April 1992.
37 For an example of this kind of political mythography peddled by the *Mail*, see 'This Tragic Marriage that could Wreck a Nation', *Daily Mail*, 15 May 1992.
38 Trewhela, 'Mistrial', op. cit., pp.37–8.
39 Zackie Achmat, 'Off the Control Track: Power, Resistance, and Representation in South African Documentaries, 1984-1994', proceedings from Media in Africa Conference, Northwestern University, Chicago, May 1994 (forthcoming).

13. The Farewell Dance
Women in the Bulgarian Transition
Dimitrina Petrova

1. Silva Rakhneva, 'Nai-Posle (At Last)', *Zhenata Dnes* (*Woman Today*), special issue, April 1991.
2. Opinion poll of the Centre for the Study of Democracy, October 1991. Various excerpts of the data have been published in the Bulgarian press.

14. From Asexuality to Gender Differences in Modern China
Min Dongchao

1. For details on these two papers see Li Yinhe, 'Asexualisation and Women's Roles in China'; Tan Shen, 'Sex Differentiation: A Perspective on Today's Women's Problems', in Women's Studies Centre of Beijing University (eds), *Papers of the First International Conference on Women's Studies of Beijing University*, Beijing, 1993.
2. Jin Yihong, *Awakening Nuwa: New Theories on the Female Concept*, Nanjing, Nanjing University Press, 1991, p.210.
3. *People's Daily* is a newspaper controlled by the Chinese Communist Party.
4. Xiong Jingming, 'Research into Government Policies Regarding Women and Social Concepts of Bringing up Children', *Sociology Studies*, Beijing, no.2, 1990.
5. Li Xiaojiang, *Eve's Search*, Zhengzhou, Henan People's Publishing House, 1988, p.165.
6. Interviews by my students, 'Mothers and Daughters', Tianjin, 1992.
7. Fen Xiaotian, 'Changes in Images of Females', *Chinese Women*, Beijing, no.7, 1992.
8. Maria Mies, *Patriarchy and Accumulation on a World Scale*, London, Zed, 1986, p.196.
9. *Chinese Women's Daily*, Beijing, 23 October 1990–31 January 1991.
10. Tan Shen and Li Xiaojiang (eds), *Women's Studies in China*, Zhengzhou, Henan People's Publishing House, 1991.
11. Wang Qi, 'Women Represent Women's Interests?', paper prepared for the ECPR joint session of workshops, Limerick University, Ireland, 1992, p.11.
12. Li Xiaojiang and Tan Shen (eds), *Multifaceted Studies of Chinese Women*, Zhengzhou, Henan People's Publishing House, 1991, p. 15.
13. Interviews by Min Dongchao, 'Chinese Intellectual Women', China, 1991-2.
14. Ibid.

15. Naked Human Nature and the Draperies of Custom
Wollstonecraft on Equality and Democracy
Kate Soper

1. Mary Wollstonecraft, *A Vindication of the Rights of Men, in a Letter to the Right Honourable Edmund Burke*, in J. Todd and M. Butler (eds), *The Works of Mary*

Wollstonecraft, New York, New York University Press, 1989, 2nd edn, vol.5, p.14. See also Karl Marx, *On the Jewish Question*, in Karl Marx and Friedrich Engels, *Collected Works*, London, Lawrence and Wishart, 1975, vol.3.
2. Mary Wollstonecraft, *A Vindication of the Rights of Woman*, Harmondsworth, Penguin Classics, 1983, p.103.
3. Ibid., p.259.
4. Ibid., p.147.
5. Ibid., pp.114–15. For an interesting discussion of Wollstonecraft s censorious views on love, which links them to the entirely sexualised conception of the feminine prevalent in her day, see Barbara Taylor, 'Mary Wollstonecraft and the Wild Wish of Early Feminism', *History Workshop*, no.33, Spring 1992, pp.197–219, especially p.208; Cora Kaplan, 'Wild Nights: Pleasures/Sexuality/Feminism', in *Sea Changes*, London, Verso, 1986.
6. Virginia Sapiro, *A Vindication of Political Virtue: The Political Theory of Mary Wollstonecraft*, Chicago and London, University of Chicago Press, 1992.
7. Ibid., p.xiv.
8. J.S. Mill, *The Subjection of Women* (1869), London, Virago, 1983, pp.25–31, 146–7.
9. Wollstonecraft, *Rights of Woman*, op. cit., p.80.
10. Taylor, 'Mary Wollstonecraft', op. cit., p.206.
11. John Barrell, *The Political Theory of Art from Reynolds to Hazlitt*, New Haven and London, Yale University Press, 1986, pp.65–6.
12. Wollstonecraft, *Rights of Woman*, op. cit., p.243.
13. Sapiro, *Political Virtue*, op. cit., p.184.
14. Interview with Jacques Derrida, *Radical Philosophy*, no.68, Autumn 1994, p.32.
15. Martha Nussbaum, 'Human Functioning and Social Justice: In Defence of Aristotelian Essentialism', *Political Theory*, vol.20, no.2, May 1992, pp.203–4.
16. Edmund Burke, *Reflections on the Revolution in France* (1790), London, Doubleday, 1961, p.19.
17. Ibid., p.90.
18. Wollstonecraft, *Rights of Men*, op. cit., p.25.
19. See in particular Ernesto Laclau and Chantal Mouffe, *Hegemony and Socialist Strategy: Towards a Radical Democratic Politics*, London, Verso, 1985; Chantal Mouffe (ed.), *Dimensions of Radical Democracy*, London, Verso, 1992; Ernesto Laclau, *New Reflections on the Revolution in our Time*, London, Verso, 1991; interviews with Laclau and Mouffe in Stuart Wilks (ed.), *Talking About Tomorrow*, London, Pluto, 1993, pp.109–22.
20. Laclau and Mouffe, *Hegemony and Socialist Strategy*, op. cit., p.152; see also p.181.
21. Ibid., pp.152–9.
22. Ibid., p.154.
23. Ibid., pp.176–93.
24. Ibid., p.181.
25. Mouffe, *Dimensions of Radical Democracy*, op. cit., p.13.

16. Mary Wollstonecraft, Feminism and Humanism
A Spectrum of Reading
Himani Bannerji

1. For a critique of feminist essentialism from the standpoint of difference, see Bell Hooks, *Ain't I a Woman? Black Women and Feminism*, Boston, South End Press, 1981, introduction, chapter 4; Patricia Hill Collins, *Black Feminist Thought: Knowledge, Consciousness and the Politics of Empowerment*, New York and London, Routledge, 1991. See also Elizabeth Spelman, *Inessential Women: Problems of Exclusion in Feminist Thought*, Boston, Beacon, 1988, preface and introduction; Dorothy E. Smith, 'Feminist Reflections on Political Economy', *Studies in Political Economy*, no.30, Autumn 1989, pp.37–59.
2. For a critique of 'woman' as a foundationalist category and a criticism of feminism based on this critique, see Judith Butler, *Gender Trouble: Feminism and the Subversion of Identity*, London, Routledge, 1990. See also Denise Riley, *'Am I that Name?': Feminism and the Category of 'Women' in History*, Minneapolis, University of Minnesota Press, 1988.
3. Mary Wollstonecraft, *A Vindication of the Rights of Woman* (1792), New York, Norton, 1967.
4. Rabindranath Tagore (1861–1942), the most influential cultural figure of India in the late nineteenth and early twentieth centuries. Tagore functioned as a major figure in moral regulation and reform in Bengal.
5. See Sumit Sarkar, *Modern India*, New Delhi, Macmillan India, 1983.
6. See Kumkum Sangari and Sudesh Vaid (eds), *Recasting Women: Essays in Indian Colonial History*, New Delhi, Kali for Women, 1989; Sumanta Bannerji, *The Parlour and the Streets: Elite and Popular Culture in Nineteenth-Century Calcutta*, Calcutta, Seagull, 1989; Joanna Liddle and Rama Joshi, *Daughters of Independence: Gender, Caste and Class in India*, New Delhi and London, Kali for Women and Zed Books, 1986. See also Himani Bannerji, 'Fashioning a Self: Educational Proposals for and by Women in Popular Magazines in Colonial Bengal', *Economic and Political Weekly of India*, 26 October 1991, Women's Studies, pp.50–62; Jasodhara Bagchi (ed.), *Indian Women: Myth and Reality*, Calcutta, Sangam, 1995.
7. Rasasundari Dasi, *Amar Jiban*, Calcutta, Dey's Publishers, 1987, pp.43–4, my translation.
8. See Meredith Borthwick, *The Changing Role of Women in Bengal, 1849-1905*, Princeton, Princeton University Press, 1984, pp.60–108; Gulam Murshid, *The Reluctant Debutante: Response of Bengali Women to Modernisation, 1849-1905*, Rajshaji, Rajshaji University Press, 1983.
9. See Sumit Sarkar, 'Rammohan Roy and the Break with the Past', in *A Critique of Colonial India*, Calcutta, Papyrus, 1985.
10. See Sangari and Vaid, 'Recasting Women: An Introduction' in *Recasting Women*, op. cit. See also Tanika Sarkar, 'Hindu Conjugality and Nationalism', in Bagchi, *Indian Women*, op. cit.
11. For this notion, see Dorothy E. Smith, *The Conceptual Practices of Power*, Toronto, University of Toronto Press, 1990.
12. See Erol Lawrence, 'Just Plain Common Sense: the "Roots" of Racism', in Centre

for Contemporary Studies, University of Birmingham, *The Empire Strikes Back: Race and Racism in 70s Britain*, London, Hutchinson, 1982.

13 For further elucidation of 'difference', see Himani Bannerji, 'But Who Speaks for Us? Experience and Agency in Conventional Feminist Paradigms', in Himani Bannerji, Linda Carty, Susan Heald, Kari Dehli and Kate McKenna (eds), *Unsettling Relations: the University as a Site of Feminist Struggles*, Toronto, Women's Press, 1991.

14 See Pratibha Parmar, 'Gender, Race and Class: Asian Women in Resistance', in *The Empire Strikes Back*, op. cit.

15 Nancy Stepan, 'Race and Gender: The Role of Analogy in Science' in David T. Goldberg (ed.), *The Anatomy of Racism*, Minneapolis, University of Minnesota Press, 1990, p.39. See also her statements on 'race', science and the construction of difference (pp.41–2).

16 See Jean-Jacques Rousseau's *The Social Contract, or Principles of Political Right*, 1762, and also Marx and Engels' *The Communist Manifesto*, 1848.

17 Virginia Sapiro, *A Vindication of Political Virtue: The Political Theory of Mary Wollstonecraft*, Chicago, University of Chicago Press, 1992.

18 See chapter 5.

19 Nancy Stepan, 'Race and Gender', op. cit., p.44.

20 See above, pp.97–8, 255n30.

21 Ferguson remarks on the association between slavery and corruption, when Wollstonecraft calls women 'slaves' in a political and civil sense; see above pp.95.

22 See Angela Davis, *Women, Race and Class*, New York, Vintage, 1981, chapters 1—3, and Hooks, *'Ain't I a Woman?'*, op. cit.

23 See Sander Gilman, 'Black Bodies, White Bodies', in Henry Louis Gates, Jr. (ed.), *'Race', Writing and Difference*, Chicago, University of Chicago Press, 1985; also his '"I am Down on Whores": Race and Gender in Victorian London' in Goldberg, *Anatomy of Racism*, op. cit. See also Stephen Gould, *The Mismeasure of Man*, New York, Norton, 1981.

24 See the works of Angela Davis, Bell Hooks, Patricia Hill Collins and Michel Wallace. Also, Gloria T. Hull *et al* have directly addressed this problem in the very title of their book, *All the Women are White, All the Blacks are Men, But Some of Us are Brave*, New York, Feminist Press, 1982. For the mysterious appearances and disappearances of women of colour in white feminist literature, see Gloria Anzaldua (ed.), *Making Faces, Making Soul/Haciendo Caras: Creative and Critical Perspectives by Women of Colour*, San Francisco, Aunt Lute Foundation, 1990.

25 For a detailed presentation of Edward Said's concept of 'orientalism', see his *Orientalism*, New York, Vintage Books, 1979, introduction, chapter 1, and *Covering Islam: How the Media and the Experts Determine How We See the World*, New York, Pantheon Books, 1981.

26 Said in *Orientalism*, op. cit. explores works of European, especially French, late eighteenth- and early nineteenth-century poets and fiction writers. Speaking of Flaubert and Nerval, he says, 'both were thoroughly steeped in aspects of European culture that encouraged...[a] perverse vision of the Orient. Nerval and Flaubert belonged to that community of thought and feeling described by Mario Praz in *The Romantic Agony*, a community for which the imagery of exotic places, the cultivation of sadomasochistic tastes,...a fascination with the macabre,

with the notion of a Fatal Woman, with secrecy and occultism, all combined to enable literary work of the sort produced by Gaultier (himself fascinated by the Orient), Swinburne, Baudelaire and Huysmans' (p.180). See also Malek Alloula, *The Colonial Harem*, translated by Myrna and Wlad Godzich, Minneapolis, University of Minnesota Press, 1986.

27 Moira Ferguson in 'Mary Wollstonecraft and the Problematic of Slavery', *Feminist Review*, no.42, Autumn 1992, pp.90–1, speaks about this in terms of Wollstonecraft's view of Africans: 'Furthermore, the blame that Wollstonecraft attaches to white women for their vanity is complicated by her assessment of the relationship between African women and dress.' She quotes a telling passage from Wollstonecraft: 'The attention to dress, therefore, which has been thought a sexual propensity, I think natural to mankind. But I ought to express myself with more precision, when the mind is not sufficiently open to take pleasure in reflection, the body will be adorned with sedulous care; and ambition will appear in tattooing or painting it. So far is this first inclination carried, that even the hellish yoke of slavery cannot stifle this savage desire of admiration which the black heroes inherit from both their parents, for all the hardly earned savings of a slave are expended in a little tawdry finery.'

28 Wollstonecraft's negative views of tradition and feudal hierarchy are best revealed, as Sapiro thinks, in her debate with Edmund Burke. See Sapiro, *A Vindication of Political Virtue*, op. cit., chapters 5, 6. See also Wollstonecraft, *Rights of Woman*, op. cit., p. 50, on Milton as a 'Mahometan' traditionalist and misogynist, and her orientalist comparison of Rousseau in chapter 5, 'Animadversions on some of the Writers who have Rendered Women Objects of Pity, Bordering on Contempt'.

29 See Francis Fukuyama, *The End of History and the Last Man*, London, Hamish Hamilton, 1992.

30 On postmodernism and its intellectual and ethical premises see Christopher Norris, *The Truth About Postmodernism*, Oxford, Oxford University Press, 1993.

31 See Peter Gay, *The Enlightenment, an Interpretation*, London, Weidenfeld & Nicolson, 1967; Karl Marx, *The Eighteenth Brumaire of Louis Bonaparte*, 1852; and Eric Hobsbawm, *The Age of Revolution*, New York, New American Library, 1962.

32 See Jane Moore, 'Sex, Slavery and Rights', in Carl Plasa and Betty Ring (eds), *The Discourse of Slavery: Aphra Behn to Toni Morrison*, New York, Routledge, 1994. Her article reduces Wollstonecraft to a minor footnote among male 'rights' theorists.

33 About Wollstonecraft's own presence in her theorising, see Moira Gatens, 'The Oppressed State of My Sex: Wollstonecraft on Reason, Feeling and Equality', in Mary Lyndon Shanley and Carole Pateman (eds), *Feminist Interpretations and Political Theory*, Philadelphia, Pennsylvania State University Press, 1991. Also see Sapiro's chapter 2, entitled 'The Reasoned, Passionate Self' in *Vindication of Political Virtue*, op. cit.

34 Wollstonecraft's *Rights of Woman* is occasioned by deformities among women produced through domination. The text as a whole is an attempt to indicate the direction of their correction. An example of Wollstonecraft's view is in the following lines: 'It is vain to expect virtue from women till they are in some degree independent of men; nay, it is vain to expect that strength of natural affection

which would make them good wives and mothers. Whilst they are absolutely dependent on their husbands they will be cunning, mean and selfish', *Rights of Woman* op. cit., p.213; also pp. 35 and 133 on mobs and slaves.

35 Wollstonecraft's opinion of property and its connection with morality comes out in chapter 9 of *Rights of Woman*, 'Of the Pernicious Effects which Arise from the Unnatural Distinctions Established in Society'; see also p.213. Sapiro's *Vindication of Political Virtue* grasps fully Wollstonecraft's critical position towards property in moral/social terms.

36 Moore's criticism in 'Sex, Slavery and Rights', op. cit., misses this Utopian dimension of Wollstonecraft's work, and thus tries to systematise her work within only one governing metaphor, or even a fully articulated theology.

Index

Achmat, Zackie 179
Acland, Mrs 135
African National Congress: (ANC) 164, 173, 174, 178, 169; Women's League 167, 175, 179
Ahmad, Sayyid 224
Aldridge, Ira 106
Alexander, Ziggi 106
All-China Women's Federation 199-200
Allgemeiner Deutscher Frauenverein (German Women's Association) 124
Anthony, Susan B. 150, 151
Araeen, Rasheed 111
Astell, Mary 23

Barbauld, Anna 91
Barker, Joseph 148
Barrell, John 212
Becker, Lydia 153
Benjamin, Walter 169, 170
Bentham, Jeremy 210
Besant, Annie 109-10, 155
Bhaba, Homi 177
Bhavnani, Kum-Kum 112
Bizos, George 167, 169, 171-2
Blake, William 121, 213
Bodichon, Barbara 124
Boris, Eileen 129, 130
Bradlaugh, Charles 155
Braidotti, Rosi 50, 60
Branch, Julia 149
Brathwaite, Kamau 114
Braun, Lily 131

Brown, Antoinette 149
Burke, Edmund 10, 28, 31, 62, 91, 215-16, 221, 239, 240

Capitalism: 1, 3, 64, 234-5; and apartheid 172; and Bulgarian women in transition to 189-91; *see* Socialism
Carpenter, Mary 123
Carroll, Lewis 50, 56-9
Centre for the Study of Democracy (Sofia) 189
Charity Organisation Society 126, 130
Chew, Ada Nield: 5, 156-60; employed by ILP, Clarion Van, Women's Trade Union League, Fabian Society, Women's Labour League and National Union of Women's Suffrage Societies 157
Chew, Doris 160
Chivalry: 3, 61, 62; Jacobin critique of 65-9, 72; Wollstonecraft and 68, 73, 74, 79
Citizenship 39, 40, 41, 42, 211-12, 220-1; *see* Women's rights
Clarkson, Thomas 90
Class and women: 158-9; relations among women 6-7, 128-33, 143-4, 157-8;

sexual oppression within working 137, 139-40; Wollstonecraft and 80-1, 83-4, 96, 102, 207, 212-13, 238, 240; *see* Feminism, Marriage
Co-operative movement 135, 137, 143, 144
Cohn, Fannia 124
Collins, Patricia Hill 113
Colonialism 170-1, 172, 177, 214, 223, 226, 227, 228; *see* Imperialism, Slavery
Committee of the Movement of Bulgarian Women 188
Common Cause 158
Condorcet 40, 43, 237
Consumption 137
Contagious Diseases Acts 163
Cowper, William 91
Craft, Ellen and William 106
Crompton, Mary 136
Cultural capital 159
Custody of Infants Act 163

Dasi, Rasasundari 226
Davies, Emily 136, 159
Davies, Margaret Llewelyn 131, 133, 134, 135-8, 139-41, 143-4
de Beauvoir, Simone 112
de Gouges, Olympe 2, 38-45

de Lauretis, Teresa 50, 59, 250n27
Deleuze, Gilles 56, 251n43
Democracy: 37, 134, 136, 140-1, 189, 207, 209, 213, 240, 242; 'radical' 218-21; see Feminism: self-representation; Liberalism
Democratic Union of Women 191
Deroin, Jeanne 150
Derrida, Jacques 214
Dewjee, Audrey 106
Diderot, Denis 42, 237
Dilke, Lady 160

Education 49, 50-1, 57-8, 125, 126-7, 136, 148-9, 152, 184, 187, 223-4, 225-6, 239
Elmy, Ben 153, 154, 155
Elmy, Elizabeth Wolstenholme 5, 152-5
Enlightenment: 2; liberty and 24; nature and 23, 233; reason and 9, 24, 238, 239; postmodern critique of 49-50, 55, 214; problematic universalism of 10, 40, 41, 213, 228, 234; Wollstonecraft's relation to 222, 228, 233, 236-7, 241-2; see Citizenship, Imagination, Liberalism
Equiano, Olaudah 91, 97-8, 230

Fabian Society 157
Falati, Xoliswa 165-6, 171
Family: in China 193-4, 198, 201, 202; language of power in 7, 122; in nationalism 163, 177; problems of heterosexual discourse of 9, 164, 170; sexual division in working-class 138-41; gendering of children 239; see Marriage, Motherhood
Fanon, Franz 170-1, 177
Fantasy 1, 2, 3-4, 30-1, 127-8; see Sensibility
Fawcett, Millicent 153
Femininity: bourgeois 122; and Bulgaria 8, 183-8; and China 8-9, 193-203; Wollstonecraft on 26; see Gender equality or difference, Sexuality
Feminism: black, 231, 233; and class 7, 144, 156, 157-60; and working-class housewives 134, 137, 138; and communism 184, 185, 194; Communist and post-Communist anti-feminism 186-9; and discourse of experience 217-20; current crisis 235-6, 241-2; divisions in Western 104, 222, 234; equality and difference 41, 45, 121; maternal 121, 208; and race 6, 104, 105, 107, 108-9, 112,117; anti-racist 115-16; and religion 22-3, 149; anti-religion 149, 154; and self-representation 40, 131, 140, 142; and temperance 149; and xenophobia 150; see Motherhood
Feminist history and tradition: anti-racist 6, 109-11, 115-16; black 6, 106-8, 113-15; exclusion from 2, 4-5, 152, 153, 154, 155, 160; oral history 121, 200-2; Wollstonecraft in 1, 3-4, 36-7, 49, 61, 102-3, 134, 148, 152, 207, 222, 228, 241-2
Feminist networks 159-60, 188
Fen Xiaotian 196
Foucault, Michel 216-17
Free Convention of the Friends of Human Progress 149
Freud, Sigmund 33
Fukuyama, Francis 235

Garvey, Marcus 114

Gatens, Moira 55
Gay and Lesbian Organisation of the Witwatersrand (GLOW) 173
Gender as unifying concept 158; see Identity
Gender equality or difference in aesthetic: 212; authorship 53-5; in Bengal 224-5, 227; in China 193-203; eighteenth-century difference 18, 34, 51-2; de Gouges and 38, 41; psychic gendering 34; Ernestine Rose and 149; Wollstonecraft and 32, 35, 53, 121, 134, 208-9, 239, 249n14
Gender of social systems 8, 9, 180-1, 182-3
General Federation of Women's Clubs 129
Godwin, William: 16-18, 59, 65; *Things as They Are, or the Adventures of Caleb Williams* 66-7, 71, 75
Goldman, Emma 112
Goldschmidt, Henriette 124
Gordon, Jan 57
Gordon, Linda 130
Greg, W.R. 123

Hall, Catherine 5
Hays, Mary 61, 71, 73, 74, 76, 103
Hegel, G.W.F. 250-1n38
Hill, Octavia 124
Hobbes, Thomas 51-2, 57, 248n9
Holcroft, Thomas 65-6, 75
Homosexuality, lesbianism, bisexuality see Sexuality
Hood, Eleanor 133
Hughes, Langston 114
Humanity and Humanism 215, 220-1, 233, 235-7, 240-1
Hume, David 115
Hurston, Zora Neale 113

Identity: 72, 213, 215, 240; feminist 2, 20, 35, 37, 237-8; fluid 6, 9, 114;

Remond, Sarah 107
Revolution: French 36, 38, 91-22, 237; San Domingo (Haiti) 89, 94, 95, 99, 102, 230, 237, 240
Reynolds, Stephen 128
Rich, Adriene 108-9
Richardson, Samuel 64, 66, 75
Riley, Denise 45
Robertson, George Croom 136
Robespierre, Maximilien 41, 43, 45
Roland, Pauline 150
Romance 1, 3, 22, 63-4, 70-5; *see* Protection
Roscoe, William 90
Rose, Ernestine 5, 147-51
Rose, William 148
Rousseau, Jean-Jacques 26, 28, 29, 30, 43, 51, 71, 73, 99, 101, 230, 237, 239
Rowbotham, Sheila 50, 250*n*27
Royal Commission on Divorce and Matrimonial Causes 131, 139, 140
Rushdie, Salman 214

Said, Edward 232, 270*n*26
Salzmann, Christian Gotthilf 93
Sapiro, Virginia 209-10, 230, 236
Seacole, Mary 106
Seipei, Stompie Moeketsi 164, 166, 169, 174
Sensibility 5, 18, 61, 62, 63, 67, 72, 73, 80, 82-3, 208, 212
Sexuality: 1, 20, 22, 27, 30, 32, 33, 71-2, 76-8, 95, 98, 256*n*39; homosexuality and homophobia 9, 164, 166-9, 170-4, 176; lesbianism and bisexuality 9, 179
Shaw, George Bernard 110
Sisterhood 122, 159, 191
Slavery: 62, 81-2, 84, 113, 232; anti-slavery 90-5, 148; colonial 62, 81-2, 84, 113, 232; discourse in Wollstonecraft 45, 52, 62-3, 89, 90, 92, 94-103, 217, 219, 229-31, 233, 236; discourse of and women's oppression 90, 155, 254*n*2; in radical political theory 229-30, 239
Smith, Amanda 107
Smith, Charlotte 103
Smith, Samuel Stanhope 97
Snitow, Ann 15
Social Democratic Federation 157
Socialism: 37, 131, 135, 148, 157, 158, 208, 235; Chinese women in transition to socialist market economy 197-8
Somerset, James 90
South African Constitution 1994 179
Stacey, Enid 136
Stanton, Elizabeth Cady 149, 150, 151
Steele, Richard 91
Stewart, Maria 113
Stone, Lucy 149

Tagore, Rabindranath 224
Talleyrand, Charles Maurice 50, 237
Taylor, Barbara 212
Trewhela, Paul 168
Truth, Sojourner 6, 112
Tuckwell, Gertrude 160

United States Children's Bureau 125, 132

Verryn, the Rev. Paul 164-9, 171-3, 176
Vigilance Association for the Defence of Personal Rights 155
Violence 62, 69, 80, 152, 154, 164-5, 267-8, 181, 190-1
Voltaire 42, 43
von Zahn-Harnack, Agnes 123

Walker, Alice 105, 113
Wheatley, Phillis 90
Wilberforce, William 93
Wollstonecraft, Mary: biography 68, 256*n*34, *n*39; love of God 15, 21, 22, 25, 35; religious views 3, 15-17, 23-5, 32, 240; texts: *The Female Reader, or Miscellaneous Pieces for the Improvement of Young Women* 91, 98; *Mary, a Fiction* 18-22, 26, 30-1, 90, 93, 212; reviews in *Analytical Review* 91, 92, 97; *A Short Residence in Sweden* 16; *Thoughts on the Education of Daughters* 16, 90, 93; *A Vindication of the Rights of Men* 16, 33, 62, 89, 92-3, 207; *A Vindication of the Rights of Woman* 16, 18, 20, 22, 26-7, 31, 35, 36, 50, 68-9, 84, 89, 94-7, 134, 207, 209, 212, 218, 219, 222-42; *The Wrongs of Woman: or, Maria* 31, 55, 61, 68, 69-72, 73-85; *see* Class, Education, Enlightenment, Feminism, Feminist history, Gender equality, Imagination, Liberalism, Orientalism, Reason, Sensibility, Sexuality, Slavery
Women's Co-operative Guild 131, 134-44
Women's Institute 144
Women's Rights 134, 139, 153, 154, 173, 179, 184, 187, 188, 194-5, 217, 236; *see* Citizenship
Women's Rights Association 149
Women's Suffrage 135, 148, 152-3, 157
Women's Trade Union League 124, 157, 159-60
Women's trade unions 135
Woolf, Leonard 141
Woolf, Virginia 112

Xiang Hua 198-9

Zetkin, Clara 131

woman/women 37, 51, 95, 168-9, 222, 241-2; *see* Imagination, Sexuality, Ernestine Rose
Ignota, *see* Elmy, Mary Wolstenholme
Imagination: 1, 2; Christian Platonist 28-9; de Gouges and 42-4; Enlightenment concept of 2, 42, 44-5; Wollstonecraft on 2, 3, 16, 19, 20, 21, 31, 71; *see* Sensibility
Imlay, Gilbert 31, 32, 33, 68
Imperialism 216, 235; *see* Colonialism
Independent Labour Party 157
Irigaray, Luce 50, 250*n*27

James, C.L.R. 109
Johnson, Amryl 112
Johnson, Dr Samuel 209
Johnson, James Weldon 114
Johnson, Joseph 33, 91, 92, 93
Jones, Mrs Ben 135
Journal des Dames 41
Jung, Carl Gustav 127-8

Kaplan, Cora 27, 53, 96
Kay, Carol 51
Key, Ellen 124
Klein, Melanie 127
Knowledge: as battleground 9; black women and theory 105, 107, 113, 117; decolonisation of 5, 108, 233; pre-colonial 226; 'discredited' 6, 104-5; *see* Reason
Kollontai, Alexandra 134

Laclau, Ernesto 218-21
Ladd-Taylor, Molly 132
Lathrop, Julia 132
Levine, Phillipa 158
Li Xiaojiang 200
Liberalism: and feminism 37, 45; Wollstonecraft's place in 10, 16, 23, 55, 208, 209, 210-11

Loane, M.E. 129
Locke, John 51, 115
Long, Edward 115
Lorde, Audre 116
Love: free love 149; Wollstonecraft on Eros 27-8; *see* Romance
Lurie, Alison 56

Macaulay, Catherine 90, 93, 99
Mandela, Nelson 9, 163, 165, 170, 174, 178, 179
Mandela, Winnie: 9, 163-4, 166; and trial 164-70, 171-2, 173-4, 175
Mark, Connie 107-8
Marriage (and divorce): 20, 27, 51, 70, 94-5, 98, 138-40, 148, 149, 153, 154, 190, 193, 195, 198-9, 201-2, 223, 225; as religous metaphor 29
Married Women's Property Committee and Act 153, 154
Marson, Una 114
Martineau, Harriet 106
Marx, Karl 207
Marxism 227, 235
McIlquham, Harriet 153, 155
McKay, Claude 110-11
Mies, Maria 197
Mill, Harriet Taylor 138
Mill, John Stuart 136, 138, 210, 224
Milton, John 21, 24, 29, 271*n*28
Moore, John 91
Morrison, Toni 104, 113
Motherhood: 122, 129-30, 131-2, 139, 140, 143-4, 158, 166, 167, 177; in Bengal 225; in Bulgaria 183-4; mothers' meetings 132, 135; national 9, 163, 168, 176, 178, 179, 243*n*6; psychoanalytic concepts of ambivalence to 127-8; social 7, 123-33; Wollstonecraft on 27, 51, 52, 70, 121, 209, 271*n*34
Mouffe, Chantal 218-21

National Union of Women's Suffrage Societies 157-8
Naylor, Gloria 113
Ngcobo, Lauretta 104, 105, 112
Nussbaum, Martha 214

Orientalism in Wollstonecraft 4, 232-3
Owen, Robert 148

Pankhurst, Christabel 157
Pankhurst, Sylvia 110-11
Parmar, Pratibha 112
Patriarchy 225, 227, 238, 240; *see* Chivalry, Protection
Poovey, Mary 27, 53, 253*n*29
Power: 10; between women 85, 252*n*2, 122, 128, 132; and difference 228, 234, 241-2
Price, the Rev. Richard 23, 24, 33, 91, 100
Professionalisation 124-7, 184
Prostitution 69, 79, 80, 154
Protection: 3, chivalric 64; Jacobin novelists 65-9; Wollstonecraft on want of as lack and desire on 69-76
Public and private spheres: 40-1, 58-9, 123, 139, 210-13, 238; in Bengal 224-5, 227; in Communism and post-Communism 185, 191-2

Race 63, 80-2, 84, 97, 228, 255-6*n*30
Radcliffe, Mary Ann 81-2
Rakhneva, Silva 187
Reading as active relationship 4, 223, 241
Reason: Alice's subversion of 56-8, 59; feminist 9; in Bengali education 223-4, 226-7; in Wollstonecraft 2, 4, 9-10, 49, 50, 53, 55, 59, 229, 237-41; Godwin on Wollstonecraft 17; *see* Knowledge